DEI and Intersectional Social Identities at Work

This book equips readers—both students and communication practitioners—with the theoretical understanding and practical skills they need to support nonprofit and for-profit organizations to create and assess their diversity, equity, inclusion (DEI), and social identity intersectionality goals.

Through applied examples of the insider activist role that the communication function plays, the book helps future and current professional communicators navigate organizations toward authentic relationship-building with internal and external audiences. It teaches that embracing DEI includes acknowledging social identity intersectionalities—recognizing that people possess multiple social identity dimensions of age, culture, ethnicity/race, faith/spirituality, gender, physical/psychological ability, sexual orientation, social class, and more. In order to illuminate the theory discussed in the book, each chapter includes thought-provoking situation-opportunity sidebars, discussion questions for drilling deeper into the issues at hand, and case studies with applied lessons about DEI issues.

This is an ideal text for advanced undergraduates and graduate courses in organizational communication, strategic communication, marketing communication, human resources, and public relations, as well as for communication practitioners working in these subdisciplines.

Donnalyn Pompper is Professor and Endowed Chair in Public Relations at the University of Oregon, USA.

Tugce Ertem-Eray is an Assistant Professor in the Department of Communication at North Carolina State University, USA.

DEI and Intersectional Social Identities at Work

A Communication Approach

Donnalyn Pompper and Tugce Ertem-Eray

NEW YORK AND LONDON

Designed cover image: SolStock/© Getty Images

First published 2024
by Routledge
605 Third Avenue, New York, NY 10158

and by Routledge
4 Park Square, Milton Park, Abingdon, Oxon, OX14 4RN

Routledge is an imprint of the Taylor & Francis Group, an informa business

Library of Congress Cataloging-in-Publication Data
Names: Pompper, Donnalyn, 1960– author. | Ertem-Eray, Tugce, author.
Title: DEI and intersectional social identities at work : a communication approach / Donnalyn Pompper and Tugce Ertem-Eray.
Description: New York, NY : Routledge, 2024. | Includes bibliographical references and index.
Identifiers: LCCN 2023059296 (print) | LCCN 2023059297 (ebook) | ISBN 9781032245287 (hbk) | ISBN 9781032245287 (pbk) | ISBN 9781003279129 (ebk)
Subjects: LCSH: Social responsibility of business. | Business communication. | Diversity in the workplace. | Group identity.
Classification: LCC HD60 .P663 2024 (print) | LCC HD60 (ebook) | DDC 658.3008—dc23/eng/20240220
LC record available at https://lccn.loc.gov/2023059296
LC ebook record available at https://lccn.loc.gov/2023059297

ISBN: 978-1-032-24529-4 (hbk)
ISBN: 978-1-032-24528-7 (pbk)
ISBN: 978-1-003-27912-9 (ebk)

DOI: 10.4324/9781003279129

Typeset in Sabon
by Apex CoVantage, LLC

Contents

PART III
**Advancing communication and positive organizational
change processes**   195

Acknowledgments

All book-length projects are a community project. For this book, we are most grateful to several friends, colleagues, and practitioners who inspired us and offered their expertise in reading chapter drafts, including: Eric Kwame Adae, Eyun-Jung Ki, Sarah Aghazadeh, Vanessa Bravo, Jacqueline Lambiase, Nneka Logan, and Jennifer Vardeman.

We also thank communication practitioners who invested their time and experiences in writing sidebars for this book: Tricia Garrison and Ru Wood.

A huge thanks to those at Routledge who supported this project: Sean Daly, Felisa Salvago-Keyes, and all team members behind the scenes.

Finally, thanks to our families, students at the School of Journalism and Communication at the University of Oregon, and donors for Endowed Chair in Public Relations support.

Part I

Exploring publics and what makes them tick

1 DEI and social identity intersectionality in organizational communication

Donnalyn Pompper

Top communicators know that making relationships and networks fruitful and useful takes a great deal of skill, practice, hard work, and advocacy. Several theories related to identity, belonging, diversity, and inclusion provide useful foundations for the practice of relationship building, which is a key component of public relations work. *Diversity* and *social identity intersectionality* are among those terms that everyone thinks they can define easily. Complexity of the socio-economic-political global world in which we live—and communicate via social media—makes what seems a simple task quite complicated. But that's actually part of the beauty of fine tuning our listening, viewing, and understanding skills—and feeling inspired and empowered to do so. Communicators are the perfect practitioners for defining organizations' success for the future, while considering the present as enveloped in a past that hasn't always been respectful or supportive of social identity difference among people. Having a positive mindset enables communicators to play a significant role in ensuring organizations authentically are diverse and that they embrace social identity intersectionality in all of the possible dimensions that interplay in organizational and social life.

This chapter offers a foundational edifice for building upon key terms and issues while outlining why they matter in the context of organizational communication practice. Sometimes students feel uncomfortable around theories, thinking theory is too abstract, hard to understand, and useless. Yet, the founding father of social psychology saw it differently. Kurt Lewin believed "There's nothing so practical as good theory" and "the best way to understand something is to try to change it" (Greenwood & Levin, 1998, p. 19). Theories about what makes us unique in terms of our individual gender, ethnicity, ability, and more help us to make sense of who we are. This is why social constructionism, social identity theory, social learning theory, and other theories offer useful tools for understanding communication's role in supporting DEI and social justice in organizations. To underscore this driving desire to support

DOI: 10.4324/9781003279129-2

Figure 1.1 Enabling people to feel that they belong in organizations means respecting all of their intersecting social identity dimensions, including employees who may identify as having a disability.

social justice and inclusion, some people and organizations they work with add a *B* representing *belonging* or a *sense of belonging mindset* to the DEI framework, too.

Coming to grips with concepts such as *multiculturalism*, *diversity*, *difference*, *social identity*, and *intersectionality* is a terrific start. The role of communication as part of these processes becomes increasingly clear as we work to understand key audiences and groups as a central function of communication among both for-profit and nonprofit organizations. There's much more to all of this than meets the eye, though. Social identity dimensions of age, class, culture, ethnicity, faith/spirituality, gender, physical/psychological ability, sexual orientation, and more intersect to uniquely shape individuals and groups. Moreover, we must avoid reductionist thinking, or any tendency to consider people solely in terms of any one social identity dimension or the same as others in some group. For example, not all people with disabilities are the same and there is a great deal of diversity among people who identify as Muslim.

Let's begin with a bit of theoretical underpinning as guide to understanding and applying conceptualizations of diversity, social identity, intersectionality—while exploring the role of communication across these dynamics. Theories are useful in helping us to describe, explain, and predict relationships among phenomena, or things that happen. This means we use theories to make sense of our lives, guide our attitudes and actions, and anticipate others' behaviors. Theories have application for explaining and predicting how we act, what we believe, and what we expect others to believe and how to act.

Social constructionism as a useful theory

Thinking critically about our decision making as individuals and how we make meaning—rooted in what happens behind the scenes and below the surface—offers an important step to fostering mutually beneficial relationships at work and in our personal lives. One way to start is to consider a theory known as social constructionism. Who we are and how we came to be the way we are can become hard-wired according to what we're taught by other people and what we discover from media.

Understanding how the world is socially constructed offers a useful theoretical lens for critiquing media and identifying ways to make media products more representative and inclusive. Moreover, recognizing that we bring the outside world into organizations when we report to work is a useful context when thinking about diversity in organizations. Social construction theory enables us to assess for ourselves what we see, hear, and experience by considering who or what was influential in shaping stories, images, policies, rules, laws, and more. Social construction theory is an interdisciplinary theory used by sociologists, psychologists, communication scholars, anthropologists, and many others for revealing and understanding people's basis for shared assumptions about reality.

Things constructed in the social world—such as the internet, sexual behavior, family recipes, ways we pray to a higher power (or not)—all are developed in conjunction with others and are subject to change over time. Each of these phenomena is molded by the opinions, attitudes, and social identities of the people who influence their creation or manufacture. People in society construct ideas or concepts that may not exist without people or language to validate those concepts or ideas. Understanding social construction when inequalities become built in can lead to change because we have the power and intelligence to critique. Because social constructionism focuses on artifacts created through social interactions and groups' shared assumptions, we can modify products like streaming programs that unfairly depict family life across faith/religion groups or offer an incomplete picture of what it's really like to be a transgender person in the workplace.

More practical theories: social identity theory and social learning theory

Society teaches us—in sometimes subtle ways and at other times overtly upfront ways—how to think about ourselves and others. Related to social constructionism is social communication theory and social comparison theory developed by a social psychologist named Leon Festinger. He hypothesized that social groups of people influence individual opinions and abilities (Festinger et al., 1950) and suggested that we are driven, instinctively, to compare themselves to others as part of our regular attention to our body and self-improvement. In other words, individual people seem to appreciate learning from those who are more experienced or successful in a specific arena. You've probably experienced this phenomenon play out whenever someone asks questions such as: "Do these pants make me look fat?" or "Does my bald spot show?"

Similar theories called social identity theory and social learning theory are useful for further understanding dynamics associated with learning as part of a group or community. Social identity theory explains how people learn to think of themselves by interpreting others' reactions to them (Van Maanen, 1979). For example, dressing in clothing considered to be out of fashion can earn a negative reaction from classmates and make us reconsider wearing that outfit again. Another psychologist, Alfred Bandura (1977), suggested we learn socially, while children, about who we are, whom we should be, and how we should act. Research findings suggest that social identity development and social learning begin at a very early age. For example, reading bedtime stories to children that contain few images of people of color and with little boys engaged in rugged activities while little girls are featured as delicate and pretty to look at offers a limited worldview on ethnicity and gender roles (Pompper & Merskin, 2020). In this way, storybook worlds are constructed based on social valuing of some groups over others while instructing readers on how they should act according to prescribed gender roles. Over the last century, a large body of scholarship has developed to help us understand processes associated with how we learn about our identity and shape ideas about others' identities. It is important to examine theories like social identity theory and social learning theory because each new development brings us closer to more clearly understanding interplay among communication and making diversity in organizations a reality.

Many researchers attribute learned benchmarking behaviors—not to genetics—but to advertising-driven desires and consumption of media images of celebrities and other people who are considered authority figures. For example, Raewyn Connell, a trans person who made a formal transition late in life, spent a career developing the field of masculinity

Figure 1.2 Learning about people's social identity dimensions begins in early child development.

studies to better understand hegemonic masculinity, or when patriarchy-shaped masculinity creates negative impacts for men and others (e.g., Connell, 2005). Investigating the root causes and effects of toxic masculinity has been the focus of several masculinity scholars in recent years (e.g., Conway, 2020). Likewise, investigations of the drive for thinness and eating disorders among women have traced links to media content and usage (e.g., Kilbourne, 2010). Basically, high school girls enact femininity by using media images of fashion models and celebrity entertainers for upward comparisons when selecting prom dresses, grooming hair, and strategically posing for photographs (Pompper & Crandall, 2014). Similarly, social media platforms such as Instagram and highly popular influencers on YouTube seem to inspire people to compare themselves with others (Jiang & Ngien, 2020).

Communication is considered a relatively young field of study when compared to psychology, sociology, and other disciplines. Yet, we have learned much in a short period of time about social constructionism—with social communication theory, social identity theory, and social learning theory to help us discover outcomes, effects, and interplay of communication behaviors with media production and consumption. A logical next step in this chapter's investigation of applied theories that serve as tools in explaining, predicting, and understanding diversity in organizational communication is to explore the concept of social identity intersectionality and some key effects.

Social identity intersectionalities, privilege, and unpacking the invisible knapsack

Exploring intersectionalities of social identity dimensions makes sense for communication practitioners. Doing so reminds us that people are complex. Intersectionality theory offers an argument for *remembering* that complexity and for *being aware of* the silos created around identity, especially by practitioners who often segment audiences. Collectively, social identity dimensions can twist, amplify, negate, and complicate one another. So far, we've skimmed the surface of thinking about the relevance of social identity dimensions of age, class, culture, ethnicity, faith/spirituality, gender, physical psychological ability, sexual orientation, and more—but later chapters in this book will explore each general category of social identity dimension in much greater depth. In many organizations, diversity, equity, and inclusion (DEI) initiatives fail to consider social identities as being composed of intersecting dimensions. Rather, DEI initiatives at work can become politicized with some managers and employees failing to see their value. For example, negative emptions affect audiences when they perceive that they are not valued because of their intersecting social identity dimensions. Read more about this in Chapter 3, "How intersectionality in social identity works . . . at work." Considering *belonging* as part of the DEI framework is helpful for public relations students and practitioners to consider as part of understanding that DEI is a core part of the work of the profession, and that despite politics, we need to embrace it because we are relationship builders. Moreover, sometimes organizations commodify or water down the importance of recognizing DEI's value by simply offering a cafeteria lunch menu celebrating Black History Month or Hispanic Heritage Week and could lead some to conclude that racist discrimination is a thing of the past (Van de Mieroop, 2016).

An important consideration now is to remember that not all people who belong to any one group are the same. There is a vast deal of difference within social groups. For example, not all Latinx people are alike and not all members of the LGBTQ+ community are exactly identical. The risk of lumping similar people together by failing to accept that all people are individuals can result in negative outcomes such as symbolic annihilation, stereotyping, out-grouping, and marginalizing.

Legal scholar Kimberlé Crenshaw (1989) introduced the concept of *intersectionality* to emphasize multiple dimensions of lived experiences among people occupying society's margin. For example, African

American/Black women share ethnic discrimination experiences in common with African American/Black men and sexism in common with many other groups of women—but also uniquely as African American/Black women and "not the sum of race and sex discrimination" (Crenshaw, 1989, p. 149). Also, African American/Black people with disabilities experience institutional discrimination which is different from the sum of racism and disablism (Miles, 2020). Some refer to intersectionality as a field of study, while others have characterized it as an analytic tool, a systematic research approach, a critical analytic strategy or lens for contesting ways social identity dimensions have been examined in the past, inspiration for advocating for equity and social justice, and inspiration for social change. In this book, we regard intersectionality as a pedagogical instrument for learning. The intersectionality concept has been embraced among communication scholars, human rights activists, political figures, lawyers, and community organizers who seek to reveal and rid society of discrimination.

While the social identity intersectionalities concept helps us to understand effects of discrimination such as being pushed to society's margins—and in some communities this takes a literal turn as people of low socio-economic status may be forced to the worst neighborhoods to live in and worst jobs to work at—it also is important to take a look at what is happening at society's main body center. Social activist and feminist scholar bell hooks (2000) explained, "To be in the margin is to be part of the whole but outside the main body" (p. xvii) and it is in the main body's center where Caucasian/White people are considered in the larger society. These processes can fuel outcomes that become normalized. For example, when organizations' management teams include no BIPOC people, the needs and concerns of BIPOC communities may not be considered in important decision-making policy meetings.

More generally, the social identity intersectionalities concept illustrates routes for enabling strategic communicators—as liaisons and boundary spanners among audiences and organizations—to keep communication lines open, even when an issue or topic is highly controversial and the subject of a Supreme Court ruling. Take a look at Sidebar 1.1.

Sidebar 1.1 Hobby Lobby, religion, and employee healthcare benefits

Tugce Ertem-Eray

Strategic communicators can keep dialog lines open—and serve as liaisons and boundary spanners among audiences and organizations—even when an issue or topic is highly controversial and the subject of a Supreme Court ruling. In 2012, an American retail chain of arts and crafts stores called Hobby Lobby found itself embroiled in a highly publicized debate that pitted the company's view on religious freedom against perceptions about personal health choices. Closer inspection of this case offers interesting perspectives on ways DEI (and belonging) involving intersections of social identity dimensions (specifically gender, age, religion/faith) can interplay and how organizations communicate internally and externally.

In the course of their day-to-day work, public relations practitioners serve as expert liaisons, as well as prescribers, communication facilitators, and process facilitators (Springston & Leichty, 1994), to ensure that communication flows clearly and smoothly among organizations and audiences. This work constitutes public relations' social responsibility (Pompper, 2015), too. This case study explores how the communication process became complicated and a source of controversy in an unlikely scene where adults and children shop for craft supplies in spaces that ordinarily connote carefree fun.

Here's what happened when one company objected to an aspect of a new law. Since 2010, the Affordable Care Act (ACA) requires most health insurance plans in the U.S. to cover contraceptive methods and counseling for all women without cost-sharing (HealthCare.gov, n.d.). This requirement has been one of the hallmark achievements of the Affordable Care Act, introduced and signed by President Barack Obama. Family planning can have significant costs attached to it for people. Without healthcare coverage, contraceptive pills can cost about $25 a month and an intrauterine device (IUD) can cost up to $900 (Dockterman, 2014). FDA-approved and ACA-covered contraception includes barrier methods like diaphragms and sponges, hormonal methods like birth control pills and vaginal rings, implanted devices like intrauterine devices (IUDs), emergency contraception like Plan B® and ella®, as well as sterilization procedures, patient education, and counseling (HealthCare.gov, n.d.). The Affordable Care Act's contraceptive coverage saved women an estimated $1.4 billion on birth control pills in its first year alone and has allowed almost 63 million women to access birth control in the U.S. (Planned Parenthood, 2019). Yet, here's the source of conflict. Nonprofit organizations with religious affiliations are *exempt* from the birth control insurance mandate.

As a for-profit company, Hobby Lobby objected to paying for such healthcare procedures for employees on religious/faith grounds. The company's mission statement includes a commitment to "honoring the Lord in all we do by operating the company in a manner consistent with Biblical principles" (Hobby Lobby, n.d.) Company founder David Green operates Hobby Lobby in conjunction with Christian principles. He opposed the contraceptive coverage mandate of the Patient Protection and Affordable Care Act and filed a lawsuit against the U.S., stating that the mandate would force the Oklahoma City-based company to provide health insurance that covers morning-after pills and other birth control products. Green and his family indicated that this healthcare law violates their religious beliefs: "The Green family's religious beliefs forbid them from participating in, providing access to, paying for, training others to engage in, or otherwise supporting abortion-causing drugs and devices" (Wertz, 2021, para. 3).

In 2014, the U.S. Supreme Court considered the case. The ruling stated that the federal government cannot require Hobby Lobby and other for-profit businesses wherein more than half of the stock is owned by five or fewer individuals to provide insurance coverage for birth control if laws conflict with the employer's religious beliefs. The Court's decision also applied to specific birth control methods of two morning-after pills like Plan B and two kinds of intrauterine devices (IUD) (Dockterman, 2014). Writing the dissenting opinion for *Burwell v. Hobby Lobby Stores, Inc, 2014*, Justice Ruth Bader Ginsburg said: "The exemption sought by Hobby Lobby and Conestoga would . . . deny legions of women who do not hold their employers' beliefs access to contraceptive coverage" (*Burwell v. Hobby Lobby Stores, Inc.*, 2014, p. 8). Ginsburg was joined by Justice Sonia Sotomayor, Justice Elena Kagan, and Justice Stephen Breyer (the only male justice who dissented): "Religious organizations exist to foster the interests of persons subscribing to the same religious faith. Not so of for-profit corporations. Workers who sustain the operations of those corporations commonly are not drawn from one religious community" *(Burwell v. Hobby Lobby Stores, Inc.*, 2014, p. 16).

In a world shaped by social media realities, just how does a strategic communicator—including public relations practitioners—ethically serve organizations *and* audiences who find themselves on opposing sides of an issue or argument? The U.S. Supreme Court ruled that some employers may impose their religious beliefs on women employees by determining which birth control methods are eligible for coverage under the company's healthcare plans. While Hobby Lobby sees this issue as religious freedom, some women (including Hobby Lobby employees impacted by the case) may see the issue as one of limiting their personal health choices. Women's rights groups protested Hobby Lobby after the decision and the protest was dubbed on a Facebook event page as "Let's Condom . . . er Condemn Hobby Lobby at their Burbank Grand Opening." Protesters handed out condoms and raised donations for Planned Parenthood. Signs said "HOBBY LOBBY IS NOT PRO RELIGION, IT'S ANTI-WOMEN" and "BIRTH CONTROL EMPOWERS WOMEN" (Cocca & Vara, 2014). A sustained tweetstorm included hashtags such as #HobbyLobby, #SCOTUS, #JointheDissent, #DrHobbyLobby, and #NotMyBossBusiness, expressing outrage about ways this decision can cause serious financial hardship. Women's rights groups fear that such a precedent will empower other for-profit, privately held companies to claim religious exceptions—and this could mean that more women would lose their rights as active citizens to control their own reproductive decisions and have to bear full financial cost of their family planning choices (Springer, 2014).

In addition to serving as boundary spanners connecting organizations and external communities, public relations practitioners serve to link organizations' management with internal audiences, as well. Indeed, employees are a key audience that serves as ambassadors for organizations providing consumer services and goods (Lipschultz, 2018; Pálenque-Suarez, 2000). Hence, knowledgeable and agreeable employees are valuable and essential to organizations' survival (Kang & Sung, 2017; Kim & Rhee, 2011), possibly enabling organizations to avert crises (Liu & Pompper, 2012). This means that face-to-face communication, listening, and continued dialogue are significant factors in building a sense of belonging and strong relationships among community groups (e.g., Rhee, 2004).

No doubt, dissent associated with this case will endure so long as employees, activists, and Hobby Lobby management do not see eye to eye on the Supreme Court's decision about employee rights and company management's expression of religious values. Diana Banister, partner and vice president of Shirley & Banister Public Affairs which provided media support for Hobby Lobby, concluded that there was much misinformation about the lawsuit that created confusion across publics (Nichols, 2014). What *is* clear is that the public relations function, in its boundary spanning and liaison capacity, is responsible for facilitating dialog, listening, and sharing information when corporate social responsibility and DEI dimensions interplay amidst degrees of conflict.

Resources

Burwell v. Hobby Lobby Stores, Inc., 573 U. S. ____ (2014). https://supreme.justia.com/cases/federal/us/573/682/

Cocca, C., & Vara, K. (2014, July 7). #NotMyBossesBusiness: Activists protest Hobby Lobby after birth control ruling. NBC. https://rb.gy/mhrbtz

Dockterman, E. (2014, July 1). 5 things women need to know about the Hobby Lobby ruling. *Time*. https://rb.gy/tnx5c7

HealthCare.gov. (n.d.). Birth control benefits. https://rb.gy/e3ceid

Hobby Lobby. (n.d.). Our story. https://rb.gy/fhyrf6

Kang, M., & Sung, M. (2017). How symmetrical employee communication leads to employee engagement and positive employee communication behaviors: The mediation of employee organization relationships. *Journal of Communication Management, 21*(1), 82–102. http://dx.doi.org/10.1108/JCOM-04-2016-0026

Kim, J.-N., & Rhee, Y. (2011). Strategic thinking about employee communication behavior (ECB) in public relations: Testing the models of megaphoning and scouting effects in Korea, *Journal of Public Relations Research, 23*(3), 243–268. https://doi.org/10.1080/1062726X.2011.582204

Lipschultz, J. H. (2018). Organizations, HR, CSR, and their social networks: Sustainability on Twitter. In D. Pompper (Ed.) *Corporate social responsibility, sustainability, & ethical public relations: Strengthening synergies with human resources* (pp. 35–52). Emerald Group Publishing Limited.

Liu, B. F., & Pompper, D. (2012). The 'crisis with no name': Defining the interplay of culture, ethnicity, and race on organizational issues and media outcomes. *Journal of Applied Communication Research, 40*(2), 127–146. https://doi.org/10.1080/00909882.2012.654499

Nichols, L. (August 1, 2014). Six questions for one PR firm supporting Hobby Lobby and the Becked Fund. *PR Week*. https://rb.gy/xl6baq

Pálenque-Suarez, E, (2000). Contribution of public relations in understanding social responsibility of organizations. *Alacaurp, 1*, 34–37.

Planned Parenthood. (2019, January 14). Court stops Trump's nationwide assault on birth control coverage. https://rb.gy/vsnoch

Pompper, D. (2015). *Corporate social responsibility, sustainability, and public relations: Negotiating multiple complex challenges*. Routledge.

Rhee, Y. (2004). The employee–public-organization chain in relationship management: A case study of a government organization. Institute for Public Relations. https://rb.gy/0oydam

Springer, A. (2014, July 2). #HobbyLobby: Feminist Twitter responds to Hobby Lobby ruling. https://rb.gy/rtu5oz

Springston, J. K., & Leichty, G. (1994). Boundary spanning activities in public relations. *Journalism Quarterly, 71*(3), 697–708. DOI: https://doi.org/10.1177/107769909407100320

Wertz, J. (2021, September 12). Hobby Lobby sues over affordable care act's 'abortion-causing' mandate. StateImpact Oklahoma. https://rb.gy/45vncs

Socialization happens at society's center, too. Using an "invisible knapsack" metaphor, Peggy McIntosh (1989) explained that "whites are taught to think of their lives as morally neutral, rather than in terms of invisible systems conferring dominance" (p. 10). Often this plays out as Caucasian/White people experiencing privilege when they enjoy advantages and benefits not shared by BIPOC groups. In her widely known essay, McIntosh (1989) chronicled how "as a participant in a damaged culture" she was unable to see White privilege as a member of "the main culture" (pp. 10–11). However, critics such as Jon Greenberg (2017) have pointed out that too often Caucasian/White people are credited for educating about White privilege when a more well-rounded perspective may be gained by also considering worldviews of BIPOC community members who, for example, may not have the privilege of enjoying a positive relationship with police, learning about their race in school, and attending segregated schools of affluence. Tom Nakayama and Robert Krizek (1995) pointed out that Caucasian/Whites' communication patterns and experiences are taken as "the norm from which Others are marked" and encouraged researchers to disengage from "normative essence" by investigating "strategies that mark the space of whiteness" (pp. 292–293). Moreover, there are plenty of examples of people enjoying multiple privileges, such as ableism regardless of other social identity dimensions such as gender, ethnicity, socioeconomic status, and more. This occurs when entire groups of people are considered less than other groups, such as when an able-bodied actor is hired to play a disabled person in a play, film, or television show, as well as when disability is framed as *tragic* or *inspirational* in media narratives (Eisenmenger, 2019).

Social identities intersect and enable us to more clearly see who experiences privilege and who does not—and to what effect. Examining how these dynamics play out in workspaces and across organizations offers a view on how these theories apply.

Managing DEI initiatives

Many organizations describe a desire to offer diverse, equitable, and inclusive employment and volunteer positions as part of their mission statement, with websites of corporations and nonprofit organizations promoting such goals. Ensuring that businesses and offices are managed and run by a large and broad pool of talented, creative people drives many organizations to pursue the benefits offered by DEI and social justice (Steimel, 2021) to profess moving beyond homophily. The social homophily thesis suggests that preserving the status quo—predominantly White/Caucasian, Christian, heterosexual—facilitates easier communication and reduces conflict and management costs (Appold et al., 1998). The thesis plays out as "similarity on socially significant attributes like ethnicity or religion" (Lazarsfeld & Merton, 1954; Melamed et al., 2020, p. 1084), as in people who seek to reduce potential conflict in relationships by surrounding themselves with people like themselves (O'Brien et al., 2020).

However, researchers offer mixed, or inconclusive findings that DEI benefits the bottom line, or profits. Just how diverse the variety of skills, knowledge, and perspectives must be to make organizations more creative, innovative, or competitive is unknown. This is called making the business case argument for supporting DEI goals—because doing so seems to make good business sense. Similarly, Steimel (2021) suggested that using a social justice argument may be even more effective. Yet, even though statistics suggest that organizations have been spending more on DEI initiatives (programs and campaigns) than ever before—$8 billion annually—many organizations still haven't delivered on a commitment to become truly diverse, equitable, or inclusive (Newkirk, 2019), given that Fortune 500 boards of directors in 2017 featured only 4.1% women of color and 9% men of color, with 65 people of color on corporate boards serving on more than one board which suggests even lower representation than may be apparent (Pompper et al., 2021).

This level of critique for investigating why and how the DEI picture remains an unclear and an unfulfilled promise is supported by our understanding of social identity theory and other explanatory frameworks introduced in this chapter. In particular, uncovering why and how mindsets and perspectives continue fueling homophily trends with bias and discrimination that keeps organizations predominantly Caucasian/White at the top through middle management offers a first step in advocating for positive systemic, infrastructural change in organizations. It also promotes and amplifies a commitment to belonging and social justice—which many characterize as a social responsibility. Read more about ESG (environment, social, governance) as part of the matrix in Chapter 5, "Social responsibility in corporations and nonprofits." For only when organizations truly support diversity across social identities and their intersectionalities will belonging and DEI become a reality. In Sidebar 1.2, consider the lifetime work of the Rev. Leon Sullivan, Jr., who inspired, nurtured, and committed himself to making *belonging* a worldwide goal as part of a movement.

Sidebar 1.2   The Rev. Leon Sullivan, Jr. and influencing public opinion to speak to power

Donnalyn Pompper

When a Black Philadelphia minister advocated for DEI using a *selective patronage* strategy, it grew into a movement in other U.S. cities and later influenced public opinion around the world to help end apartheid in South Africa. Perhaps no more poignant example of a commitment to *belonging* has so profoundly and positively influenced our world population.

The Rev. Leon Sullivan, Jr. founded and led the first Opportunities Industrialization Centers of America, Inc. (OIC), a nonprofit organization for employing and training programs for underserved communities. Beginning in 1958, the Rev. Sullivan led 400 spiritual leaders working in solidarity to convince Philadelphia-area business owners to hire more Black managers or else face consequences of pulpit-advocated economic withdrawal (boycotts) among community members. The strategy was to organize and pressure for social change—and it worked—with the slogan "Don't buy where you can't be hired." Pastor of Zion Baptist Church, Sullivan (1998, p. 12) explained:

> I found out that with most companies there was a thin line between making money and losing money and that the profit margins of some of the largest corporations were less than 3 percent . . . All of them depended on the black customer to stay in business.

Later in the 1970s, as a member of General Motors' board of directors, the Rev. Sullivan led an activist movement to convince business leaders that achieving moral goals belongs within "the realm of business" (Sullivan, 1998, p. 51). He wrote the Sullivan Principles (later called the Principles of Equal Rights), detailing ways to end unjust laws by advocating for organizations' adopting operating guidelines such as non-segregation of races, equal and fair pay and employment practices for all employees, developing training programs to prepare nonwhites for managerial jobs, and improving the quality of employees' lives outside the work environment. By the 1980s, the Rev. Sullivan worked for ending apartheid in South Africa and the release of Nelson Mandela by convincing businesses internationally to apply economic pressure in South Africa.

The power of disrupting *business as usual* in order to accomplish moral goals is one way the Rev. Sullivan's activism worked to harness the power of business to affect positive change for social justice. Historically, the Rev. Sullivan's selective patronage campaign was perhaps one of the most successful consumer boycotts designed to grab the attention of corporate managements moving too slowly in hiring African American/Black employees in certain positions.

Concerned about unemployment and poor living conditions among Black communities, the Rev. Sullivan inspired 400 spiritual leaders in Philadelphia and other major U.S. cities in solidarity to strategically visit managers at corporations that were not hiring African American/Black people in certain jobs and if the visit proved unsuccessful in persuading managers to change their ways, the spiritual leaders used the pulpit to encourage parishioners to participate in selective patronage "Don't buy where you can't work" campaigns (Sullivan, 1969, 1998). Today, the principles of equal rights are at work globally as the legacy of this Baptist minister, civil rights leader, and social activist who organized job training for marginalized people, General Motors board of directors member, and anti-apartheid activist. He spoke truth to power and turned the tide of public opinion.

Resources

Sullivan, L. H. (1969). *Build brother build*. Macrae Smith Company.
Sullivan, L. H. (1998). *Moving mountains: The principles and purposes of Leon Sullivan*. Judson Press.

What is DEI?

Diversity, *equity*, and *inclusion* are words we hear used in many places and contexts—in both positive and negative ways. Plenty of disagreement surrounds these terms and there is no one uniform definition for them. In organizational contexts, some researchers conceptualize work group diversity in terms of variety, separation, and disparity (Biemann & Kearney, 2010). Others consider demographic, informational, and personality attributes as another way to define diversity (Van Knippenberg & Schippers, 2007). According to Cox (2001), diversity is

> the variation of social and cultural identities among people existing together in a defined employment or market setting" (p. 3) [wherein] "social and cultural identity refers to personal affiliations with groups that research has shown to have significant influence on people's major life experiences.
>
> (p. 4)

The acronym DEI (diversity, equity, inclusion) has emerged in recent years—with no one person credited with conjoining the terms—to expand on ways we think about diversity by adding dimensions of equity and inclusion. For example, thinking about ways to diversify a workforce while also making it equitable and inclusionary are important considerations for employees' quality of life at work and opportunities to advance and maximize their potential. Another way to think about defining diversity is to consider one organizational theorist's straightforward assessment that there must be as much diversity within an organization as there is outside it for the organization to be optimally effective (Weick, 1979). Back in the 1980s, diversity became a popular buzzword and a widely circulated *Workforce 2000* report published by the Hudson Institute for the U.S. Department of Labor was hotly debated as a context for framing policy discussions. The report predicted labor shortages and anticipated that by 2000, five-sixths of U.S. workers would be women, African American/Black, Latino/a, and immigrants (Johnston & Packer, 1987). Fast forward four decades, journalist Pamela Newkirk (2020) suggested that workplace diversity initiatives have proved unsuccessful in bringing equality to major institutions and industries in the U.S. This could mean that organizational contexts make little more than a buzzword out of diversity (Allen, 2011), with some forgetting that the underlying and original intent of diversity is antidiscrimination (Newkirk, 2019).

Further sharpening our view on how DEI actually happens (or not) in organizations requires a deeper investigation of internal and external factors that interplay.

An inside look at organizations

Whether nonprofit or for-profit organizations adhere to strategic or altruistic motivations, DEI has become big business. The diversity consultant industry has boomed within the past decade and organizational hiring/promotion of people to serve as *diversity professional* has flourished, too (Newkirk, 2019). While these measures could be indicators that organizations authentically want to improve their hiring and promotion infrastructures, others have suggested that lip service to DEI programs minimizes potentially negative outcomes in courts of law is more often the motivation since "the diversity apparatus doesn't have to work—it just has to exist—and it can help shield a company against successful bias lawsuits" (Newkirk, 2019). Overall, organizations are ill equipped to avoid homophily because they lack the practice and perhaps the willingness to succeed at authentic DEI with Caucasian/White majorities preferring to maintain their privilege in organizations rather than endure what some perceive as reverse discrimination (Lindemann et al., 2020). Reverse discrimination is the favoring of groups who are/have been discriminated against.

Results of social science research on diversity in teams conducted over the past 65 years suggest numerous benefits associated with organizational diversity, even though equal access and opportunity remain optimistic but necessary goals while the glass ceiling persists (Catalyst, 2020). Management consultant and diversity advocate Marilyn Loden introduced the glass-ceiling term a little over 40 years ago to describe an invisible organizational barrier that keeps women and BIPOC groups from rising to top management ranks in organizations (100 Women, 2017). From a greater-good, or ethical-moral grounds standpoint, enabling employees to achieve their maximum potential without roadblocks of organizational bias and discrimination is the right thing to do (Baselga-Pascual et al., 2018). According to The Business Roundtable of nearly 200 major U.S. corporations (Fitzgerald, 2019), a corporation's purpose is "investing in employees, delivering value to customers, dealing ethically with suppliers and supporting outside communities." Thus, human resource executives suggest that main benefits of diversity among employee teams—as they positively reflect on the bottom line, consistent with business case arguments—include good use of talent, deep marketplace understanding, and enhanced problem-solving abilities and creativity (Robinson & Dechant, 1997).

Organizations have found that embracing DEI in the executive suite is a prerequisite for organization-wide DEI programs' success across ranks. Recent research on CEO activism, or corporate social advocacy, formalizes a growing trend of corporate concerns for the greater good, including authentic DEI (e.g., Chatterji & Toffel, 2018; Dodd & Supa, 2015). Observers have attributed CEOs' direct and public engagement with social issues like DEI to a period early in former U.S. President Donald Trump's administration when a travel ban to the U.S. was exacted against citizens of seven Muslim countries and several CEOs took to social media to oppose the executive order (Weber Shandwick, 2017). Similarly, Apple CEO Tim Cook publicly opposed a bill in Indiana in 2015 and advocated for Republican Governor Mike Pence to sign a revised version of the law that made it clear that it would not allow discrimination based on sexuality (Senzee, 2015).

Yet from a strategic, business case standpoint, accurately measuring how increased diversity of organizations and work teams affects work processes and performance outcomes remains a challenge (e.g., Kochan et al., 2003). One set of research findings suggests that disrupting homophily can negatively impact social integration and communication, increasing group conflict when organization members resist change (e.g., Webber & Donahue, 2001). Such an outcome may be one reason why some organizations have begun publishing dashboards, accountability reports, and DEI strategic plans—to illustrate progress on important goals, like DEI work. Some academic researchers encourage organizations to reframe their strategic perspective if the ethical/moral argument does not provide enough evidence that DEI thinking is the best course of action. Mannix and Neale (2005) suggested that rather than working to directly link DEI to performance, researchers instead should focus on links between DEI and group processes by encouraging and rewarding change, for example. Similarly, other researchers have advocated for organizations to change from the inside at top levels, with corporations reconfiguring their boards of directors to make them more diverse (Newkirk, 2020; Pompper et al., 2021). Human resources departments charged to manage employees can help organizations to evolve from homophily to spaces where DEI is embraced, too. For example, Marques (2010) advocated for greater attention to "diversity-focused communication flow" among HR and other departments (p. 444) and Appelbaum and colleagues (2015) emphasized that DEI initiatives for genuine employee connections makes everyone feel appreciated and welcome.

Another route for organizations to consider when plotting a forward course in tearing down barriers created by homophily is to consider social justice (Steimel, 2021) and employees' intersecting social identities: avoiding any tendency to overgeneralize and categorize social groups, but remembering that each human being consists of multiple social identity dimensions of age, class, culture, ethnicity, faith/spirituality, gender, physical/psychological ability, sexual orientation, and more as they intersect to uniquely shape us. Results of the 2020 U.S. Census suggest that families across the U.S. have *grown more diverse* (Tavernise et al., 2021) and that census takers took advantage in a census form change allowing them to report on their social identity in greater detail. Considering just the social identity dimension of race, for a moment, the number of non-Hispanic Americans identifying as multiracial spiked by 127% since 2010 with many people of mixed race reporting a wide range of identities (Tavernise et al., 2021). Considering the even wider range of social identity dimensions, ways these intersect, and the fact that we bring our "whole self" to work (Creed & Scully, 2000, p. 392), it is more important than ever to understand how permeable walls are that may appear to separate organizational culture from the outside (Ringel et al., 2018).

External factors driving organizations' internal DEI efforts

Social norms and media narratives are just as much a part of organizational culture as the break room and the company intranet in driving internal DEI goals and outcomes. Increasingly, organizations face scrutiny for what they do and don't do to make infrastructural change that replaces homophily with authentic DEI. Chief in driving such analysis are media and social movements like #MeToo and #BlackLivesMatter that bring attention to bias, discrimination, and stalled DEI efforts.

Widely publicized industry awards and world's-most-admired-companies lists offer a platform for observing which for-profit organizations have recognized DEI benefits and amplify their efforts in negotiating systemic change, satisfying employees, and attracting top talent. Starbucks' closure of retail outlets in 2019 so that employees could participate in unconscious bias in the workplace training—after a Philadelphia employee called the police on African American/Black men sitting in the store without buying anything—elevated public discourse about workplace bias (Polonskaia & Royal, 2019).

Company leaders seek to increase their rankings on *Fortune* magazine most-admired lists and industry scorecards to impress not only employees, but other audiences, like stockholders (Jung & Pompper, 2014). The media and information firm, Reuters, created a Diversity and Inclusion Index to rank more than 5,000 publicly traded companies according to factors that define diverse and inclusive workplaces. Companies then use a good score to publicize their brands. The Global Reporting Index, for corporations' social responsibility reporting, also includes a DEI ranking score. Similarly, organizations also hope to avoid negative publicity resulting from embarrassing missteps that could reveal a less-than-authentic DEI commitment, such as when a Victoria's Secret chief marketing officer apologized for comments he made during an interview with *Vogue* magazine about why a transsexual could not represent the women's lingerie brand (Winchel, 2018).

Figure 1.3 People who identify as transsexual want to feel that organizations represent them accurately, that organizations respect them, and that they
feel as though they belong.

Consumer boycotts, such as those discussed in Sidebar 1.2, and stock-
holder activism pressure companies to change their behaviors consistent
with goals of social movements. For example, in 2014, Cover Girl's "get
your game face on" campaign earned the scorn of domestic violence activists who created a social media meme by altering an ad to feature a black
eye on the model wearing a Baltimore Ravens jersey in the wake of an elevator video showing Ravens running back Ray Rice knocking his fiancée
unconscious (Elejalde-Ruiz, 2014). The image used in the Photoshopped
Cover Girl ad was a highly powerful protest against the NFL when the
nonprofit organization inaccurately reflected on timing of when it saw the
elevator videotape (Richards, 2014). Social media participants demanded
that Cover Girl seek firing of NFL commissioner Rodger Goodell, but as of
the date of this book, this has not happened.

Social norms and media narratives are powerful external factors driving
DEI attention across organizations and around the world via social media
platforms.

Communication and difference

In recent years, workplaces have become more inclusive of difference
(opposite of homophily) among employees by dismantling degrees of
bureaucratic rigidity of the 20th century. Creating an inclusive and equitable organization shaped by belonging where we work and volunteer

while dismantling homophily and building DEI depends on information, respect, and communication skills. Essentially, communication aids in the construction of social identity and its performance through enforcement, renegotiation, and management (e.g., Ashcraft & Allen, 2003; Ashcraft & Mumby, 2004), involving interplay with difference as a "central organizing principle of the workplace" (Mumby, 2013, p. 229). In other words, having a communication perspective is necessary for shaping structures and work practices (Ashcraft, 2011) in support of difference.

Social identities, or *difference* (Orbe & Harris, 2001), is socially constructed and communicatively transmitted via talk in interpersonal situations, texts, and other mediated forms. However, not all social identities are considered the same, with some more and less valued than others. These dynamics make understanding of social identity intersectionality and even something as simple as filling out a questionnaire like the U.S. Census form even more complicated! At their roots, social identity dimensions are connected to power and what many define as *normal*; a central feature that will be examined in great detail throughout this book, particularly in Chapter 4, "Power differentials in organizations and society."

Increasingly, organizations have interpreted effects of globalization and rapid economic, social, and political change as risk and lessened control. Read more deeply about this in Chapter 2, "Factoring in globalization, (mis)trust, risk, and sociopolitical contexts." It is important to recognize that audiences have greatly influenced organizations as people exchange opinions and share information about organizations across social media. In particular, corporations translate these massive changes as potential sources of conflict that amplify risks to their reputation. Therefore, efforts to enact control on the internal goings-on within organizations seem somewhat within organizations' reach and control. Preserving the status quo (things as usual)—according to a social homophily thesis—can appear to facilitate ease in communication, diffuse conflict, and reduce management costs (Appold et al., 1998). Yet efforts to keep any workforce homogeneous are inconsistent with general population trends and are perceived as discriminatory for breaking with the spirit of Title VII of the Civil Rights Act of 1964. Simply put, it is illegal to discriminate in the workplace under laws enforced by the U.S. Equal Employment Opportunity Commission (EEOC). Yet, thousands of people report job discrimination to the government each year (Jameel & Yerardi, 2019) and organizations continually fail to reflect (on the inside) the populations they serve on the outside.

Communication is the basis for managing DEI in organizations. Communication can be reduced to a tug of war over power—who has it and doesn't want to let go and who doesn't have it but wants it. Whereas using communication to change, negotiate, and share power often is the more productive route. Diversity, as encouraged and supported via infrastructural and system change in organizations to allow greater access and social justice for all, should grow—and public relations practitioners can offer leadership to make this happen (Edwards, 2015).

Concluding thoughts

Public relations practitioners who accept and celebrate intersectionalities of people's social identity dimensions offer significant value to organizations they work with—and society overall. Applying theory as a practical tool helps public relations practitioners to accomplish this goal. Indeed, this talent is intrinsic to what it means to be a socially responsible and ethical public relations practitioner. While *audience segmentation* has become an engrained facet of constructing and amplifying messages, this work must be accomplished without stereotyping or inadvertently doing harm, such as offending a community's history or present lived experiences. Understanding and applying theories explored in this book enables public relations practitioners to avoid building and fortifying silos that continue to marginalize, symbolically annihilate, or narrowly define communities and groups. Overall, recognizing differences between audience segmentation that is done respectfully and mindfully is very different from audience segmentation that defaults to hackneyed and false stereotypes.

Theory also assists in recognizing ways social identity dimensions intersect to produce complex realities that we must clearly understand when communicating about and representing social identity dimensions interpersonally in organizations and across media platforms. Recognizing and revising infrastructural systems that preserve privilege—such as White/ Caucasian-ness, heterosexuality, and able-bodiedness (to name a few examples)—involves unpacking the invisible knapsack as an integral component of managing DEI and putting organizations in the best position to support and amplify social justice. Embracing the external forces driving internal DEI efforts requires respect for belonging, understanding, and willingness to assume risks associated with constant change. Dismantling homophily and its glass ceiling in support of social justice inside organizations and within the scope of organizations' influence is hard work worth doing. Yet, at the same time, public relations practitioners must avoid universality thinking about publics—regardless of their social identity dimensions. Thinking about publics as one-size-fits-all when making decisions and establishing policies that affect them is a serious shortcoming among organizations and these issues are covered in greater detail in Chapter 6, "Universality thinking about publics and its pitfalls."

Next, in Chapter 2, "Factoring in globalization, (mis)trust, risk and sociopolitical contexts," we offer fundamentals for becoming more knowledgeable and confident about developing competence when counseling organizations about DEI, belonging, and social justice. Being prepared for informal discussions, as well as organizations' policy-making table, is the responsibility of every professional communicator. Hence, examining backdrops to why and how organizations cling to homophily that relies on deep-rooted -isms like sexism and racism will offer meaningful examinations of why some organizations cling to the past rather than embracing our multicultural world and its challenges. Embracing diversity and accepting the implications of audiences' intersecting social identity dimensions are outcomes of degrees of trust and risk (both real and perceived). Combined, these factors significantly impact relationship building across individuals, groups, and organizations—for an overall goal of building/enhancing belonging.

Key words

BIPOC—Acronym for Black, Indigenous, and People of Color who are individuals from historically excluded groups, particularly people of low income (Estien et al., 2021). In many organizational spaces, BIPOC experience systemic racism and implicit bias that materializes in challenges in achieving their maximum potential and advancing professionally. According to the *Merriam-Webster* dictionary, BIPOC has replaced POC (People of Color) to acknowledge that not all people of color face the same kinds or degrees of social injustice (BIPOC, 2021).

DEI—Acronym for diversity, equity, and inclusion used as part of programs designed to reveal and remedy implicit bias in organizations and industry. For example, the philanthropic community prepared a nationwide report addressing gains and how far "we still have to go" to make philanthropy socially just (Olivo et al., 2016).

Diversity—In organizational settings, diversity may be defined in terms of separation, disparity, and variety (Harrison & Klein, 2007). The U.S. Department of Defense created a Board on Diversity and Inclusion to foster workplaces "where diversity and individual differences are valued and leveraged to achieve the vision and mission of the organization . . . to avoid stereotypical responses and behavior" (Brown et al., 2021, p. 36).

Equity—Measuring degrees of diversity in organizations can include evaluating how equal opportunities are for success and advancement among all employees and volunteers. It can refer to the specific tools and accommodations each person needs. For example, some people may need to work from home due to a medical condition in order to fulfill their potential at their job (Soken-Huberty, n.d.)

Inclusion—Degrees of employee and volunteer perceptions that they and people like them feel an authentic part of their organization offers one measure of authentic diversity in organizations. Research methods such as interviews and surveys help organizations to assess how people feel about inclusion in their workplace (Brown et al., 2021).

Intersectionality—As a tool for activism in ensuring people's social identity dimensions are respected in organizations, the foundations for this political and intellectual movement are built in Kimberlé Crenshaw's critique of the U.S. legal system and treatment of Black women (Grzanka, 2014). Others consider the Combahee River Collective Statement of 1977 as its inspiration. This Black feminist organization critiqued ways that a White feminist movement was "not addressing their particular needs" or intersectional social identities of gender, ethnicity, and sexual orientation (The Combahee, 2016).

Invisible knapsack—In her assessment of White privilege, Peggy McIntosh (1989) used this metaphor to describe "unearned assets" that White people are born with but may not realize they have—which BIPOC people do not enjoy. She wrote, "White privilege is like an invisible weightless knapsack of special provisions, maps, passports, codebooks, visas, clothes, tools and blank checks" (McIntosh, 1989, p. 10).

Professional communicator—This refers to people who co-create meaning (Krippendorf, 1994) using oral, written, visual, and digital forms of information as part of their employment or volunteer work since "effective communication ensures a smooth flow of ideas, facts, decisions, and advice" (Definition, n.d.). Professionals are people who work to meet "the societal need for expertise and credentialism" as they link individuals with the larger society (Leeper & Leeper, 2005, p. 645). Professional communicators are highly valued for their accuracy, clarity/brevity, and more (Definition, n.d.)

Reductionism—This perspective is one that should be avoided—as when considering one social identity set or experiences as representing a collective group's overall social and cultural interpretation or reality. The diversity of people's experiences must not "render social life in terms of just one analytic strategy" (Atkinson & Delamont, 2008, p. 688), but rather consider each person's unique reality according to the social identity dimensions that constitute them.

Social communication theory—Rooted in the social cultural tradition, communication is a process involving concepts like social structure, norms, rituals, collective belief systems, and identities. People's view of reality is shaped by the language they use since infancy (Griffin, 2003).

Social constructionism—Communication theorist and media critic James Carey posited that humans create symbols and then "take up residence in the world we have produced" (Carey, 1989, p. 30). Symbols convey large amounts of information quickly and succinctly—through writing and images—and over space and time (Leeds-Hurwitz, 1993). As such, language is used to change the world.

Discussion questions for deep engagement

1. On a piece of paper, list your own social identity dimensions. How do they intersect to make you unique? Which dimensions suggest you might have privilege (or not)—and why or why not?
2. Consider your earliest memory in as much detail as you can. Thinking about how you feel about this memory, in what ways do words and images help you to recall it? In other words, how are the images and feelings shaped by your own social identity and the culture you grew up in? How is your memory—and the way you feel about it now—socially constructed?
3. The next time you go to school, shopping, work, or to your place of worship, take a mental note of how much diversity you see. Consider how you're defining diversity. What does what you see say about those organizations—and your perspective?
4. Visit the Instagram or other social media site of someone you really admire. How are they communicating about their own social identity? How might their site be influencing others?
5. Google any social identity dimension like "sexual orientation" and select the Images link. What kinds of symbols do you see? How diverse are the people in the images that appear? What are the words you see being used to represent "sexual orientation"?

Resources

100 Women: 'Why I invented the glass ceiling phrase.' (2017, December 13). BBC. Downloaded August 15, 2021 from https://www.bbc.com/news/world-42026266

Allen, B. J. (2011). *Difference matters: Communicating social identity*, 2nd ed. Waveland Press, Inc.

Appelbaum, L., Walton, F., Southerland, E. (2015). An examination of factors affecting the success of underrepresented groups in the public relations profession. Report, City College of New York.

Appold, S. J., Siengthai, S., & Kasarda, J. D. (1998). The employment of women managers and professionals in an emerging economy: Gender inequality as an organizational practice. *Administrative Science Quarterly*, 43, 538–565. DOI: 10.2307/2393675.

Ashcraft, K. L. (2011). Knowing work through the communication of difference: A revised agenda for difference studies. In D. K. Mumby (Ed.), *Reframing difference in organizational communication studies: Research, pedagogy, practice* (pp. 3–30). Sage.

Ashcraft, K. L., & Allen, B. J. (2003). The racial foundation of organizational communication. *Communication Theory*, 13, 5–38. DOI: https://doi.org/10.1111/j.1468-2885.2003.tb00280.x

Ashcraft, K. L., & Mumby, D. K. (2004). *Reworking gender: A feminist communicology of organization*. Sage.

Atkinson, P., & Delamont, S. (2008). Analytic perspectives. In N. K. Denzin and Y. S. Lincoln (Eds.) *Collecting and interpreting qualitative materials* (pp. 285–311). Sage.

Bandura, A. (1977). *Social learning theory*. Prentice Hall.

Baselga-Pascual, L., Trujillo-Ponce, A., Vahamaa, E., & Vahamaa, S. (2018). Ethical reputation of financial institutions: Do board characteristics matter? *Journal of Business Ethics*, 148, 489–510. DOI: https://doi.org/10.1007/s10551-015-2949-x

Biemann, T., & Kearney, E. (2010). Size does matter: How varying group sizes in a sample affect the most common measures of group diversity. *Organizational Research Methods*, 13(3), 582–599. DOI: 10.1177/1094428109338875

BIPOC. Merriam-Webster.com Dictionary, Merriam-Webster. Downloaded August 27, 2021 from: https://www.merriam-webster.com/dictionary/BIPOC.

Brown, B., Carlucci, R., & Stewart, S. (2021). Holding ourselves accountable: Building scorecards for diversity and inclusion. *Phalanx*, 54(2), 36–43.

Carey, J. W. (1989). *Culture as communication: Essays on media and society*. Unwin Hyman.

Catalyst (2020). Women in management. Downloaded August 15, 2021 from: https://www.catalyst.org/research/women-in-management/

Chatterji, A. K., & Toffel, M. W. (2018, January–March). The new CEO Activists. *Harvard Business Review*, 78–89. Retrieved from: https://hbr.org/2018/01/the-new-ceo-activists

Connell, R. W. (2005). *Masculinities*. University of California Press.

Conway, S. (2020). Poisonous pantheons: God of War and toxic masculinity. *Games and Culture*, 15(8), 943–961. DOI: 10.1177/1555412019858898

Cox, T. (2001). *Creating the multicultural organization: A strategy for capturing the power of diversity*. Jossey-Bass.

Craig, R. T. (1999). Communication theory as a field. *Communication Theory*, 9(2), 119–161. DOI: https://doi.org/10.1111/j.1468-2885.1999.tb00355.x

Creed, W. E. D., & Scully, M. A. (2000). Songs of ourselves: Employees' deployment of social identity in workplace encounters. *Journal of Management Inquiry*, 9, 391–412. DOI: https://doi.org/10.1177%2F105649260000900410

Crenshaw, K. W. (1989). Demarginalizing the intersection of race and sex: A Black feminist critique of antidiscrimination doctrine, feminist theory and antiracist politics. *University of Chicago Legal Forum 1989*, 139–167. DOI: https://rb.gy/3xgq2h

Definition (n.d.) Definition and top eight features of professional communication. hrdevelopmentinfo.com Accessed August 27, 2021 from https://rb.gy/ncgkao

Dodd, M. D., & Supa, D. (2015). Testing the viability of corporate social advocacy as a predictor of purchase intention. *Communication Research Reports*, 32(4), 287–293. DOI: http://dx.doi.org/10.1080/08824096.2015.1089853

Edwards, L. (2015). *Power, diversity and public relations*. Routledge.

Eisenmenger, A. (2019). Ableism 101: What it is, what it looks like, and what we can do to fix it. Blog downloaded August 12, 2021 from https://rb.gy/viy9qc

Elejalde-Ruiz, A. (2014). Cover Girl 'game face' ad becomes part of NFL scandal. *Chicago Tribune*. Downloaded August 14, 2021 from https://rb.gy/njnhq5

Estien, C. O., Myron, E. B., Oldfield, C. A., Alwin, A., & Ecological Society of America Student Section (2021). Virtual scientific conferences: Benefits and how to support underrepresented students. *Bulletin of the Ecological Society of America*, 102(2), 1–12. DOI: https://www.jstor.org/stable/10.2307/27000722

Festinger, L., Schachter, S., & Back, K. W. (1950). *Social pressures in informal groups*. Harper.

Fitzgerald, M. (2019). The CEOs of nearly 200 companies just said shareholder value is no longer their main objective. Downloaded August 21, 2019 from https://cnb.cx/2QMr345.

Greenberg, J. (2017). 10 examples that prove White privilege exists in every aspect imaginable. *Yes! Solutions Journalism*. Downloaded August 12, 2021 from https://rb.gy/rbejqx

Greenwood, D. J., & Levin, M. (1998). *Introduction to action research: Social research for social change*. Sage.

Griffin, E. (2003). *A first look at communication theory* (5th ed.). McGraw Hill.

Grzanka, P. R. (2014). Introduction. In P. R. Grzanka (Ed.) *Intersectionality: A foundations and frontiers reader* (pp. xi–xxvii). Westview Press.

Harrison, D. A., & Klein, K. J. (2007). What's the difference? Diversity constructs as separation, variety, or disparity in organizations. *Academy of Management Review*, 32, 4, 1199–1228. DOI: https://doi.org/10.5465/amr.2007.26586096

hooks, b. (2000). *Feminist theory from margin to center*, 2nd ed. South End Press.

Jameel, M., & Yerardi, J. (2019). Workplace discrimination is illegal. But our data shows it's still a huge problem. *Vox*. Downloaded August 25, 2021 from https://rb.gy/vq7iq8

Jiang, S., & Ngien, A. (2020). The effects of Instagram use, social comparison, and self-esteem on social anxiety: A survey study in Singapore. *Social Media & Society*, 1–10. DOI: https://doi.org/10.1177%2F2056305120912488

Johnston, W. B., & Packer, A. H. (1987). *Workforce 2000: Work and workers in the 21st century*. Hudson Institute.

Jung, T., & Pompper, D. (2014). Assessing instrumentality of mission statements and social-financial performance links: Corporate social responsibility as context. *International Journal of Strategic Communication*, 8(2), 79–99. DOI: https://doi.org/10.1080/1553118X.2013.873864

Kilbourne, J. (2010). *Killing us softly 4: Advertising's image of women*. Media Education Foundation.

Kochan, T., Bezrukova, K., Ely, R., Jackson, S., Joshi, A., Jehn, K., Leonard, J., Levine, D., & Thomas, D. (2003). The effects of diversity on business performance: Report of the diversity research network. *Human Resource Management*, 42, 3–21. DOI: https://doi.org/10.1002/hrm.10061

Krippendorf, K. (1994). A recursive theory of communication. In D. Crowley and D. Mitchell (Eds.), *Communication theory today* (pp. 78–104). Polity Press.

Lazarsfeld, P. F., & Merton, R. K. (1954). Friendship as a social process. In M. Berger, T. Abel, and C. H. Page (Eds.), Freedom and control in modern society (pp. 18–66). Van Nostrand.

Leeds-Hurwitz, W. (1993). *Semiotics and communication: Signs, codes, cultures*. Lawrence Erlbaum Associates, Publishers.

Leeper, K. A., Leeper, R. V. (2005). Professional and professionalism. In R. L. Heath (Ed.), *Encyclopedia of public relations* (pp. 645–647). Sage.

Lindemann, B., Grossman, P., Weirich, G. (2020). *Employment discrimination law*. 6th ed. ABA Book Publishing.

Mannix, E., & Neale, M. A. (2005). What differences make a difference? The promise and reality of diverse teams in organizations. *Psychological Science in the Public Interest*, 6(2), 31–55. DOI: https://doi.org/10.1111/j.1529-1006.2005.00022.x

Marques, J. F. (2010). Colorful window dressing: A critical review on workplace diversity in three major American corporations. *Human Resource Development Quarterly*, 21(4), 435–446. DOI: https://doi.org/10.1002/hrdq.20045

McIntosh, P. (1989). White privilege: Unpacking the invisible knapsack. *Peace and Freedom*, July/August, 10–12. Wellesley College Center for Research on Women.

Melamed, D., Simpson, B., Harrell, A., Munn, C. W., Abernathy, J. Z., & Sweitzer, M. (2020). Homophily and segregation in cooperative networks. *American Journal of Sociology*, 125(4), 1084–1127. DOI: https://doi.org/10.1086/708142

Miles, A. L. (2020). Disability: What have Black people got to do with it? *Black Perspectives*. Downloaded August 25, 2021 from https://rb.gy/3m7er3

Mumby, D. K. (2013). *Organizational communication: A critical approach*. Sage.

Nakayama, T. K., & Krizek, R. L. (1995). Whiteness: A strategic rhetoric. *Quarterly Journal of Speech*, 81, 291–301. DOI: https://doi.org/10.1080/00335639509384117

Newkirk, P. (2019). Diversity has become a booming business. So where are the results? *Time*. Downloaded August 14, 2021 from https://time.com/5696943/diversity-business/

Newkirk, P. (2020). *Diversity Inc.: The fight for racial equality in the workplace*. Bold Type Books.

O'Brien, B. G., Barreto, M. A., & Sanchez, G. R. (2020). They're all out to get me! Assessing inter-group competition among multiple populations. *Politics, Groups, and Identities*, 8(5), 867–893. DOI: https://doi.org/10.1080/21565503.2019.16 29305

Olivo, S., & Weissblum, C. R. (2016). Less talking, more doing: Operationalizing diversity, equity, and inclusion in philanthropy. Philanthropy New York. Accessed August 27, 2021 from https://rb.gy/yetdae

Orbe, M., & Harris, T. M. (2001). *Interracial communication: Theory into practice*. Wadsworth.

Polonskaia, A., & Royal, M. (2019). How the world's most admired companies drive D&I. *Human Resource Executive*. Downloaded August 15, 2021 from https://rb.gy/gnjped

Pompper, D., & Crandall, K. (2014). The erotic-chaste dialectic and the new southern belle code at the high school prom: Feminine gender role stress across ethnic and socio-economic factors. *The Journal of Popular Culture*, 47(5), 937–951. DOI: https://doi.org/10.1111/jpcu.12180

Pompper, D., Ertem-Eray, T., Amevor, E., Diop, L., Nadel, S., & Adae, E. K. (2021). Diversity at the big table: A snapshot of Fortune 500 boards of directors. In D. Pompper (Ed.) *Public relations for social responsibility: Affirming DEI commitment with action* (pp. 51–69). Emerald Group Publishing Limited.

Pompper, D., & Merskin, D. (2020). The more things change? Social identity representations among 'The 50 Best Kids' Books Published in the Last 25 Years'. *Journal of Popular Culture*, 53(5), 1135–1159. DOI: https://doi.org/10.1111/jpcu.12959

Richards, K. (2014). This Photoshopped Cover Girl ad is the most powerful protest against the NFL we've seen. *Business Insider*. Downloaded November 23, 2023 from https://www.businessinsider.com/photoshopped-nfl-covergirl-ad-2014-9

Ringel, L.; Hiller, P. & Zietsma, C. (2018). Toward permeable boundaries of organizations? In L. Ringel, P. Hiller, & C. Zietsma (Eds.), *Research in the Sociology of Organizations* (pp. 3–28). Emerald Publishing.

Robinson, G., & Dechant, K. (1997). Building a business case for diversity. *Academy of Management Executive*, 11(3), 21–31. DOI: https://doi.org/10.5465/ame.1997.9709231661

Senzee, T. (2015). Tim Cook's Apple and Mike Pence's Indiana: One's the future, the other the past. *Advocate*. Downloaded August 15, 2021 from https://rb.gy/oa7k7e

Soken-Huberty, E. (n.d.) Examples of equality and equity in the workplace. Human Rights Careers. Accessed August 27, 2021 from https://rb.gy/fpopzo

Steele, C. M., & Aronson, J. (1995). Stereotype threat and the intellectual test performance of African-Americans. *Journal of Personality and Social Psychology*, 69(5), 797–811. DOI: https://doi.org/10.1037//0022-3514.69.5.797

Steimel, S. J. (2021). Beyond the business case for diversity and inclusion: Approaches to promoting organizational diversity. *Communication Teacher*, 35, 3, 197–201, DOI: 10.1080/17404622.2021.1923771

Sullivan, L. H. (1998). *Moving mountains: The principles and purposes of Leon Sullivan*. Judson Press.

Tavernise, S., Mzezewa, T., & Heyward, G. (2021). Behind the surprising jump in multiracial Americans, several theories. *New York Times*. Downloaded August 15, 2021 from https://www.nytimes.com/2021/08/13/us/census-multiracial-identity.html

The Combahee River Collective Statement (2016). Verso. Accessed August 27, 2021 from https://rb.gy/0uipsb

Van de Mieroop, K. (2016). On the advantage and disadvantage of Black history month for life: The creation of the post-racial era. *History and Theory*, 55, 1, 3–24. DOI: https://www.jstor.org/stable/24809580

Van Knippenberg, D., & Schippers, M. C. (2007). Work group diversity. *Annual Review of Psychology*, 58, 515–541. DOI: http://dx.doi.org/10.1146/annurev.psych.58.110405.085546

Van Maanen, J. (1979). Reclaiming qualitative methods for organizational research: A preface. *Administrative Science Quarterly*, 24, 520–526. DOI: https://doi.org/10.2307/2392358

Webber, S., & Donahue, L. (2001). Impact of highly and less job-related diversity on work group cohesion and performance: A meta-analysis. *Journal of Management*, 27, 141–162. DOI: https://doi.org/10.1177%2F014920630102700202

Weber Shandwick. (2017). CEO activism in 2017: High noon in the C-suite. https://www.webershandwick.com/uploads/news/files/ceo-activism-in-2017-high-noon-in-the-c-suite.pdf

Weick, K. E. (1979). *The social psychology of organizing*, 2nd ed. Addison-Wesley.

Winchel, B. (2018). Victoria's Secret exec apologizes after interview gaffe. *Ragan's PR Daily*. Downloaded August 15, 2021 from https://rb.gy/5neyet

2 Factoring in globalization, (mis)trust, risk, and sociopolitical contexts

Tugce Ertem-Eray

Upon the foundation built so far in the previous chapter's introduction of key terms and issues relative to DEI—and why they matter in the context of communication practice—this chapter offers the fundamentals for counseling organizations operating as part of the globalization trend. The reason why we offer this backdrop is so that readers may more easily understand the complexity of what happens when organizations fail to embrace DEI. Specifically, when organizations do not make people feel that they belong and that their social identity dimensions (and ways they intersect) are respected, audiences hold back on extending their trust in and to those organizations. Today, this dynamic is a risk that organizations cannot afford to take. Therefore, building a sense of belonging and real relationships connecting organizations and audiences must be a priority.

So, just what is globalization? **Globalization** is a process by which people across vast physical distances become connected in more and different ways (Lechner & Boli, 2019). One effect of this process is that people of various cultures and walks of life encounter one another more than ever before in human history. Organizations of all sizes, whether for-profit or nonprofit, operate amidst this reality. Enabling audiences to feel genuinely respected is no small order, given that organizations—especially corporations—long have operated with goals of mostly reducing conflict that could interrupt operations (Rao, 2011). Merely trying to reduce conflict is not nearly enough for embracing DEI, so this chapter dives deeply into the globalization phenomenon to underscore its relevance to embracing DEI within organizations and across audiences.

A key impact of globalization that has significantly impacted organizations' attention to DEI is the reality of the globalization trend in accelerating multiculturalism in organizations and across audiences impacted by organizations (Hong & Cheon, 2017). **Multiculturalism** is a term broadly used to refer to a culturally heterogeneous population (Van de Vijver et al., 2008). The international division of labor, the spread of various cultures,

DOI: 10.4324/9781003279129-3

and immigration in the workplace are all outcomes associated with globalization. In many ways, these are great opportunities for sharing and learning since the coexistence of different cultural communities in the workplace and other spaces offers opportunities to celebrate multiculturalism. Multiculturalism also includes respecting ways cultural groups coexist in the organization while maintaining their distinct identity. Because globalization trends require communicators to understand how individuals shaped across cultures coexist within the workplace, this chapter offers advice on how to develop intercultural competence for embracing cultural diversity. Developing intercultural competency helps communication practitioners understand cultures, reduce their fear of cultures, make them want to learn more about cultures, and feel that they have become more tolerant of immigrants (Ertem-Eray, 2021). Therefore, this chapter helps communication practitioners understand the importance of creating an environment in which everyone can live and work harmoniously by offering a focused examination of globalization's implications such as multiculturalism.

No discussion about globalization and multiculturalism is complete without acknowledging that ethnocentrism is the antithesis (opposite) of multiculturalism. Ethnocentrism is a mindset which thwarts DEI efforts, as covered later in this chapter. Ethnocentric perspectives mean failure to appreciate cultural diversity within the workplace. Such outlooks often are marked by use of negative stereotypes that lead to misunderstandings, bias, discrimination, and other manifestations of unequal treatment of cultural groups in organizations. Because some organizations fail to change with the times while globalization has accelerated cultural diversity within the workplace, negative outcomes shaped by ethnocentrism endure (Ely & Thomas, 2020). Organizations must avoid amplifying ethnocentric values and negative stereotypes while accepting cultural diversity. One way to do this is to improve intercultural communication competence and to support acculturation. These are two crucial frameworks used to understand and respect cultural differences among people in the workplace—and they form the basis for sections later in this chapter.

The alternatives to fostering belonging among all people where organizations have a say are daunting, indeed. Organizations' failure to embrace DEI without recognizing the differences among audiences' cultural identity dimensions can result in those audiences' decreased trust toward organizations and increased risks for the organizations, such as reputational damage, loss of sales, and finding less talented staffing pools (Pratt, 2023)—such as when fewer people want to work for organizations mired in a past unaccepting of DEI. For example, young people declare that diversity and inclusion in the workplace are a *requirement* for them, not a *preference* (Miller, 2021).

Overall, this chapter covers these key areas for a comprehensive view of globalization, (mis)trust, risk, and sociopolitical contexts: 1) historical context of globalization, 2) multiculturalism and barriers to acceptance at work, 3) nurturing intercultural communication competence, 4) actions for organizations, and 5) concluding thoughts.

Historical context of globalization

Around the world, globalization trends have greatly influenced workplace demographics and transformed society, economics, and politics. First viewing globalization through an economic lens before examining its social implications makes good sense. According to Anthony Giddens (1990), globalization is the spread of modernization, or "the world capitalist economy" (p. 68), the nation-state system, the world military order, and the international division of labor. This means that all nation-states push their economic interests into the international arena and this can end up expanding the most powerful nations' cultures along with their economic interests. For example, globalization has involved the spread of European culture through settlement and colonization (Waters, 1995). These processes involve complex changes and adaptation, or what some critics characterize as Western cultural imperialism (Thussu, 2019). This means that in the pursuit of profit, corporations have enabled the culture of the most powerful nations to reshape or replace indigenous nations' culture—such as native people learning consumer lifestyles by watching U.S.-based media that is supported by advertising (e.g., Grixti, 2011). Critics suggest this outcome negatively impacts indigenous cultures who become forced to adopt Western values (e.g., Campbell, 2010).

Since the 1990s, researchers have expanded the globalization implications conversation beyond economics to more deeply scrutinize the trend's social implications. Chiefly, international corporations have greatly benefitted from globalization trends (Thussu, 2019) and discovered a need to manage increased cultural diversity within the workforce. Many corporations have responded by adopting new policies and guidelines for employees. Instituting employee diversity training programs, hiring consults with expertise in their implementation, and forming committees and work groups are some of the actions corporations have pursued to protect culturally diverse employees from discrimination, appreciate multiple viewpoints (McFarlin, 2019), and proactively reduce the risk of workplace discrimination and harassment claims filed in courts of law (Johnson et al., n.d.)

While there may be multiple definitions of globalization because it has many layers, dimensions, and applications, the various arenas of scrutiny have one thing in common—people become more connected around the world and grow more aware of their connections. Globalization trends mean having new opportunities to perform volunteer work, spread faith/belief systems, sample various entertainment media adapted from international formats, and manage far-flung supply chains to transfer products to stores around the globe (Lechner & Boli, 2019). Moreover, people are becoming more connected due to globalization and one symptom that nearly everyone can relate to is the spread and expansion of social movements beyond physical borders. For example, the Occupy movement connected people around the world as protesters targeted Wall Street and economic inequality perpetuated in D.C. politics (Anderson, 2021). The Occupy movement shares ties with many social movements in Latin America such as the Landless Workers Moment in Brazil which has created alternative communities to contest neoliberal policies and demand free-market capitalism, regressive taxation, and restore social services (Goudarzi et al., 2022). McKane (2014) expanded the argument to link the Occupy movement with the Global Justice Movement which works to ensure that all people can benefit from the technological potential now available. In 2017, the #MeToo movement grew to a global, survivor-led movement against sexual violence after actress Alyssa Milano invited sexual harassment and assault victims to share their sotries via social media (Brown, 2022). Even though the Occupy and #MeToo movements began in the U.S., with the help of social media, globalization trends have enabled these social movements to spread around the world. Importantly, various cultures add their unique lived experiences to the context. Adding personalized nuances to social movement protests tailors movements with cultural footprints and reveals unique concerns and needs.

Globalization and its multiculturalism effects include other benefits, too. Organizations that are culturally diverse are perceived as insightful and open-minded. Because globalization has accelerated multiculturalism, organizations rich in DEI can take pride in employees and managers who bring their talent, diverse perspectives, and problem-solving skills to work with them every day. In the U.S., for example, the Silicon Valley region has enjoyed unprecedented success in creating an environment for establishing technology businesses. This geographic area has become a hotbed of ideas generated by people hailing from a wide variety of cultures who respect differences in human beings and create equal opportunities for all regardless of their national origin (Urban Times, n.d.). The most significant factor in Silicon Valley's success has been its unique environment that champions having people with diverse skills and backgrounds who do not know one other to come together and form trust bonds and take chances together (Hwang, 2012). Internally, globalization trends can inspire organizations to change systems and infrastructures to foster a more belonging environment.

For example, Johnson & Johnson has created employee resource groups to connect and engage diverse employees across the company with a goal of creating an inclusive work environment and culture—especially across management levels for even more women and BIPOC community representation (SocialTalent, n.d.).

Multiculturalism and barriers to acceptance at work

Survival instinct responses have inspired migrations around the globe since the beginning of human existence, but the multiculturalism impacts of globalization have captured the popular imagination more recently as organizations strive to keep up with and stay ahead of social change effects linked to globalization trends. The term *multicultural* indicates cultural plurality in a specific context (Arasaratnam, 2013) and the coexistence of different cultural groups within the same political society who choose to maintain their distinct identity without completely assimilating (Raz, 1998). Use of *multiculturalism* to characterize these phenomena emerged in Canada in 1971 to recognize the importance of immigration and the blending of multiple cultures (Sloan et al., 2018). The concept has gained increased attention in the U.S. due to greater demographic diversity and a growing realization that organizations should not ignore minority groups' unique

Figure 2.1 The annual Carnaval in Rio de Janeiro in Brazil attracts the world's attention, as people representing multiple cultures participate.

experiences (Ryan et al., 2007). Despite the length of time researchers have been studying globalization trends and multicultural outcomes, paths forward in supporting organizations struggling to adapt to DEI practices has been complicated by forces shaping ethnocentrism, homophily, stereotypes, and intercultural conflict.

Historically, the 19th century witnessed the large-scale movement of people within and out of Europe to countries such as Argentina, Canada, and the U.S. (Raz, 1998). For example, 1.5 million people left Ireland for the U.S. in the wake of the Potato Famine, a period of starvation and disease from 1845 to 1852. Beginning in the 1850s, during the North American gold rush and the discovery of significant gold deposits, large numbers of Asians began arriving on the continent (Ancestry, n.d.). Amidst many large migrations, however, dominant populations usually seek to protect their privilege and preserve power hierarchies for social order (Sloan et al., 2018). Assimilation during this large-scale movement of people did not unfold easily because migrants were considered inferior people (Modood, 2013). In the U.S., the 1882 Chinese Exclusion Act limited the number of Chinese immigrants because they were seen as a threat to the U.S. labor market. This was the first time in U.S. history that an immigration law specifically targeted an ethnic group (Ancestry, n.d.). Raz (1998) has argued that "in a way, multiculturalism is one of the strands in modern political thought which is trying to undo some of the harm done by nationalism" (p. 195).

Interrogating multiculturalism offers an opportunity to peel back layers of numerous and complex power relations—including the systems and infrastructures that stifle debate, foster separatism, and deny minority communities. When DEI is considered as disrupting the status quo, then out-groups experience fears about security, employment, and resources (Sloan et al., 2018). For example, Turkish citizens complain about Syrian refugees undermining employment prospects for Turkish workers in Turkey (Makovsky, 2019). Thus, it is important to understand ways that ethnocentrism thwarts organizations' ability to embrace DEI.

Next, addressed are four specific yet related sets of challenges that threaten organizations' attempts to make DEI programs successful: ethnocentrism, homophily, stereotypes, and intercultural conflict.

Ethnocentrism

In a context of multiculturalism, **ethnocentrism** is a harsh value judgment steeped in a belief that anyone's own culture is superior to other cultures. The term *ethnocentrism* is rooted in two Greek words: *ethno* which means "one's own ethnic or cultural group" and *centrism* which means "one's own group should be looked upon as the center of the world" (Ting-Toomey & Chung, 2005, p. 234). Ethnocentrism in organizations can play out as discriminatory attitudes and behaviors that position one's own group (the in-group) as superior and out-groups as inferior (LeVine & Campbell, 1972). Ethnocentrism depends on group boundaries that are typically defined by one or more observable difference characteristics such as language, physical features, or religion (Hammond & Axelrod, 2006). Ethnocentric behaviors negatively impact ways in-group members communicate with out-groups who have different cultural backgrounds in a multicultural environment (Tagle, 2021). Therefore, ethnocentrism is considered a defense mechanism for preserving privilege and characterizes fear of change (Ting-Toomey & Chung, 2005). Overall, ethnocentric behaviors resist multiculturalism and DEI programs, directing negativity toward out-groups.

Effects of ethnocentrism in organizations are multiple and negative, possibly leading to a tarnished organizational image and reputation (Ely & Thomas, 2020). For example, ethnocentric attitudes and behaviors create tension in a multicultural workplace which could result in corroded teamwork, misunderstandings across employee groups, decrease in productivity, absenteeism, employee turnover, and disrespect of out-group values, customs, norms, and traditions. Such results negatively impact organizations' bottom line (Panicker & Sharma, 2021) and cause great human hurt and suffering (Banks, 2016).

Promoting cultural diversity, reducing conflicts among intergroup interactions, and accepting different cultures by embracing multiculturalism can motivate people to overcome ethnocentrism (Berry & Kalin, 1995). Moreover, higher levels of multiculturalism in organizations possibly leads to reduced feelings of ethnocentrism (Dong et al., 2008) as people can begin to empathize with other people's perspectives (Makedon, 1996). Sometimes, organizations featuring diverse demographics turn greater profits and can enter and capture new markets better (Glynn, 2022). Therefore, it is important to support elimination of ethnocentrism within workplaces. Having and respecting culturally diverse employees means representing all voices and differences within the organization. People from different backgrounds and experiences can share ideas and find new solutions to issues. Organizations also can send a message to the communities they serve that they value cultural diversity. Therefore, organizations must manage ethnocentrism in the workplace through employing a diverse workforce while offering cultural training, teambuilding exercises, job rotation, and enforcing policies that support workplace DEI. Indeed, the role of cultural differences in misunderstandings across organizations and their employees working around the globe can have significant implications. Check out Sidebar 2.1 to discover what happened at Apple during the pandemic.

Sidebar 2.1   Apple and pandemic working conditions in China

Tugce Ertem-Eray

Cultural differences can be a source of fun, but they also can contribute to frictions across organizations and their employees working around the globe. Because popular American brands are distributed in many nations, this means U.S. culture has spread globally. This case study of Apple, Inc., a U.S.-based global corporation, offers an example of how a popular American brand can risk losing consumer trust when manufacturing its products beyond U.S. shores during a pandemic.

Figure 2.2 Apple maintains about 46 retail stores in mainland China.

The COVID-19 pandemic forced American brands to pay greater attention to relationships with employees working beyond U.S. shores. Here's the story. In 2020, the COVID-19 pandemic crisis served as a reminder for organizations to be bold in their ambition to embrace DEI (Anand, 2022). Apple discovered just how important it is to carefully nurture supportive work environments as part of its manufacturing processes in China—while building and maintaining relationships across culturally diverse audiences.

Apple, Inc is one of the world's largest technology companies by revenue (Ponciano, 2022). Every September, Apple, Inc. announces release of its latest iPhones, and a few weeks later, new iPhones are shipped from China to customers around the world (Mickle et al., 2022). Yet, in October 2022, Apple faced manufacturing challenges at a Foxconn iPhone factory in Zhengzhou, China, a metropolis on the Yellow River, the capital of east-central China's Henan province—and the manufacturing and shipping process ground to a halt.

The problems began when workers struggled to leave the iPhone factory campus operated by Foxconn, one of Apple's biggest partners, in connection with the COVID-19 pandemic. When COVID-19 cases started to spike in Zhengzhou, Foxconn enclosed approximately 200,000 workers inside the factory so they could produce the iPhones (Mickle et al., 2022). Hundreds of workers joined the protests, with some of them smashing surveillance cameras and windows. Some workers complained about the organization's plan to delay bonus payments and others shared stories about how they were forced to share dormitories with colleagues who had tested positive for COVID-19 (Reuters, 2022). Even though Apple offered bonuses to employees who returned to work, violent protests broke out (Liu, 2022). Overall, the COVID-19 conditions and poor work conditions—including a shortage of food—made workers want to leave the factory campus (Reuters, 2022). As a result, the production slowdown in China facilitated Apple in warning investors about the negative impact of the worker protests on future iPhone shipments (Mickle et al., 2022).

Multinational organizations must attend to culture and other demographics, as well as government policies in the country where their businesses are located (Kent & Taylor, 2011; Swann, 2018). The Chinese government's strict *zero COVID* policy caused a slowdown in production, flee of employees, and a decrease in sales. Furthermore, it created a huge backlash for the organization on social media from publics criticizing Apple. For example, one Twitter user questioned how a company worth more than $2.3 trillion could treat employees by enclosing them inside the workplace during a pandemic. Social media platforms offer a real-time barometer on public opinion, as another Twitter user posted: "Further cements my loyalty to a different phone manufacturer. Apple is evil for staying silent" (Carbonaro, 2022, para. 1, 2).

This case underscored an imperative that global organizations ponder multiple considerations when their products are manufactured outside of the U.S.

Resources

Anand, R. (2022). *Leading global diversity, equity, and inclusion. A guide for systemic change in multinational organizations.* Berrett-Koehler Publishers.

Carbona, G. (2022, November 25). Apple criticized over worker conditions at China iPhone plant. *Newsweek.* https://rb.gy/iham2. Accessed June 26, 2023.

Kent, M., & Taylor, M. (2011). How intercultural communication theory informs public relations practice in global settings. In N. Bardhan & C. K. Weaver (Eds.), *Public relations in global cultural contexts: Multi-paradigmatic perspectives* (pp. 50–76). Routledge.

Liu, J. (2022, November 26). Apple has a huge problem with an iPhone factory in China. *CNN.* https://rb.gy/utd0e. Accessed June 26, 2023.

Mickle, T., Che, C., & Wakabayashi, D. (2022, November 7). Apple built its empire with China. Now its foundation is sh,owing cracks. *The New York Times.* https://rb.gy/duydq. Accessed June 26, 2023.

Ponciano, J. (2022, May 12). The world's largest tech companies in 2022: Apple still dominates as brutal market selloff wipes trillions in market value. *Forbes.* https://rb.gy/cc0s3. Accessed June 26, 2023.

Reuters. (2022, November 23). Huge Foxconn iPhone plant in China rocked by fresh worker unrest. *Reuters.* https://rb.gy/ethbd. Accessed June 26, 2023.

Swann, P. (2018). *Cases in public relations management: The rise of social media and activism.* Routledge.

Homophily

Research findings concur that people in organizations most often are attracted to and associate with people who are similar to themselves (e.g., Kossinets & Watts, 2009; Reagans, 2005). Similarity along social identity dimensions such as age, ethnicity/race, faith/religion, and gender contributes to strong relationships among people in organizations (Reagans, 2011) that can improve communication exchanges and create a more trustworthy environment (Lazarsfeld & Merton, 1954). **Homophily** can be one of the factors in organizations for employees to distinguish their in-group or out-group status (Carmon et al., 2010). Even though there are degrees of comfort to be gained by linking with similar people at work, sometimes these acts and processes bolster in- and out-group boundaries making career advancement difficult or impossible for some people. Homophily is perpetuated in organizations, for example, when White/Caucasian male managers consistently hire other people who look like them (Pompper, 2014).

Consequently, homophily can foster a negative environment for out-group individuals. When individuals feel they are not part of the in-group because of their intersecting social identity dimensions, they may feel isolated from the organization to the degree that they feel as though they do not belong and lose trust in the organization. These dynamics also can foster perceptions that out-group members are treated unfairly. Thus, homophily can be unwelcoming to immigrants and individuals who have different cultural patterns than an organization's employee majority. These feelings can result in a lack of trust, high turnover, and lawsuits. A homogeneous workplace that limits DEI is not only an unfair practice, morally and legally, but it is unwise because such organizations miss out on valuable employee perspectives that ends up diminishing organizations' competitive edge in the marketplace (Pieterse et al., 2013). Job applicants driven to find employers who value DEI often turn to *best places to work for DEI* lists that use criteria such as use of a global DEI advisory board, unconscious bias training for employees, reviewing pay across positions to ensure equity, aligning DEI plans with results, monitoring percentages of social identity dimensions among employees, and programs for promoting belonging (Velazquez & Steines, 2023).

Stereotypes

Ethnocentric perspectives that hinder acceptance of multiculturalism in work spaces often are typified by negative stereotype use. Stereotypes play out in misunderstandings and blatant discriminatory behaviors that promote unequal treatment among diverse cultural groups. In the U.S., the journalist Walter Lippmann (1997) introduced the concept of *stereotype* in his book *Public Opinion*: "we tend to perceive that which we have picked out in the form stereotyped for us by our culture" (p. 81). In general, a **stereotype** is defined as "beliefs about the characteristics, attributes, and behaviors of members of certain groups" (Hilton & von Hippel, 1996, p. 240). They are pictures of what we create about a group of individuals depending on our beliefs and expectations about their characteristics or behaviors (Ting-Toomey & Chung, 2005). Stereotypes often are amplified across news media products as journalists subliminally impose values through use of language (Fowler, 1991). For example, news reporters amplified negative stereotypes while reporting on Donald Trump's characterizing of the COVID-19 virus as "Chinese virus" and "Kung flu" (Cole & Pompper, 2020).

Demeaning stereotype use that discriminates against ethnic and minority groups undermines organizations' DEI efforts. Organizational psychologists have indicated that workplace discrimination regularly involves a manifestation of prejudice and stereotypes about immigrants and other cultural out-groups (Dietz, 2010; Ryan et al., 2007; Wolsko et al., 2000). For example, stereotyping immigrants as incompetent or unfeeling supports negative workplace attitudes toward immigrants (Bradley-Geist & Schmidtke, 2018), making them targets for prejudice and discrimination (Krings et al., 2014). Ultimately, stereotyping behaviors support poor communication, misunderstandings, and unequal workplace treatment outcomes such as inequitable salary scales and career advancement barriers. For example, more Caucasian/White people work in the highest-paying occupational categories as compared to BIPOC groups (U.S. Bureau of Labor Statistics, 2021). Stereotyping also can create unequal treatment among customers and patients (Galanti, n.d.).

Intercultural conflict

Workplace conflict linked to intercultural challenges also can serve as a DEI barrier in organizations. When individuals operate according to their cultural patterns, or interact in ways that differ from or are inconsistent with another culture group's behaviors, there may be complications beyond usual tensions due to intercultural conflict negotiation styles (Brett, 2018; Brew & Cairns, 2004). For example, Mexican managers think that U.S. managers are rude in their relationships with each other and employees, interpreting disagreement in management meetings as a personal insult (Martin & Nakayama, 2018). Therefore, culture-sensitive insights are essential to anticipating and resolving intercultural conflicts in the workplace. Without culture-sensitive knowledge, individuals cannot be able to evaluate behaviors in an intercultural conflict interaction because they continue to use their ethnocentric lenses (Ting-Toomey, 2009).

Now that the scope of the globalization trend and its impact on organizations in terms of multicultural realities—with both benefits and challenges—has been outlined, the next parts of this chapter address two approaches to understanding and respecting cultural differences among people in the workplace in support of organizations' DEI efforts. Both approaches are essential for communicators counseling organizations operating amidst the globalization trend.

Nurturing intercultural competence

Because the world has changed dramatically with peoples' heightened awareness of a need to embrace multiculturalism as an outcome of globalization, we know that encountering new people across cultures happens everywhere now throughout communities and workplaces. Essential is respectful and informed **intercultural communication** (Lustig & Koester, 2006), or "communication between people from different national cultures" (Gudykunst, 2005, p. 179). Moreover, *intercultural* must be extended beyond geophysical national boundaries to include additional social identity dimensions among people, including ethnicities and beliefs (Arasaratnam & Doerfel, 2005).

Communication competence is a social judgment that depends on the context, the interactions between participants, and the goals associated with these interactions (Lustig & Koester, 2006). To be competent in communication means being successful in "interaction that is perceived as effective in fulfilling certain rewarding objectives in a way that is also appropriate to the context in which the interaction occurs" (Spitzberg, 1988, p. 68). In other words, being a competent communicator means an ability to be effective in achieving desirable outcomes and using appropriate messages that are expected in a given context (Wiseman, 2003). Therefore, **intercultural communication competence** involves knowledge, motivation, and skills to interact with people from other cultures effectively and appropriately (Wiseman, 2003). Possessing intercultural communication competence skills is essential for organizations' communication staff members.

Being an effective intercultural communicator involves possessing excellent communication skills, of course, but it also involves knowledge and insights rooted in a willingness to learn about a wide variety of cultures. For example, because every intercultural interaction includes differences among **cultural patterns** such as beliefs, values, norms, and social practices which affect the perception of competence, organizations' communications team members must be willing to discover key audiences' cultural patterns, knowing that variety and nuances of difference mean that not all cultural members necessarily share the *same* cultural patterns.

Developing intercultural communication competence that is respectful and informed can prove time consuming, but it is time well invested. To begin, communicators must consider people as unique individuals who may or may not match up to a typical profile of a specific culture member. Yet, all cultural representatives should be able to offer organizational communicators essential insights to better understand fundamental aspects of cultures as part of the process of developing intercultural competence (Lustig & Koester, 2006). For example, in the case of the deadly Marburg Virus, international health workers representing a variety of nonprofit organizations work with local people to implement effective containment strategies and respect local burial customs (Swann, 2018). Discovering cultural patterns and having skills to communicate—even with an interpreter—supports local communities' health during crises.

Certainly, respectful and informed intercultural communication steeped in competence, compassion, and respect for cultural patterns lends an open-minded approach and path forward to embracing multiculturalism outcomes in organizations that are linked to globalization trends.

Acculturation

While some intercultural encounters may be brief—such as sitting next to an international student in class—some intercultural encounters offer opportunities for long-term relationship building—such as when DEI-embracing organizations work at building employee and volunteer bases that eschew ethnocentric tendencies. Sometimes **acculturation** can take several generations to play out (Murray et al., 2014). Acculturation is defined as what happens "when groups of individuals having different cultures come into continuous first-hand contact, with subsequent changes in the original culture patterns of either or both groups" (Redfield et al., 1936, p. 149). Acculturation begins when cultural groups interact with each other (Berry, 2008), processes which cause cultural and psychological changes across groups. It is a process that causes a degree of identity change when individuals move from a familiar environment to an unfamiliar one (Ting-Toomey & Chung, 2005).

Outcomes of groups coming together in organizations can take many shapes (Berry, 2008). *Assimilation* occurs when people engage in regular routine day-to-day interaction with other groups. *Separation* occurs when people prefer to hold on to their original culture and do not look for interaction with others. *Integration* occurs when people want to maintain their original culture but at the same time look for day-to-day interactions with other groups. *Marginalization* occurs when people are not interested in cultural maintenance or having relations with others. Often people who integrate adapt better to situations than people who acculturate by way of assimilation, separation, or marginalization (Sam & Berry, 2010). Understanding these nuances can help organizations' communicators to prepare for realities of day-to-day work further developing their intercultural competencies.

Having an *integration* mindset can lend significant support for success of DEI programs in organizations. Integration processes involve changes across groups as the out-group adopts the basic cultural patterns of the larger society, and the in-group adapts the organization to better meet the needs of all groups within the organization. Having an integration attitude seems to bring less stress and the best acculturation for all groups (Thissen, 2021), since those new to organizations can assume characteristics of their new culture while they can value their original culture. Thus, organizations must be open and inclusive toward DEI among key audiences including employees and customers. For example, organizations can begin by examining how varying cultures make decisions, build relationships, and communicate with one other. Overall, organizations that invest in developing cultural competence across employee groups reap benefits of culturally appropriate practices (Thissen, 2021).

The next section discusses specific actions organizations take to embrace DEI, making it a reality rather than a wish-list item included in their mission or vision statements.

Actions for organizations

Organizations committed to DEI make plans and monitor progress so that their wishes can become reality. Action plans can include: engaging in true dialogue with out-group individuals and listening, becoming intercultural allies, promoting social justice within the organization, and embracing DEI in global practices.

Dialogue and listening

Globalization trends marked by inevitable multicultural work environments require relationship building across cultures and physical spaces, forcing organizations to take action with tangible steps for actually achieving DEI. Engaging in respectful dialogue with out-group individuals to discover their perceptions and needs speaks volumes about how highly some organizations value people (Martin & Nakayama, 2018). Organizations must show employees that their input always is taken seriously. Employees who perceive that their input is valued are more likely to become vocal (Forbes, 2023). Talking through and exchanging ideas about tension-filled topics and engaging in conversations is "useful for families, small groups, businesses, communities, organizations" as a route toward navigating conflict (Schirch & Campt, 2007, p. 5). Dialogue enhances communication for building and maintaining relationships across varying cultural patterns (Sloan et al., 2018).

There are several strategies for harnessing the power of listening and building a listening culture in organizations. Researchers suggest that the best dialogue begins with listening because listening promotes sharing and reciprocity (Martin & Nakayama, 2018; Starosta & Chen, 2005). Listening affects the satisfaction, team spirit, determination, productivity of employees, a sense of togetherness (Lloyd, Boer & Voelpel, 2017; Reed, Goolsby & Johnston, 2016), and perceptions that customers and employees are partners with organizations in achieving shared goals (Place, 2019). Listening encourages respect and goes a long way in building organization–public trust. Building a listening culture in organizations means listening to *everyone and all groups*, being patient to hear what is said, acknowledging what is said, and collectively discussing further steps based on ideas generated during the dialogue (Forbes, 2023). One way to realize the vision of a listening culture at work is to produce a social media platform of cultural expression, "enabling a dialogue across and within cultures, both minority and majorities on what constitutes such shared values and rights, and for the redefinition of the identities of multicultural nations in the West" (Bailey & Harindranath, 2007, p. 299). Moreover, organizations may use digital technologies to support respectful listening, specifically among marginalized audiences (Place, 2021) because these technologies can offer useful tools to obtain feedback among participants (Place, 2022). Building listening centers to amplify opportunities for listening among culturally diverse identities, as well as developing policies and implementing structural changes to create a fair environment for all groups can help, too (Place, 2022).

Becoming intercultural allies

In addition to promoting dialogue and listening as tangible steps toward achieving DEI, organizations also can build infrastructures and set into motion programs and policies that establish organizations as intercultural supporters and allies. This important work means embracing the complexities of intercultural communication, addressing power issues, and fostering a real sense of belonging across audiences associated with organizations. Becoming an intercultural ally involves a willingness to form partnerships among people representing various social identities who work together promoting peace, social justice, and/or cultural understanding (DeTurk, 2017).

Organizations must prove a commitment to intercultural relationships despite any inconveniences associated with managing difficult situations and potential for misunderstanding given culture difference. Organizations first must recognize that they need to help audiences overcome fear that organizations have most or all the power (as employers, bankers, landlords, food manufacturers, etc.). Organizations' communicators should learn and use the basics of non-verbal communication—interculturally, depending on

Figure 2.3 Organizational members must keep dialogue fluid to discover the most useful and respectful means for exchanging information, ideas, and opinions across cultural divides.

the context and individuals/groups involved—for mutually beneficial dialogue that is respectful and fruitful. For example, various cultures uniquely perceive eye contact, handshaking, gesturing, and etiquette in meetings and dining. A sense of time, deadlines, and degrees of formality at work also have cultural dimensions that possibly could lead to miscommunication or offense (Reynolds, 2018). Organizations that work hard to manage and address cultural dimensions by letting publics know how much they are valued and respected communicates a willingness to meet audiences halfway (Collier, 2015; Martin & Nakayama, 2018). For example, organizations can scrutinize their communication styles to understand whether they foster a *command and control* style or a *connected* style that is rooted in an exchange of information, ideas, and opinions (Tassone, 2017). Organizations' communicators and other leaders can consider how power differentials inadvertently may inspire some audiences to shy away from achieving their full potential by not taking advantage of support resources available in organizations.

Consider the case study of Oreo's #stayhomestayplayful campaign to discover how the brand connected with consumers and increased the sense of belonging among culturally diverse audiences.

Sidebar 2.2   Oreo campaigned for unprecedented global connections

Tugce Ertem-Eray

The globalization trend has connected people in unprecedented ways, shining a huge spotlight on the benefits and challenges of multiculturalism across organizations the world over (Arasaratnam, 2013). So, creative communicators responsible for promoting the Oreo cookie developed a campaign to bring people together during the COVID-19 pandemic (Stein, 2020). Here is their case study.

Oreo is a brand of sandwich cookie introduced by Nabisco in 1912. It currently is owned by Mondelez International since 2012. The cookie consists of two cocoa biscuits with a sweet fondant filling. In 1928, Oreo cookies went global, rolling into Central and Latin America. Today, Oreo cookies can be found in more than 100 countries with the mission to playfully connect people around the world (Oreo, n.d.).

When the COVID-19 pandemic hit, the Oreo team pondered how they could use their creativity and playfulness to bring people together around the world (Stein, 2020). The global team first turned to China for guidance since China was the first country to deal with COVID-19. The "Stay Home, Stay Playful" concept was created by the team in the Middle East and Africa. The tagline is a simple edit of Oreo's existing "Stay Playful" campaign, which was created by the U.S. team in 2019 (Stein, 2020) and also spread to Australia, New Zealand, and the E.U. Latin America markets also looked at adapting the content to Spanish (Stein, 2020).

In a series of posts on social media platforms such as Instagram, Facebook, and Twitter, Oreo provided ideas to people for playful activities during the lockdown. They introduced the Oreo Playbook which includes activities designed to help people find another way to stay playful during the lockdown. These activities included baking recipes such as Oreo brownies, having fun with indoor camping, finding new ways for improving Zoom calls, creating homemade air filters, and making one's own escape room. People who participated in these activities used the #stayhomestayplayful hashtag to inspire those around the world to share their attempts (Digitas, 2020).

For example, the #stayhomestayplayful campaign was published in the U.K. in April 2020 by the ad agency Digitas. The goal was to build human connections through warmth, playfulness, and fun (Nikiforidis, 2020). The campaign had 2M reach on every Instagram activity, a 5.95% Instagram story engagement rate, 9M reach on every Facebook activity through the campaign period, 50K Facebook organic reach, and +100% increase in predicted clicks on Twitter 18K vs. 9K in the UK (Digitas, n.d.).

During the COVID-19 pandemic publics expected brands to share positive and user-generated content that brings people together and creates communities around brands. Social media content also inspired people with hope and uplifting stories (Gallegos, 2021). People wanted to think that "we're all in this together" during the COVID-19 pandemic and brands who reflected this idea in their communication plans with an emphasis on globalization and multiculturalism stayed connected with their publics. The Stay Home Stay Playful ad reached 7.2K views on YouTube and included families across cultures as they were in quarantine dealing with the challenges of spending quality time with their family and keeping in touch with their friends (Cabra, 2020). This campaign connected the brand with its publics and increased the sense of belonging across culturally diverse publics (Gallegos, 2021).

Resources

Arasaratnam, L. A. (2013). A review of articles on multiculturalism in 35 years of IJIR. *International Journal of Intercultural Relations*, 37(6), 676–685. https://doi.org/10.1016/j.ijintrel.2013.09.006

Cabra, C. (2020, April 10). OREO stay home stay playful commercial song. https://commercial-song.net/2020/04/oreo-stay-home-stay-playful-commercial-song/. Accessed September 6, 2023.

Digitas. (2020, April 29). OREO gets playful in lockdown in new campaign by Digitas UK. *Little Black Book*. https://mediashotz.co.uk/oreo-gets-playful-in-lockdown-for-new-campaign-by-digitas-uk/. Accessed September 6, 2023.

Digitas. (n.d.). #stayhomestayplayful. https://www.creativebrief.com/agency/digitas/case-studies/stayhomestayplayful?cta-ref=cta-agencies. Accessed September 6, 2023.

Gallegos, J. A. (2021, January 20). Lessons from UGC in 2020 – and how it can help you in 2021. *Social Media Today*. https://www.socialmediatoday.com/news/lessons-from-ugc-in-2020-and-how-it-can-help-you-in-2021/593678/. Accessed September 6, 2023.

Modood, T. (2013). *Multiculturalism*. Wiley.

Nikiforidis, L. (2020, October 7). Why OREO's latest campaign centers on the need to build human connections through shared enjoyment and fun. *creativebrief*. https://www.creativebrief.com/bite/trend/guest-trend/why-oreos-latest-campaign-centres-need-build-human-connections-through-shared-enjoyment-and-fun Accessed September 6, 2023.

Oreo. (n.d.). About us. https://www.oreo.com/about-us. Accessed September 6, 2023.

Ryan, C. S., Hunt, J. S, Weible, J. A., Peterson, C. R., & Casas, J. F. (2007). Multicultural and colorblind ideology, stereotypes, and ethnocentrism among Black and White Americans. *Psychology Faculty Publications*, 84. https://digitalcommons.unomaha.edu/psychfacpub/84.

Stein, L. (2020, April 9). Oreo's local-first, globally connected COVID-19 strategy around playfulness. *Campaign US*. https://www.campaignlive.com/article/oreos-local-first-globally-connected-covid-19-strategy-around-playfulness/1679976. Accessed September 6, 2023.

In addition to demonstrating intercultural allyship, another means to advance DEI action in organizations is to discover and take to heart key audiences' lived experiences, historically (Martin & Nakayama, 2018). In other words, history books' stories traditionally have been told by healthy and wealthy heterosexuals (usually Caucasian/White males). Expanding the viewfinder on a people's history by examining their culture over time and how it has been treated sociopolitically offers a unique opportunity to understand groups' contemporary context that may be rooted in the past. For example, organizations well educated about the histories of BIPOC communities, ethnic groups, women, people with disabilities, and LGBTQ+ communities (Sloan et al., 2018) and social identity intersectionalities can move organizations forward in achieving their DEI goals when they understand issues, factors, and variables that have spelled bias and discrimination for certain groups across generations. Organizations need to accept rather than question individuals' lived experiences shaped by power inequalities over time—even when doing so means questioning one's own worldview (Martin & Nakayama, 2018). During crises, organizations often forget the impact of the past in shaping marginalized groups' present perceptions of organizations (Liu & Pompper, 2012). For example, social researchers have long realized the negative impact of the unethical Tuskegee Syphillis Experiment (1932–1972) legacy in U.S. history and how/why some members of African American/Black communities still distrust public health authorities (Newkirk, 2016).

Promoting social justice

Organizations also can do much more than offer lip service to **social justice** goals, missions, and visions while transforming workplaces to embrace

DEI. To promote social justice, organizations need to acknowledge that oppression, inequities, and privilege co-exist—with degrees of harm and discomfort depending upon one's social position. Organizations that listen and encourage the hard, uncomfortable conversations open space for multiple voices that have been silenced or marginalized, historically (Martin & Nakayama, 2018). Rather than ignoring out-group individuals, progressive organizations shaped by globalization trends with multiculturalism outcomes find ways to understand, acknowledge, and embrace cultural differences to promote social justice within organizations (Ryan et al., 2007).

While people living and working in the U.S. continue to be socialized for competition that promotes individualism over collectivism, the pull yourself up by your bootstraps idiom has been debunked as a myth (Quart, 2023, para. 1). This means that the American Dream of "getting ahead on only your energy and steam, without help from your family, government, or community" also has revealed itself as a nightmare shaped by economic disparity separating *haves* from *have-nots* (Quart, 2023, para. 1). Rather, organizations that support collective well-being and egalitarianism among in-group and out-group individuals (Sloan et al., 2018) and leaders that set a positive tone by engaging in real multiculturalism practices stay ahead of negative trends and earn the respect and trust of their constituents, including employees (Sloan et al., 2018). For example, companies that engage with unconscious bias training workshops for employees actually walk the walk by developing awareness of unconscious bias that can creep into recruiting and hiring practices (Aperian Global, n.d.).

Embracing DEI in global practices

Operating amidst globalization trends means global for-profits, nonprofits, and non-governmental organizations (NGOs) work across geo-physical boundaries and must adjust their operational practices and strategies for achieving real DEI accordingly. The **European Union Platform of Diversity Charters** was established by the EU commission within the first decade of the 21st century. Organizations who sign it do so with a commitment to DEI opportunities for their staff (Moosmüller, 2016). A significant stumbling block is the gap separating practices in organizations' home nations that may not translate well abroad, as Anand (2022) characterized in describing her experiences as a DEI officer and the pitfalls of imposing U.S. practices on the rest of the world. Because a power differential still separates headquarters and subsidiaries, some organizations still undervalue autonomy among subsidiaries' potential. Ethnocentrism is playing out in these dynamics—a belief that the headquarters' perspectives are best and that there may be little to learn from local cultures

(Moosmüller, 2016). In particular, corporations that offer expatriate work abroad programs encourage their employees to enhance their intercultural competencies and sometimes use these programs as pipelines to management levels (Pompper, 2017). Another way to accommodate cultural difference and embrace it while learning about it is through global exchange programs (Place, 2019). For example, Boston Consulting Group, an American global management consulting firm, enables employees to participate in extended-stay assignments (typically one year) among its worldwide offices. Similarly, Deloitte, a British multinational professional services network, has partnerships in 150 countries and provides employees with international assignments that vary from short-term projects to longer-term strategic roles (Kastner, n.d.).

Even though operating and thriving in a multicultural global world is not without its challenges, there are multiple opportunities, too, for expanding horizons and enhancing intercultural competency skill sets. Organizations simply may engage in dialogue with lots of listening, as well as by becoming an intercultural ally promoting social justice, and paying attention to and respecting cultural differences.

Concluding thoughts

The purpose of this chapter is to understand the fundamentals of the myriad ways globalization with a multiculturalism imperative offers a backdrop of challenges and opportunities for for-profit organizations, nonprofits, and non-governmental organizations. Developing intercultural competence is no longer merely a desirable goal, but an imperative. Tracing the early history of globalization to illustrate how globalization creates a multicultural environment for organizations was followed by a close examination of the concept of multiculturalism with interrogation of challenges ranging from ethnocentrism to stereotypes to illustrate how important it is for organizations to embrace DEI and social justice. Forward-thinking organizations can create systematic change in social and economic spheres, beginning with intercultural communication competence which includes knowledge, motivation, and skill to build and maintain relationships with people across cultures within and among organizations. These factors can help to minimize the negative attitudes, stereotyping, and ethnocentrism that can negatively affect the workplace environment.

A workplace shaped by an embrace of DEI is beneficial for employees, employers, customers, suppliers, and many other audiences. Organizations that embrace cultural diversity in the workplace are more likely to recruit, retain, have organizational commitment, individual empowerment, job satisfaction, and build relationships with their employees.

Workplace DEI also means active engagement with diverse publics attached to the workforce (Damelang & Haas; 2012; Neault & Mondair, 2011; Wolfson et al., 2011).

Next, Chapter 3, "How intersectionality in social identity works . . . at work," focuses on lived experiences of individual people and groups—according to social identity dimensions and ways they intersect.

Key words

Acculturation—Redfield and colleagues (1936) explained that acculturation means the effects of what happens when groups of individuals representing various cultures come into continuous first-hand contact. The net result includes changes in culture patterns within groups.

Cultural patterns—Shared beliefs, values, norms, and social practices produce repeated, steady reactions over time (Dunaway, 2023).

Ethnocentrism—This is an attitude that one's own group, ethnicity, or nationality is superior to others.

European Union Platform of Diversity Charters—This was created in 2010 to help public and private sector organizations across the European Union design and implement effective diversity and inclusion policies (European Commission, n.d.).

Globalization—This term refers to the processes by which people across vast physical geo-political distances become more connected in "more and different ways" (Lechner & Boli, 2019, p. 2).

Homophily—In social networks, people tend to align themselves or seek acquaintance among those with whom they share common characteristics, such as culture, socio-economic status, and more.

Intercultural communication—This is "a symbolic, interpretive, transactional, contextual process in which people from different cultures create shared meanings" (Lustig & Koester, 2006, p. 46).

Intercultural competence—Intercultural competence involves knowledge, motivation, and skills to interact with people from other cultures effectively and appropriately (Wiseman, 2003).

Intercultural conflict—When there are frictions among two or more cultural groups, opportunities for developing mutually beneficial relationships are diminished. Intercultural conflict in the workplace usually starts with different expectations and is based on cultural ignorance or misunderstanding (Ting-Toomey & Oetzel, 2001).

Multiculturalism—Often, multiculturalism refers to social identity dimension, or demographic feature, such as ethnicity or culture. Also, policymakers use the term when wording new policies designed to manage cultural diversity.

Social justice—Social justice is defined as full participation in society and the balancing of benefits and burdens by all citizens, resulting in equitable living and a just ordering of society (Buettner-Schmidt & Marie L. Lobo, 2012).

Stereotype—A stereotype is a generalized belief about a group of individuals; usually negative and critical (Kanahara, 2006).

Workplace DEI—Work spaces fostered by organizations that embrace diversity, equity, and inclusion celebrate all people, including openness about all aspects of culture and other social identity dimensions (Neault & Mondair, 2011).

Discussion questions for deep engagement

1. How would you describe your own interactions with people from other cultures? Is yours a *command and control* style or a *connected* style that is rooted in an exchange of information, ideas, and opinions? For additional insights, consult Tassone (2017).
2. How would you describe your own cultural identity?
3. What is the culture composition in your workplace? Which groups hold the power? How do you see power playing out (those who have it and those who do not)?
4. What policies and practices are used in your school or workplace to maintain or dismantle homophily?
5. How can you serve as an intercultural ally? Offer three specific actions you can take.

Resources

Anand, R. (2022). *Leading global diversity, equity, and inclusion: A guide for systemic change in multinational organizations*. Berrett-Koehler Publishers.

Ancestry. (n.d.). U.S. immigration in the 1800s. Ancestry® Family History Learning Hub. https://www.ancestry.com/c/family-history-learning-hub/1800-us-immigration#:~:text=The%20high%20immigration%20statistics%20in,in%20the%201840s%20and%201850s. Accessed October 2, 2023.

Anderson, J. A. (2021, November 15). Some say Occupy Wall Street did nothing. It changed us more than we think. *Time*. https://time.com/6117696/occupy-wall-street-10-years-later/ Accessed October 2, 2023.

Aperian Global. (n.d.). Interrupting bias among top leaders at Carlsberg. *Aperian Global*. https://www.aperianglobal.com/case-studies/interrupting-bias-among-top-leaders/. Accessed June 27, 2023.

Arasaratnam, L. A. (2013). A review of articles on multiculturalism in 35 years of IJIR. *International Journal of Intercultural Relations*, 37(6), 676–685. https://doi.org/10.1016/j.ijintrel.2013.09.006

Arasaratnam, L. A., & Doerfel, M. L. (2005). Intercultural communication competence: Identifying key components from multicultural perspectives. *International*

Journal of Intercultural Relations, 29(2), 137–163. https://doi.org/10.1016/j.ijintrel.2004.04.001

Bailey, O. G., & Harindranath, R. (2007). Ethnic minorities, cultural difference and the cultural politics of communication. *International Journal of Media & Cultural Politics*, 2(3), pp. 299–316. https://doi.org/10.1386/macp.2.3.299_1

Banks, A. J. (2016). Are group cues necessary? How anger makes ethnocentrism among Whites a stronger predictor of racial and immigration policy opinions. *Political Behavior*, 38(3), pp. 635–657. DOI: https://www.jstor.org/stable/48693835

Berry, J. W. (1980). Acculturation as varieties of adaptation. In A. Padilla (Ed.), *Acculturation: Theory, models and some new findings* (pp. 9–25). Westview Press.

Berry, J. W. (1997). Immigration, acculturation and adaptation. *Applied Psychology: An International Review*, 46(1), 5–34. https://doi.org/10.1111/j.1464-0597.1997.tb01087.x

Berry, J. W. (2008). Globalisation and acculturation. *International Journal of Intercultural Relations*, 32(4), 328–336. https://doi.org/10.1016/j.ijintrel.2008.04.001.

Berry, J. W., & Kalin, R. (1995). Multicultural and ethnic attitudes in Canada: An overview of the 1991 national survey. *Canadian Journal of Behavioral Science*, 27, 301–320. https://psycnet.apa.org/doi/10.1037/0008-400X.27.3.301.

Bradley-Geist, J. C., & Schmidtke, J. M. (2018). Immigrants in the workplace: Stereotyping and discrimination. In Adrienne J. C. and Eden B. K. (Eds.), *The Oxford Handbook of workplace discrimination* (pp. 159–176). Oxford Library of Psychology. https://doi.org/10.1093/oxfordhb/9780199363643.013.12.

Brett, J. (2018). Intercultural challenges in managing workplace conflict—a call for research. *Cross Cultural & Strategic Management*, 25(1), 32–52. https://doi.org/10.1108/CCSM-11-2016-0190.

Brew, F. P., & Cairns, D. R. (2004). Do culture or situational constraints determine choice of direct or indirect styles in intercultural workplace conflicts? *International Journal of Intercultural Relations*, 28, 331–352. https://doi.org/10.1016/j.ijintrel.2004.09.001

Brown, A. (2022). More than twice as many Americans support than oppose the #MeToo movement. Pew Research Center.

Buettner-Schmidt, K., & Lobo, M. L. (2012). Social justice: A concept analysis. *Journal of Advanced Nursing*, 68(4), 948–958. https://pubmed.ncbi.nlm.nih.gov/22032609/.

Campbell, A. M. (2010). Screening culture: Is Western media to blame for tainting traditional Third World values? Pell Scholars and Senior Theses. 57. https://digitalcommons.salve.edu/pell_theses/57.

Carmon, A. F., Miller, A. N., Raile, A. N. W., Roers, M. R. (2010). Fusing family and firm: Employee perceptions of perceived homophily, organizational justice, organizational identification, and organizational commitment in family businesses. *Journal of Family Business Strategy*, 1(4), 210–223.

Cole, C. & Pompper, D. (2020, October). *A new generation of fear: A critical race theory analysis of Asian Americans' reaction to "Chinese Virus" and "Kung Flu" in the age of COVID-19*. Global Fusion Conference, Carbondale, IL.

Collier, M. J. (2015). Partnering for anti-poverty praxis in Circles, USA: Applications for critical dialogic reflexivity. *Journal of International and Intercultural Communication*, 8(3), 208–223.

Damelang, A., & Haas, A. (2012). The benefits of migration: cultural diversity and labour market success. *European Societies*, 14(3), 362–392. https://doi.org/10.1080/14616696.2012.676758.

DeTurk, S. (2017). Intercultural alliance. Critical intercultural communication theories, issues, and concepts. In Y. Y. Kim (Ed.), *The International Encyclopedia of Intercultural Communication*. Wiley Blackwell.

Dietz, J. (2010). Introduction to the special issue on employment discrimination against immigrants. *Journal of Managerial Psychology*, 25(2), 104–112. https://doi.org/10.1108/02683941011019320.

Dong, Q., Day, K. D., & Collaço, C. M. (2008). Overcoming ethnocentrism through developing intercultural communication sensitivity and multiculturalism. *Human Communication*, 11(1), 27–38.

Dunaway, D. (2023). *Intercultural communication*. LibreTexts.

Ely, R. J., & Thomas, D. A. (2020). Getting serious about diversity: Enough already with the business case. *Harvard Business Review*. Downloaded November 24, 2023 from https://hbr.org/2020/11/getting-serious-about-diversity-enough-already-with-the-business-case.

Ertem-Eray, T. (2021). U.S. students' perceptions of international teaching assistants in the public relations field. *Journal of Public Relations Education*, 7(1), 122–152.

European Commission. (n.d.). EU platform of diversity charters. https://commission.europa.eu/strategy-and-policy/policies/justice-and-fundamental-rights/combatting-discrimination/tackling-discrimination/diversity-and-inclusion-initiatives/eu-platform-diversity-charters_en#:~:text=Role%20of%20the%20Platform,-The%20EU%20Platform&text=By%20signing%20a%20charter%2C%20the,origin%2C%20religion%20or%20sexual%20orientation. Accessed June 23, 2023.

Forbes. (2023, May 31). 20 smart ways managers can foster more open dialogue in the workplace. *Forbes*. https://www.forbes.com/sites/forbescoachescouncil/2023/05/31/20-smart-ways-managers-can-foster-more-open-dialogue-in-the-workplace/?sh=40b5a15b7097. Accessed October 2, 2023.

Fowler, R. (1991). *Language in the news: discourse and ideology in the press*. Routledge.

Galanti, G.-A. (n.d.). Understanding cultural diversity in healthcare. Case studies. https://ggalanti.org/case-studies-field-reports/. Accessed June 27, 2023.

Giddens, A. (1990). *The consequences of modernity*. Polity.

Glynn, P. (2022, September 19). 17 diversity in the workplace statistics every company needs to know. *InsightGlobal*. https://insightglobal.com/blog/diversity-in-the-workplace-statistics/. Accessed June 28, 2023.

Goudarzi, S., Badaan, V., & Knowles, E. D. (2022). Neoliberalism and the ideological construction of equity beliefs. *Perspectives on Psychological Science*, 17(5), 1431–1451. https://doi.org/10.1177/17456916211053311.

Grixti, J. (2011). Indigenous media values: Cultural and ethical implications. In R. S. Fortner and P. M. Fackler (Eds.), *The handbook of global communication and media ethics* (pp. 342–363). Blackwell Publishing.

Gudykunst, W. B. (2005). *Theorizing about intercultural communication*. Sage.

Hammond, R. A., & Axelrod, R. (2006). The evolution of ethnocentrism. *Journal of Conflict Resolution*, 50(6), 926–936. https://doi.org/10.1177/0022002706293470.

Hilton, J. L., & von Hippel, W. (1996). Stereotypes. *Annual Review of Psychology*, 47, 237–271. https://doi.org/10.1146/annurev.psych.47.1.237.

Hong, Y., & Cheon, B. K. (2017). How does culture matter in the face of globalization? *Perspectives on Psychological Science*, 12(5), 810–823. https://doi.org/10.1177/1745691617700496.

Hwang, V. (2012, April 26). To replicate Silicon Valley's success, focus on culture. *The Washington Post*. https://www.washingtonpost.com/business/onsmall business/to-replicate-silicon-valleys-success-focus-on-culture/2012/04/25/gIQAzFQkhT_story.html. Accessed July 20, 2023.

Johnson, R., Phillips, L., & Douglass, N. (n.d.) How DEI consulting can mitigate risk and avoid D&O and EPL lawsuits. Gallagher. Downloaded November 24, 2023 from https://www.ajg.com/us/news-and-insights/2021/sep/diversity-equity-and-inclusion-an-important-loss-prevention-tool/.

Kanahara, S. (2006). A review of the definitions of stereotype and a proposal for a progressional model. *Individual Differences Research*, 4(5), 306–321.

Kastner, M. (n.d.). 7 companies that will send you abroad for a year or two. *Monster*. https://www.monster.com/career-advice/article/companies-jobs-work-abroad-0816. Accessed October 2, 2023.

Kossinets, G., & Watts, D. J. (2009). Origins of homophily in an evolving social network. *American Journal of Sociology*, 115(2), 405–450. https://psycnet.apa.org/doi/10.1086/599247.

Krings, F., Johnston, C., Binggeli, S., & Maggiori, C. (2014). Selective incivility: Immigrant groups experience subtle workplace discrimination at different rates. *Cultural Diversity and Ethnic Minority Psychology*, 20(4), 491–498. https://pubmed.ncbi.nlm.nih.gov/25133409/

Lazarsfeld, P. F., & Merton, R. K. (1954). Friendship as social process: A substantive and methodological analysis. In T. Abel & C. H. Page (Eds.), *Freedom and control in modern society* (pp. 8–66). Nostrand.

Lechner, F. J., & Boli, J. (2019). *The globalization reader*. Wiley.

LeVine, R. A., & Campbell, D. T. (1972). *Ethnocentrism*. Wiley.

Lippmann, W. (1997). *Public opinion*. Macmillan.

Liu, B. F., & Pompper, D. (2012). The 'crisis with no name': Defining the interplay of culture, ethnicity, and race on organizational issues and media outcomes. *Journal of Applied Communication Research*, 40(2), 127–146. DOI: https://doi.org/10.1080/00909882.2012.654499.

Lloyd, K. J., Boer, D., & Voelpel, S. C. (2017). From listening to leading: Toward an understanding of supervisor listening within the framework of leader-member exchange theory. *International Journal of Business Communication*, 54(4), 431–451. https://doi.org/10.1177/2329488415572778.

Lustig, M. W., & Koester, J. (2006). *Intercultural competence: Interpersonal communication across cultures*. Pearson.

Makedon, A. (1996). What multiculturalism should not be? http://alexandermake don.com/articles/multiculturalism.html#:~:text=Unlike%20ethnocentrism%2C%20which%20to%20a,are%20even%20opposite%20to%20ours. Accessed June 28, 2023.

Makovsky, A. (2019, March 13). Turkey's refugee dilemma. *CAP*. https://www.americanprogress.org/article/turkeys-refugee-dilemma/. Accessed June 6, 2023.

Marriott International (n.d.). *Diversity & Inclusion—Corporate*. https://www.marriott.com/diversity/corporate-diversity.mi. Accessed June 6, 2023.

Martin, J. N., & Nakayama, T. K. (2018). *Intercultural communication in contexts*. McGrawHill Education.

McFarlin, K. (2019). The effects of globalization in the workplace. *Chron*. https://smallbusiness.chron.com/effects-globalization-workplace-10738.html. Accessed June 6, 2023.

McKane, R. (2014). The globalization of social movements: Exploring the transnational paradigm through collection action against neoliberalism from Latin

America to the Occupy movement. *Pursuit – The Journal of Undergraduate Research at The University of Tennessee*, 5(1), Article 11. Available at: https://trace.tennessee.edu/pursuit/vol5/iss1/11.

McPherson, M., Smith-Lovin, L., & Cook, J. M. (2001). Birds of a feather: Homophily in social networks. *Annual Review of Sociology*, 27, 415–444. https://doi.org/10.1146/annurev.soc.27.1.415

Miller, J. (2021). For younger job seekers, diversity and inclusion in the workplace aren't a preference. They're a requirement. *The Washington Post*. Downloaded November 24, 2023 from https://www.washingtonpost.com/business/2021/02/18/millennial-genz-workplace-diversity-equity-inclusion/.

Modood, T. (2013). *Multiculturalism*. Wiley.

Moosmüller, A. (2016). Cultural diversity in multinational corporations. In C. Braedel-Kühner & A. P. Müller (Eds.), *Re-thinking diversity multiple approaches in theory, media, communities, and managerial practice* (pp. 121–132). Springer.

Murray, K. E., Klonoff, E. A., Garcini, L. M., Ullman, J. B., Wall, T. L., & Myers, M. G. (2014). Assessing acculturation over time: A four-year prospective study of Asian American young adults. *Asian American Journal of Psychology*, 5(3), 252–261. DOI: 10.1037/a0034908. PMID: 25558310; PMCID: PMC4280080.

Neault, R. A., & Mondair, S. (2011). Supporting workplace diversity: Emerging roles for employment counselors. *Journal of Employment Counseling*, 48(2), 72–80. https://doi.org/10.1002/j.2161-1920.2011.tb00116.x.

Newkirk, V. R. (2016). A generation of bad blood. *The Atlantic*. Downloaded November 25, 2023 from https://digitalpublications.brown.edu/projects/race-public-health-in-america/resource/bad-blood.

Panicker, A., & Sharma, A. (2021). Ethnocentrism: Enemy of productive and happy multicultural workplace. *Turkish Journal of Computer and Mathematics Education*, 12(5), 756–760. https://doi.org/10.17762/turcomat.v12i5.1481.

Pieterse, A. N., Knippenberg, D. V., & Dierendonck, D. V. (2013). Cultural diversity and team performance: The role of team member goal orientation. *Academy of Management Journal*, 56(3), 782–804. http://dx.doi.org/10.5465/amj.2010.0992.

Place, K. R. (2019). Listening as the driver of public relations practice and communications strategy within a global public relations agency. *Public Relations Journal*, 12(3), 1–18. https://prjournal.instituteforpr.org/wp-content/uploads/katieplace_listening.pdf.

Place, K. R. (2021). 'People are more than just a statistic': Ethical, care-based engagement of marginalized publics on social media. *Journal of Media Ethics*, 36(3), 1–13. https://doi.org/10.1080/23736992.2021.1937175.

Place, K. R. (2022). Toward a framework for listening with consideration for intersectionality: Insights from public relations professionals in borderland spaces. *Journal of Public Relations Research*, 34(1–2), 4–19. https://doi.org/10.1080/1062726X.2022.2057502.

Pompper, D. (2014). *Practical and theoretical implications of successfully doing difference in organizations*. Emerald Group Publishing Limited.

Pompper, D. (2017). Management with glass borders: Women and expatriate experiences. In J. P. Fyke, J. Faris and P. M. Buzzanell (Eds.), *Cases in organizational and managerial communication: Stretching boundaries* (pp. 121–126). Routledge.

Pratt, L. (2023, June 29). What are the dangers of not embracing diversity in business? *Future Business*. https://future-business.org/dangers-of-not-embracing-diversity/#:~:text=By%20not%20embracing%20diversity%2C%20businesses,can%20have%20a%20negative%20impact. Accessed September 2, 2023.

Quart, A. (2023, March 10). Bootstrapping has always been a myth. The new American dream proves it. *Time*. Downloaded November 25, 2023 from https://time.com/6261476/bootstrapping-myth-new-american-dream/.

Rao, V. (2011). A brief history of the corporation: 1600 to 2100. *Ribbonfarm*. Downloaded November 24, 2023 from https://www.ribbonfarm.com/2011/06/08/a-brief-history-of-the-corporation-1600-to-2100/.

Raz, J. (1998). Multiculturalism. *Ratio Juris*, 11(3), 193–205.

Reagans, R. (2005). Preferences, identity, and competition: Predicting tie strength from demographic data. *Management Science*, 51(9), 1374–1383. https://psycnet.apa.org/doi/10.1287/mnsc.1050.0389.

Reagans, R. (2011). Close encounters: Analyzing how social similarity and propinquity contribute to strong network connections. *Organization Science*, 22(4), 835–849. https://www.jstor.org/stable/20868899.

Redfield, R., Linton, R. & Herskovits, M. J. (1936). Memorandum for the study of acculturation. *American Anthropologist*, 38, 149–152. https://doi.org/10.1525/aa.1936.38.1.02a00330

Reed, K., Goolsby, J. R., & Johnston, M. K. (2016). Listening in and out: Listening to customers and employees to strengthen an integrated market-oriented system. *Journal of Business Research*, 69(9), 3591–3599. https://psycnet.apa.org/doi/10.1016/j.jbusres.2016.01.002.

Reynolds, K. (2018). 13 benefits and challenges of cultural diversity in the workplace. *Hult International Business School*. https://www.hult.edu/blog/benefits-challenges-cultural-diversity-workplace/. Accessed October 2, 2023.

Ryan, C. S., Hunt, J. S, Weible, J. A., Peterson, C. R., & Casas, J. F. (2007). Multicultural and colorblind ideology, stereotypes, and ethnocentrism among Black and White Americans. *Psychology Faculty Publications*, 84. https://digitalcommons.unomaha.edu/psychfacpub/84.

Sam, D. L., & Berry, J. W. (2010). Acculturation: When individuals and groups of different cultural backgrounds meet. *Perspectives on Psychological Science,* 5(4), 472–481. https://doi.org/10.1177/1745691610373075.

Schirch, L., & Campt, D. (2007). *The little book of dialogue for difficult subjects*. Good Books.

Sloan, L. M., Joyner, M. C., Stakeman, C. J., & Schmitz, C. L. (2018). *Critical multiculturalism and intersectionality in a complex world*. Oxford University Press.

SocialTalent. (n.d.). 9 companies around the world that are embracing diversity in a big way. *SocialTalent*. https://www.socialtalent.com/blog/diversity-and-inclusion/9-companies-around-the-world-that-are-embracing-diversity. Accessed June 27, 2023.

Spitzber, B. H. (1988). Communication competence: Measures of perceived effectiveness. In C. H. Tardy (Ed.), *A handbook for the study of human communication* (pp. 67–105). Ablex.

Starosta, W. J., & Chen, G.-M. (2005). Intercultural listening: Collected reflections, collated refractions. In W. J. Starosta & G.-M. Chen (Eds.), *Taking stock in intercultural communication: Where to now?* (pp. 274–285). National Communication Association.

Swann, P. (2018). *Cases in public relations management: The rise of social media and activism*. Routledge.

Tagle, A. (2021). Reducing ethnocentrism through multiculturalism and social learning in multicultural societies. *International Journal of Multidisciplinary: Applied Business and Education Research*, 2(11), 1235–1242. https://www.ijmaberjournal.org/index.php/ijmaber/article/view/226.

Tassone, S. (2017, June 23). How to identify and banish power differentials to advance more women to leadership roles. *Forbes*. https://www.forbes.com/sites/forbescoachescouncil/2017/06/23/how-to-identify-and-banish-power-differentials-to-advance-more-women-to-leadership-roles/?sh=7113c94c141d. Accessed October 2, 2023.

Thissen, J. (2021, April 14). To acculturate or not to acculturate. *Culture Resource Center*. Downloaded June 28, 2023 from https://www.linkedin.com/pulse/acculturate-joost-thissen.

Thussu, D. K. (2019). *International communication: Continuity and change*. Bloomsbury Academic.

Ting-Toomey, S. (2009). Intercultural conflict competence as a facet of intercultural competence development. Multiple conceptual approaches. In D. K. Deardorff (Ed.), *The SAGE Handbook of intercultural competence* (pp. 100–120). Sage.

Ting-Toomey, S., & Chung, L. C. (2005). *Understanding intercultural communication*. Roxbury Publishing Company.

Ting-Toomey, S., & Oetzel, J. H. (2001). *Managing intercultural conflict effectively*. Sage.

Urban Times. (n.d.). Promoting diversity in a globalized world. *Smartcitiesdive*. https://www.smartcitiesdive.com/ex/sustainablecitiescollective/promoting-diversity-globalized-world/129576/#:~:text=Globalisation%20has%20also%20led%20to,than%20societies%20which%20promote%20monoculture. Accessed June 27, 2023.

U.S. Bureau of Labor Statistics. (2021, November). Labor force characteristics by race and ethnicity, 2020. https://www.bls.gov/opub/reports/race-and-ethnicity/2020/home.htm. Accessed July 20, 2023.

Van de Vijver, F. J. R., Breugelmans, S. M., & Schalk-Soekar, S. R. G. (2008). Multiculturalism: Construct validity and stability. *International Journal of Intercultural Relations, 32*(2), 93–104. https://doi.org/10.1016/j.ijintrel.2007.11.001.

Velazquez, R. & Steines, M. (2023). Eight companies with the best diversity and inclusion programs. Built-in. Downloaded November 25, 2023 from https://builtin.com/diversity-inclusion/companies-with-the-best-diversity-and-inclusion-programs.

Waters, M. (1995). *Globalization*. Routledge.

Wiseman, R. L. (2003). Intercultural communication competence. In W. B. Gudykunst (Ed.) *Cross-cultural and intercultural communication* (pp. 191–208). Sage.

Wolfson, N., Kraiger, K., & Finkelstein, L. (2011). The relationship between diversity climate perceptions and workplace attitudes. *The Psychologist-Manager Journal, 14*(3), 161–176. https://doi.org/10.1080/10887156.2011.546170.

Wolsko, C., Park, B., Judd, C. M., & Wittenbrink, B. (2000). Framing interethnic ideology: Effects of multicultural and colorblind perspectives on judgments of groups and individuals. *Journal of Personality and Social Psychology, 78*(4), 635–654. https://doi.org/10.1037/0022-3514.78.4.635.

3 How intersectionality in social identity works . . . at work

Tugce Ertem-Eray

Making DEI a reality in organizations sometimes pivots on carefully scrutinizing and revising (as necessary) the policies and systems that structure and make up an organization. Carefully considering exactly how people and the social identity dimensions that make them *unique* play out within the organization's infrastructure so that everyone receives fair and equitable treatment must be central to every organization's goals. In other words, understanding social identity dimensions and ways they intersect is central to understanding how to enable people to feel that they belong in/with organizations. This kind of work can take a great deal of time and in business, time means money—even for nonprofits and NGOs. Yet, failure to do this challenging work could be interpreted to mean that an organization's commitment to actually making DEI true and real is lacking if the organization is unwilling to invest the resources required to affect systemic infrastructural change. On the one hand, stating that an organization respects people can seem easy. On the other hand, organizations and the people associated with them don't know what they don't know. When people feel that they don't belong and negative feelings develop, organizations risk losing (or not gaining in the first place) the trust necessary for organizations to operate successfully for the long haul.

Especially strong negative emotions can emerge among audiences when they perceive they are not valued and/or are disrespected because of their intersecting social identity dimensions. Organizations have to position themselves as respectful workplaces where multiple and intersecting social identities are appreciated. Otherwise, normalized **hegemonic** worldviews can foster poor employer–employee relationships, lower employee productivity, diminish employee creativity, and fuel community activism (including resistance, protest, and boycott) designed to discredit and damage organizations' reputations. Moreover, organizations should be structured to celebrate the value that **difference** brings to the party. Whether organizations subscribe to a **business case** way of thinking—that DEI translates to greater profits—or that work among nonhomogeneous teams is "simply

DOI: 10.4324/9781003279129-4

smarter," numerous research findings suggest that working with people of multiple varieties can "challenge your brain to overcome its stale ways of thinking and sharpen its performance" (Rock & Grant, 2016, para. 3).

This chapter builds upon the concept of social identity introduced in Chapter 1, "DEI and social identity intersectionality in organizational communication" by applying theory for a deeper understanding of how intersectionality plays out in organizations. Globally, research findings suggest that organizations with inclusive practices make people feel heard and employee pools composed of a variety of "genders, races, and nationalities" inspire "intellectual potential" for keeping employees' biases in check as they question "their assumptions"—which ultimately makes employee teams smarter and organizations more successful (Rock & Grant, 2016, para. 11). Indeed, *innovation* and *DEI* have become synonymous in the new millennium. Yet, organizations may not fully comprehend the value or importance of fully understanding and accommodating the concept of *intersectionalities*. Therefore, this chapter addresses these key areas: 1) the social identity concept, 2) applying intersectionality in organizations, 3) advancing intersectionality in organizations, 4) how to be inclusive at work, and 5) concluding thoughts.

The social identity concept

Social identity, as a concept, focuses on physiological and social processes attached to ways people self-categorize in relation to their group memberships. Understanding this concept is central to recognizing the multiple facets of DEI issues in organizations. Social identity is "the individual's knowledge that he [sic] belongs to certain social groups together with some emotional and value significance to him [sic] of the group membership" (Tajfel, 1972, p. 31). A **social group** consists of "two or more individuals who share a common social identification of themselves or, which is nearly the same thing, perceive themselves to be members of the same social category" (Turner, 1982, p. 15). These two definitions are testament to ways our social identity and social group membership are linked. Just how people define themselves relates directly to ways they consider characteristics of the social group that they consider themselves members of (Abrams & Hogg, 1990b). Overall, this view offers a window on people's psychological state.

Considering a social identity approach involves accepting that society consists of social categories for humans along dimensions such as ethnicity/race, faith/religion, gender, sexual orientation, socio-economic class, and more. Recognizing ways these categories are defined, applied in everyday usage, give shape and structure to organizations, and measure up against one another are useful exercises for underscoring complexity of these processes. As social identity dimensions, each social category stands in power- and status-relation to one another and sheds light on dynamics that human beings, or society, bring to the conversation (Abrams & Hogg, 1990b), or the social state.

Social identity theory explains how individuals position themselves with regard to groups (Tajfel & Turner, 1986). It is a useful theory for scrutinizing how social identity dimensions play out in organizations—such as who eats lunch together, who volunteers to participate on teams, and who gets invited to social events. Social identity theory is also useful for understanding phenomena in organizations such as hiring and firing, promotions, bias, and discrimination. Another important dynamic under the social identity theory umbrella that is associated with social group membership is a person's status in groups. Social identity theory explains how in-groups and out-groups form (Tajfel & Turner, 1986) in organizations—just who belongs in the group and who does not. Organizations can become repositories for negative attitudes about *the other* which contribute to systemic discrimination and can become embedded in formal organizational policies and informal relations which follow people across their life course. Social identity theory also explains how people learn to think of themselves by interpreting others' reactions to them (Van Maanen, 1979).

Social identity groups and their categories shape society and each is imbued with degrees of power, prestige, and status when compared with other groups (Stets & Burke, 2000). People we think of as similar to ourselves are considered part of an *in-group*. People whom we think of as different from ourselves we consider to be members of an *out-group* (Stets & Burke, 2000). Often, people consider these social identity categories in contrast with one another—and there can be significant power dimensions attached to group membership. For example, dominant contrast social categories have created the binary dualisms of: male/female, masculine/feminine, heterosexual/homosexual, abled/disabled, East/West, atheist/religious, and domestic/foreign (Gardiner, 2002). Moreover, an individual can be a member of multiple social categories such as being a male Black Muslim (Abrams & Hogg, 1990b). Ultimately, categorization and group membership affects how people see themselves, too (Hornsey, 2008).

Social identity theory is a useful theoretical framework for analyzing how differences interplay within the workplace. As revealed in Chapter 1, "DEI and social identity intersectionality in organizational communication," organizations mostly fail to consider social identity differences because Caucasian/Whiteness is considered the dominant standard in organizations. For example, in 2017, Fortune 500 companies' boards of directors members were overwhelmingly Caucasian/White men with only 4.1% women of color and 9% men of color (Pompper et al., 2021). Even though the number of BIPOC and female students are increasing across the U.S., 73%

of college presidents are Caucasian/White men (Bauer-Wolf, 2023). In the National Foodball League (NFL), only one player has publicly come out as gay or bisexual while being an active player (Middlehurst-Schwartz, 2021). These are but a few examples and by no means offer an exhaustive list of ways social identity dimensions are symbolically annihilated in organizations or media representations.

Social identity dimensions and how people consider them is a fluid, dynamic process that also changes over time and must be considered in context. Recognizing this fact can help organizations to create and nurture diverse, equitable, and inclusive environments for working and volunteering. Consider that not all social identity dimensions are visible, either. For example, a person's mental ability, ethnic or cultural background, sexual orientation, or faith/religion system may not be easily recognized. Moreover, every individual has multiple social identities which intersect and play out in our relationships. Context always matters (Center for Creative Leadership, 2023). Recognizing that each person is a culmination of multiple intersecting social identities can help organizations to create more inclusive and respectful spaces.

Applying intersectionality in organizations

As introduced in Chapter 1, "DEI and social identity intersectionality in organizational communication," legal scholar Kimberlé Crenshaw (1989) presented the concept of intersectionality with an emphasis on individuals' multidimensional lived experiences. Scholars, policy makers, communicators, and activists from a wide variety of fields and ideologies have applied intersectionality to inform their work these past few decades. The concept is useful for interrogating ways that social identities dimensions and their intersectionalities come into play in cases of bias and discrimination in organizations. Collins and Bilge (2020) proposed a general description of the concept:

> Intersectionality investigates how intersecting power relations influence social relations across diverse societies as well as individual experiences in everyday life. As an analytic tool, intersectionality views categories of race, class, gender, sexuality, nation, ability, ethnicity, and age—among others – as interrelated and mutually shaping one another. Intersectionality is a way of understanding and explaining complexity in the world, in people, and in human experiences.
>
> (p. 2)

Intersectionality has promoted the complex understanding of individual identities. Intersectionality focuses on how individuals' identities intersect, how they differ from one situation to another, and how these situations are shaped by intersecting power relations. Intersectionality scholars question perceived group homogeneity, essentialist categories, and argue that there are substantial intra-group differences, too. Researchers who embrace multiple social identity dimensions as constituting an individual posit that each dimension is not some layer that is piled or added on. Rather, uneven power distribution in a society complicates situated identities by more firmly entrenching some people at the center and others in the margin (hooks, 1984). On a basic level, this means that an individual can identify themselves as simultaneously Chicana and a lesbian (Collins & Bilge, 2020). Intersectionality is an understanding that social identity dimensions are socially constructed and cannot be isolated from each other. These social identity dimensions also are unique to personalities, experiences, and relationships. Therefore, the intersectionality concept can be applied and used as an analytic tool to reform institutions, organizations, and policies in order to achieve social justice. For example, in recent years, many organizations have encouraged their employees to "bring your whole self to work" to create more inclusion within the workplace (Haymon & Wang, 2020).

In day-to-day life, the intersectionality concept can be applied as an analytic tool to solve workplace dilemmas since there seems to be broad agreement in the U.S. that inclusivity and fairness are desired qualities for organizations (Cox & Lancefield, 2021). For example, creating inclusive workplaces where employees may choose to pray or meditate at work can present challenges since not everyone shares the same belief system, and some people consider faith/religion as more of a private activity that has no place at work. Organizations such as the Tanenbaum Center for Interreligious Understanding offers allyship training and initiatives to support organizations working through these challenges (tanenbaum. org). Organizations must consider including more underrepresented employees in decision-making—while simultaneously remembering that people represent multiple social identity categories at any given time. No one person is just their gender, just their socio-economic status, or just their ethnicity or culture. Embracing the power of intersectionality thinking can enable organizations to avoid misunderstandings and accusations of **tokenism**.

Organizations that understand and apply the intersectionalities concept as a tool have realized benefits for themselves and people associated with the organization. For example, large corporations that form partnerships with and develop outreach programs by lending employees' expertise, offering skills training, and following up with ongoing coaching can benefit small business owners and entrepreneur groups across underrepresented groups. Such efforts involve bringing together people representing a variety of backgrounds to design, develop, and market new products built on the powerful foundation of intersectionality thinking (Haymon & Wang, 2020).

Overall, intersectionality is an important concept to understand how individual social identity dimensions play out in organizations and serve as a tool for problem solving and creating inclusive spaces.

Advancing intersectionality in organizations

Organizations should strive to mirror the demographic composition of the audiences they serve. In other words, to be a moral and successful organization, there should be as much diversity (across social identity dimensions and their intersectionalities) *within* an organization as there is *outside* organizational walls (Ely & Thomas, 2020). DEI not only promotes creativity within the workplace but also nurtures an environment that encourages people to be better decision makers and problem solvers, as well as innovators, explorers, and discoverers (Phillips, 2014). Thus, organizations across globalization trends with multicultural networks must find ways to maximize benefits of social identity categories and ward off limitations of bias and discrimination effects of in-grouping and out-grouping. The question is how? How do organizations advance intersectionality thinking to create more DEI at work?

Understanding privilege

In-groups at the center of decision making in organizations must acknowledge their own **privilege**. Privilege comes in many forms and an individual can experience more than one axis of privilege simultaneously—such as being a Caucasian/White, educated, middle-class, able-bodied, male U.S. citizen. People's failure to accept and understand privilege and how it operates behind the scenes can make them emotionally deficient since they are unable to develop empathy for those who do not have privilege (Amaechi, 2020) and unaware that lack of DEI in organizations is even problematic. Caredda (2022) mentioned that as a Caucasian/White and taller-than-average male he can go out any time of day without worrying about his safety walking home late or he can wear more or less what he wants because of his gender identity. Similarly, Tulshyan (2022) emphasized that if an individual has said, "But I don't see color," then they probably are among an ethnic/racial majority (p. 23).

Yet, individuals acknowledging their privilege does not mean their life is easy or their pain any less legitimate than someone else's. Recognizing privilege does not minimize an individual's lived experiences or hardships. Rather, acknowledging how privilege plays out in humans' lives enables humans to notice why some lives are harder than they should be (Amaechi, 2020). Recognizing privilege can help people realize the systematic advantages and disadvantages that individuals experience in the workplace. For example, job hunting is not the same experience for everyone. Individuals who come from the *wrong address* in town, or their parents are in jail, or if they cannot afford public transportation often can mean they won't get the job (Caredda, 2022). However, it is possible to do something to challenge social systems and organizations' infrastructures (policies and procedures) when people recognize the importance of considering the role of privilege. Individuals need to confront their own privilege to be able to make a meaningful change as part of their DEI commitment (Tulshyan, 2022). This could start with listening, as mentioned in Chapter 2, "Factoring in globalization, (mis)trust, risk, and sociopolitical contexts." Listening intently, without interrupting or comparing personal experiences to the stories of individuals who have been marginalized in their workplaces can help build and maintain an inclusive environment within organizations (Tulshyan, 2022). For example, one CEO who launched a reverse mentoring program invited managers to choose employees to mentor—mentees of social identities that vary from their own—so managers could discover employees' lived experiences (Fuchs et al., 2018).

Exploring social identity intersectionalities

Despite legal protections in the U.S., gender and age—and ways these social identity dimensions intersect with others—very well may constitute cores of the most concerning bias and discrimination issues experienced in organizations today. Title VII of the Civil Rights Act in the U.S. prohits an employer from treating a person differently or less favorably because of their gender is prohibited. Yet, gender discrimination comes in many forms for working women today, with 42% of U.S. women declaring that they have faced job discrimination because of their gender (Parker & Funk, 2017). The Age Discrimination in Employment Act of 1967 (ADEA) protects people aged 40 and over from employment discrimination based on age. Yet, ageism in the form of interpersonal encounters, internalized ageism, harassment, exclusion, denied opportunities, and hiring bias endures (EEOC, n.d.) So, despite protections in courts of law, there are many people who experience negative outcomes of their social identity as part of their work life. Gender and age stand out as being two of the most basic personal characteristics, or social identity dimensions (Wilks & Félix Neto, 2012). Therefore, the focus of this section is to further scrutinize age and gender social identity dimensions, ways they intersect, and how these intersectionalities play out in the workplace. Sidebar 3.1 offers a case study on the role of the Equal Employment Opportunity Commission (EEOC) in supporting legal protections for U.S. employees by considering the issue of raising the minimum wage to benefit people who are underrepresented or marginalized in conjunction with multiple intersecting social identity dimensions.

Sidebar 3.1 Fight for $15 gets at the heart of intersecting social identity dimensions

Tugce Ertem-Eray

Raising the minimum wage is especially important for people who are underrepresented and/or marginalized according to their inter-secting social identity dimensions. The worldwide campaign for increasing the minimum wage to $15 has been a tool for lifting low-income employees out of poverty—especially people who identify as members of BIPOC communities who are women. African American/Black and Latinx households are more likely to report difficulty paying expenses compared to Caucasian/White households (Derenon-court et al., 2020). Therefore, a broad increase in the U.S. minimum wage particularly benefits African American/Black and Latinx house-holds (Derenoncourt et al., 2020). More specifically, women who are

Figure 3.1 Demonstrators participated in a Fight for $15 protest outside a McDonald's restaurant in Las Vegas.

mothers are better able to support their families when the minimum wage increases (Boesch et al., 2021).

According to the U.S. Equal Employment Opportunity Commission (n.d.), pay discrimination appears in the workplace when an employee is paid differently from other employees because of their social identity dimensions, including age, (dis)ability, ethnicity/race, faith/religion, gender, and national origin. Pay discrimination in the workplace affects employees' lives every day, and employers across industries often engage in wage discrimination while ignoring state and federal laws (Fenton, 2022).

The Fight for $15 campaign started in 2012 with 200 fast-food workers walking off the job to ask for $15/hr and union rights in New York (Fightfor$15, n.d.). Then the movement went global in over 300 cities on six continents with fast-food workers, home health aides, childcare teachers, airport workers, adjunct professors, retail employees, and other underpaid workers protesting (Fightfor$15, n.d.). In May 2014, fast-food workers struck in 150 U.S. cities and 33 countries around the world for $15/hr and union rights. April 2015 saw the largest strike of low-wage employees across multiple industries who said they were underpaid as they demanded respect and a voice on the job.

Even though the U.S. Congress has failed to increase the hourly minimum wage since 2009, states and companies have raised wages in the wake of the Fight for $15 campaign across the U.S. By April 2016, California and New York won the $15/hr fight for more than 10 million workers. In September 2022, California passed the FAST Recovery Act, which brought multiple reforms to the state's fast-food industry (Fightfor$15, n.d.). To date, the campaign has seen an increase in the minimum wage to $15/hr in California, Connecticut, Illinois, Massachusetts, New York, New Jersey, Maryland, Florida, and Washington, D.C., as well as in Seattle (Fightfor$15, n.d.). In Pennsylvania, nursing home and hospital workers also have seen minimum wage increases (Fightfor$15, n.d.). Also, Nebraska has embraced a $15 minimum wage, and Hawaii has approved an $18 minimum wage (Greenhouse, 2022).

A National Employment Law Project policy analyst explained how inspirational the movement's success is: "It has helped 26 million workers across the U.S. win $150bn per year in additional pay. Its impact on workers of color is significant. About 12 million workers of color have benefited and their additional earnings are $76bn a year" (Greenhouse, 2022, para. 4). Although the 10-year Fight for $15 campaign has seen a reduced Black–White wealth gap in some states across the U.S., employees in the South still have a long way to go (Kaplan & Hoff, 2022). Overall, the campaign won raises for millions of employees across the country, and the activists continue the fight.

The successful fight for $15 campaign begun in the U.S. saw in increase in the minimum wage specifically to support society's underrepresented and marginalized according to multiple intersecting social identity dimensions. Several social protest events captured media attention (Greenhouse, 2022). Even though the campaign succeeded in increasing the minimum wage for many employees across the U.S. and made a difference in their lives, there is still a long way to go to prevent pay discrimination because of employees' intersecting social identity dimensions of age, ethnicity/race, gender, national origin, and more. Organizations must support DEI programs to support their members, including employees. Increasing the minimum wage is one way to support underrepresented or marginalized people.

Resources

Boesch, D., Bleiweis, R., & Haider, A. (2021, February 23). Raising the minimum wage would be transformative for women. *CAP.* https://rb.gy/66oum. Accessed July 21, 2023.

Derenoncourt, E., Montialoux, C., & Bahn, K. (2020, October 29). Why minimum wages are a critical tool for achieving racial justice in the U.S. labor market. https://rb.gy/lkznj. Accessed July 21, 2023.

Fenton, M. K. (2022, May 16). Pay discrimination in the workplace: Am I protected? https://rb.gy/2wy8p. Accessed July 21, 2023.

Fightfor$15. (n.d.). Why we strike. https://fightfor15.org/why-we-strike/. Accessed July 21, 2023.

Greenhouse, S. (2022, November 23). 'The success is inspirational': the Fight for $15 movement 10 years on. *The Guardian.* https://rb.gy/w8399. Accessed July 21, 2023.

Kaplan, J., & Hoff, M. (2022, November 29). A 10-year fight to raise the minimum wage has slashed the Black–White wealth gap in half in some states. The South still has a long way to go. *Insider.* https://rb.gy/qv1sn. Accessed July 21, 2023.

U.S. Equal Employment Opportunity Commission. (n.d.). Pay Discrimination—FAQs. https://www.eeoc.gov/youth/pay-discrimination-faqs. Accessed July 21, 2023.

Gender inequality

Gender fluidity seems to be increasingly recognized in organizations respecting that there are individuals who identify themselves as possessing a gender social identity that resides beyond the traditional gender binary (Dray et al., 2020). Pronouns also are becoming an important aspect of DEI in the workplace because they are part of an individual's professional identity (Kiesewetter, 2021). Employees may prefer using gender expansive pronouns such as *they, them,* and *theirs,* instead of the more traditional *he, him, his, she, her, hers.* Other inclusive honorifics such as *Mx* instead of *Ms.* or *Mr.* pronouns also are personal and using desired pronouns within the workplace is seen as a form of mutual respect and recognition (HRC, n.d.). Having an organizational culture that provides pronouns in different settings such as email, name badges, and business cards not only reduces the risk of disrespect among people, but also communicates an inclusive environment.

Now for the bad news. Gender disparity among the U.S. workforce (and arguably around the globe) is a fact (e.g., Wooll, 2021). Evidence mounts in unequal pay, disparity in promotions, incidents of sexual harassment, racism, and unequal treatment as compared to male co-workers when women are considered less competent and possessing fewer leadership qualities. The salary gender gap for the past 20 years remains an issue in the U.S. with women earning only 82 cents for every dollar that men make (Kochhar, 2023). During the COVID-19 pandemic, gender disparities widened in the workforce. For example, more women aged 25 and older who have no education beyond high school left the labor force than men (Fry, 2022). Also, globally, more than a quarter of women who were working before the pandemic were out of work in September 2021 (Gregory, 2022).

Gender inequality also presents itself in more nuanced ways, such as fewer opportunities for women who are mothers (Wooll, 2021). According to Pew Research Center findings, about two-thirds of working mothers in the U.S. feel pressure to focus on their household responsibilities (Aragao, 2023) and so women engaged in unpaid second shift work as family caregivers and homemakers endures (Hochschild, 1989). Nike, an American footwear manufacturing multinational corporation, faced a lawsuit from four women employees who said the organization violated state and U.S. equal pay laws by creating a work environment that allowed harassment. As a result of this lawsuit, one of Nike's top human resources executives acknowledged that Nike had failed to promote enough women (Helmore, 2018). Such acknowledgments could offer a starting point for powerful organizations to engage in infrastructional change that embraces true DEI (Short, 2018).

More specifically, BIPOC women continue to face workplace discrimination linked to their intersecting gender, ethnicity/race, and sexual orientation social identity dimensions (e.g., Kramer, 2020; Wooll, 2021). For example, African American/Black executives are 30% more likely to think of leaving employers as compared to their Caucasian/White counterparts (Pandey, 2020), perhaps since Black women experience the stress of feeling compelled to constantly operate in "survival mode" at work with 75% of 1,431 African American/Black women indicating that their organization does not pay enough attention to their skills and 63% indicating that they don't think they will get a promotion within their current organizations—so it may feel easier to switch to a new job (Jackson, 2022). Overall, organizations' DEI programs may not be enough without infrastructural change. DEI programs must invest in intersectional thinking and promote the advancement of underrepresented populations such as BIPOC and LGBTQ+ women who experience among the most marginalized workplace realities (Tulshyan, 2022). Thus, organizations must move beyond one-size-fits-all DEI programs and approaches by engaging in intersectionalities thinking.

Age discrimination

People in the U.S. are living longer, and employers have become increasingly aware of the aging labor force in the U.S.—and worldwide. The life expectancy of the average person in the U.S. has increased from age 76.8 to age 78.7 years (Irby, 2020), so organizations must adapt to demographic changes like this in order to embrace DEI in organizations. Yet, many employees consistently file lawsuits accusing employers of ageism. Bias in the form of age stereotyping and discrimination has increased over the years as older people prefer to continue to work longer in the life course (White et al., 2018). Even though **ageism** is against individuals who are considered too young or too old, the brunt of negative effects seem to impact older individuals more seriously (McNair & Flynn, 2006).

Research findings suggest that older workers are valuable resources given their history and longevity with organizations that gives them perspective and insight to guide decision making (Moore & Moore, 2014). Other studies suggest that older workers exhibit higher levels of work motivation and job involvement than younger workers (Ng & Feldman, 2010). Yet, older workers often are stereotyped as being less capable, harder to train, less adaptable, less flexible, more resistant to change (Posthuma & Campion, 2009), and technology averse (Olson, 2022). Older employees become susceptible to stereotype threats which can have negative psychological effects on their mental health that ultimately result in costly organizational losses in the form of absenteeism (Manzi et al., 2018).

Age intersects with other social identify dimensions so that discriminatory outcomes in organizations play out uniquely among employees in the workplace. Gender social identity dimensions, as well as ethnic/culture/race dimensions intersect in ways that make ageism a reality for people at work. For example, women showing visible aging signs are isolated from projects or professional development opportunities due to biases associated with age discrimination (Diehl et al., 2023; Place, 2021). At the other end of the age spectrum, younger women are considered too inexperienced and middle-aged women are seen to have too many family burdens (Diehl et al., 2023; Pompper, 2011). Findings of a multi-national study suggested that 77% of research participants stated their organization's DEI initiatives did not include strategies for avoiding gendered ageism (Marcus, 2021).

When age and gender social identity dimensions intersect with ethnicity/race social identity dimensions, the outlook is even more nuanced in the U.S. and the U.K. For example, African American/Black workers experience age discrimination most when they are younger, but rates fall during middle age and rise again as workers near retirement (Van Dam, 2021). Older African American/Black people in the U.S. tend to have extreme difficulty finding a new job later in life as compared to their Caucasian/White counterparts (Choi, 1997). Similarly, 13% of older African American/Black individuals say they face discrimination in not being hired for a job and not being promoted, as compared to Caucasian/White peers (Gonzales et al., 2021). In the U.K., both older Caucasian/White and African American/Black British men and women experience occupational access constraints and are paid less than younger Caucasian/White British men (Drydakis et al., 2022). African American/Black British men and women experience higher levels of job discrimination than Caucasian/White British men and women, overall (Drydakis et al., 2022).

Clearly, organizations have their work cut out for themselves if they are serious about making DEI a reality by making deep infrastructural changes in the way organizations operate. Engaging with social identity intersectionality thinking and encouraging managers to take stock of their own privilege are two paths forward.

How to be inclusive at work

Workplaces where DEI foci exist as an intrinsic part of the work culture is more than sum of policies, programs, headcounts, and business case arguments. A DEI commitment must permeate the entire organization with a work climate environment ruled by respect for diverse needs and perspectives (Bush, 2021). Therefore, a DEI commitment also includes an understanding of and commitment to social identity intersectionalities.

Respecting intersectional social identity dimensions

Being inclusive at work begins with respecting ways social identity dimensions intersect—and how these dynamics play out in people's lives across organizations. Everyone's voice and opinions are central to a living and breathing DEI commitment in organizations. For example, creating spaces for prayer/faith and meditation offers an authentic follow-through beyond merely stating in a mission or vision statement that organizations welcome people of all faith systems. Offering a prayer or meditation room is tangible evidence that an organization respects its employees' various faith/religion backgrounds. Gogo, an in-flight internet service provider, asked their employees for their opinions about prayer rooms for the offices and followed through with employee-designed spaces. Today, Gogo's prayer rooms include a foot-washing station for Muslim employees and three include a kneeling bench (Gurchiek, 2018). Bak USA, a manufacturer of mobile computers, also created a prayer room for employees who represent 14 different nationalities. The organization is conscious of a diverse workforce and wanted to make it an inclusive space where everyone feels comfortable bringing all of their intersecting social identity dimensions with them to work (Gurchiek, 2018).

Figure 3.2 Respecting organizational members who desire space for prayer, reflection, and meditation offers an authentic follow-through beyond merely stating in a mission or vision statement that organizations welcome people of all faith systems.

Another example of respecting intersectional social identity dimensions at work involves acknowledging holiday celebrations across cultures, such as Bodhi Day, Ramadan, Diwali, Kwanzaa, Omisoka, Christmas, and Hanukkah since cultures view these celebrations as an expression of their culture's values. Organizations can use their intranet system to make sure all organizational members are aware of upcoming faith-based holiday celebrations so that they may be respectful to work around such days when scheduling meetings and other events (McClendon, 2022). Moreover, organizations should configure organization-wide planning committees to make sure all cultures, celebrations, and religions/faiths are accurately represented and respected. Having diverse representation on all committees that govern organizations—and not just generic DEI committees—can ensure that employees' varied social identity dimensions are included. Carter (2021) also recommended that organizations consider compensating employees for organization-wide committee participation as evidence that the organization has made DEI a top priority and is doing all that is possible to make DEI a reality. Take a look at Sidebar 3.2 to discover how a hospital's cancer awareness campaign turned into a massively successful amplification of its embrace of social identity intersectionalities that was fun and unique.

Sidebar 3.2   Success spawns a sequel: Providence St. Vincent's pink glove dance video campaign

Tugce Ertem-Eray

Organizations must offer work spaces where employees feel valued and respected as they bring their whole selves to work, including all of their intersecting social identity dimensions. Appreciating multiple social identities is an important step for organizations to authentically embrace DEI, increase employee productivity and creativity, and enhance their reputation. Providence St. Vincent Medical Center in Portland, Oregon, is one such case study of how an organization communicates about its DEI ways.

Providence St. Vincent Medical Center became known as a destination where people wanted to work because of a wide-appealing video it posted, "The Pink Glove Dance," as part of its cancer awareness campaign in 2009. More than 200 employees across hospital job responsibilities throughout the organization wore pink gloves, gathered together, and danced on a video that went viral, spreading the word about breast cancer awareness (Boule, 2009; Krem Staff, 2009).

The three-and-a-half-minute video includes employees representing a wide variety of social identity dimensions, including age, ethnicity/race, gender, and socio-economic status—as employees representing varying occupations including nurses, doctors, cafeteria workers, cleaning service staff, lab technicians, and more. Even though the goal of the video was to create awareness about breast cancer, it also demonstrated how an organization can create an inclusive workplace environment. In the wake of the video's release, applicants sought job opportunities at the hospital system, and people wanted to move to Portland and work at what looks like the happiest hospital in the world (Boule, 2009). Moreover, the video created engagement among the hospital's employees from a variety of backgrounds and social identities as part of the fun and unique breast cancer awareness campaign.

Providence St. Vincent Medical Center put the video on YouTube with the name "The Pink Glove Dance" and the video went viral on the internet with more than 13 million views (Boule, 2009; Krem Staff, 2009) and inspired so many pink glove dance videos and events around the world (Menees, 2012). The pink gloves were introduced to generate breast cancer awareness and sold to raise funds for breast cancer research (Roan, 2009). "The Pink Glove Dance" features Jay Sean's song "Down" and employees from every area of the hospital, the CEO, nurses, doctors, cooks, cleaning services, and lab technicians, even a patient or two danced throughout the original video (see https://www.youtube.com/watch?v=zOJxX7mNGwM). Apparently, phone calls of support poured in as well as thousands of letters from around the world. Martie Moore, a nurse at Providence said: "One gentleman called and said he lost his wife in 2005 and he felt like he'd been alone for a long time and he saw this video and it reminded him that people care, and he called just sobbing" (Krem Staff, 2009, para. 5). Fans posted videos on YouTube saying thanks to the hospital, thousands of people commented on the YouTube video, and Martie Moore was interviewed on ABC World News, CNN, and Fox News (Boule, 2009).

In October 2010, 4,000 healthcare workers and breast cancer survivors produced a sequel (see https://www.youtube.com/watch? v=cTyIhMLp3FA), and in 2011, the first national Pink Globe Dance Video competition was held sponsored by Medline Industries. There were 139 entries from hospitals, nursing homes, schools, and other organizations, and the competition became a national phenomenon (Menees, 2012). People also commented about how inclusive the video is. For example, one of the users indicated how fun it is dancing with *everyone* while one of them stated seeing the togetherness in all of this is more worth than a paycheck. One of them mentioned, "Let's bring the guys in. Cancer ain't just a woman's disease."

Even though this campaign started with one hospital and 200 employees, it expanded all around the world including 80,000 participants globally with more than 20 million online views. The campaign unites clinicians with their patients and communities in the fight against cancer (Medline Industries, Inc., 2013). This case is not only an example of a successful cancer awareness campaign but also indicates the role people can play in an inclusive organization when they feel as though they belong and their intersecting social identity dimensions are embraced and valued.

Resources

Boule, M. (2009, December 13). Providence St. Vincent's 'pink glove' dancers go viral for breast cancer awareness. *The Oregonian*. https://www.oregonlive.com/news/oregonian/margie_boule/2009/12/providence_st_vincents_pink_gl.html Accessed July 20, 2023.

Krem Staff. (2009, December 16). Providence "Pink Gloves" video a viral sensation. *KREM*. https://www.krem.com/article/news/health/providence-pink-gloves-video-a-viral-sensation/293-413310498. Accessed July 20, 2023.

Medline Industries, Inc. (2013, November 19). Third annual Medline pink glove dance viral video contest reaches 20 million views; millions raised for breast cancer education and prevention. *PR Newswire*. https://www.prnewswire.com/news-releases/third-annual-medline-pink-glove-dance-viral-video-contest-reaches-20-million-views-millions-raised-for-breast-cancer-education-and-prevention-232044781.html. Accessed July 21, 2023.

Menees, C. (2012, October 10). Pink Glove Dance raises breast cancer awareness. *NWTN Today*. https://www.nwtntoday.com/2012/10/10/pink-glove-dance-raises-breast-cancer-awareness/. Accessed July 21, 2023.

Pink Glove Dance. https://www.youtube.com/watch?v=zOJxX7mNGwM. Accessed July 20, 2023.
Pink Glove Dance. Pink Glove Dance: The Sequel. https://www.youtube. com/watch?v=cTyIhMLp3FA. Accessed July 20, 2023.
Roan, S. (2009, December 1). This pink-gloved hospital is rockin'. *Los Angeles Times*. https://www.latimes.com/archives/blogs/booster-shots/story/2009-12-01/this-pink-gloved-hospital-is-rockin. Accessed July 20, 2023.

Another way organizations may demonstrate respect for members and their intersectional social identity dimensions is to offer lactation rooms and diaper-changing facilities to support breastfeeding in the workplace and childcare support for guests and/or employees who are permitted to bring their children to work. Regardless of size, it is organizations' responsibility to help employees who are child caregivers to transition back to work by creating a comfortable and safe space (Lewis, 2023). Women have been criticized and shamed for nursing their babies in public for years (Doonan, 2022). Even though it only became legal in 2018 (in all 50 states) to nurse babies in public, women still consider quitting their jobs for more breastfeeding-friendly jobs (Mazziotta, 2018). There are ethnicity/race dimensions to the breastfeeding in public phenomenon, too, as "suboptimal breastfeeding is more pervasive in Black communities in the U.S." (Asiodu et al., 2021, p. 447). Hence, organizations must take responsibility for creating an inclusive environment for employees and others who are mothers as their gender, ethnicity/race, and culture social identity dimensions intersect. For example, Marriott International renovated its lactation room equipped with multi-use pumps and breastfeeding supplies and curtains separating each station to create a private space for women using the rooms (Kahn, 2016).

So, respecting audiences' intersectional social identity dimensions is a central feature of organizations respecting DEI at work.

Role of leadership

Ensuring that actions such as these that illustrate respect for intersecting social identity dimensions actually become a reality—like prayer/meditation rooms and lactation spaces at work—often pivots on an organization's leadership team and *their* degrees of commitment to making DEI a reality. Leadership teams in organizations can include the chief executive officer, president, vice presidents, legal officer, human resources head and cut across physical geographic locations such as international locations. An organizational culture that values social identity intersectionality is not possible without supportive leadership. An organization's leadership team inspires an inclusive mindset that can permeate the work environment by valuing all individuals' talents, work styles, and collaboration with others (Tulshyan, 2022).

Sometimes processes associated with developing and demonstrating respect for intersecting social identity dimensions can begin with leadership team members being OK with feeling uncomfortable—and then discovering what they don't know. As mentioned earlier in this chapter, in-groups at the center of decision making in organizations must acknowledge their own privilege. Developing greater acknowledgment of leadership privileges and biases may be uncomfortable—but it's also necessary for fostering and nurturing a DEI work environment. Leaders should reflect on what they don't know about the challenges marginalized communities face. Here's where formal data collection and analysis can help. See an expanded discussion about applying research skills in the service of DEI in Chapter 8, "Future directions for developing competence as a diversity and difference change manager." Leaders who put themselves into the shoes of employees and other people touched by an organization can better discern deficiencies in perspectives typically overlooked when establishing organizational policy or making decisions with DEI implications (and what doesn't?) (Tulshyan, 2022). Leaders experiencing privilege who do not consider the challenges marginalized communities face operate from a deficit standpoint. They don't know what they don't know. People most impacted by challenges are the ones who may be most qualified to participate in designing barrier-free future work (Praslova, 2022). Thus, including wide social identity dimension representation among committees charged to do an organization's planning, designing, and assessment is imperative—and an earmark of strong leadership.

As a matter of routine and follow-through on their DEI commitment, oranizations' leaders must seek feedback to discover audiences' perceptions of their leaders' actions. DEI-related actions must be considered authentic and not just lip service. Organizations can conduct anonymous surveys, hold town hall meetings, use feedback platforms, schedule one-on-one meetings with employees, and engage in reverse mentoring to encourage employees to offer feedback (Carruthers, 2022). Leaders must grow from their mistakes and acknowledge that change takes time. It is important to take time to listen and learn to avoid making only minimal changes within the organization. For example, in 2020, when George Floyd, an African American/Black man, was murdered by a Caucasian/White policeman and the #BlackLivesMatter movement spread around the globe, many organizations took to social media to proclaim solidarity condemning racism. Yet, far fewer implemented actual follow-up actions to ensure their own organizations' commitment to DEI was doing all it could do (Tulshyan, 2022).

Organizational justice in hiring and promoting process

Following through on a commitment to build an inclusive work environment, leaders must take stock of their own privilege in order to respect organizational members' intersectional social identity dimensions. Overall, this commitment also involves offering fair and equitable hiring and promotion processes that eradicate microaggressions, maximize microaffirmations, and ensure organizational justice. **Organizational justice** means fairness and equality across organizations' policies, procedures, interactions, and outcomes—including members' interpersonal relationships and their perceptions (e.g., Baldwin, 2006; Bies & Moag, 1986). Organizations must offer a foundation for creating **equal opportunities** for everyone—consistent with laws and moral commitments. For example, organizations must be certain that hiring tools and procedures do not inadvertently exclude individuals with physical or mental impairments, such as autistic applicants unable to maintain eye contact in conjunction with formal interviews (Praslova, 2022). Some corporations provide unconscious bias training, promote mentorship programs, and engage in retention programs to maintain employees of under-represented groups—such as women, LGBTQ+ people, African American/Black, Latinx, veterans—after hiring (Myers, 2022).

Once on the job, however, some employees seeking promotion experience degrees of challenges related to their social identity dimensions in the form of bias and discrimination (e.g., Beeson, 2009)—despite any formal policy manuals that organizations create and use. Fundamentally, some employees perceive the criteria for promotion vague (Martinez, 2021). Also, one of the reasons employees cite for leaving a job is lack of career development and advancement potential (Chodyniecka et al., 2022). Organizations can support both of these challenges by eradicating bias from promotion processes, providing clear promotion guidelines, and offering career advancement support (Cooks-Campbell, 2022). Grondelle (2021) found that a consultancy organization seeking to develop a DEI-committed culture needed to revise promotion procedures to redress imbalanced criteria emphasizing technical skills over relationship-building skills.

Addressing microaggressions and microaffirmations

Ridding organizations of behaviors known as microaggressions—while encouraging microaffirmations—is yet another means for ensuring organizational justice. **Microaggressions** thwart attempts to develop DEI commitment in organizations. Microaggressions are "subtle snubs, slights, and insults directed toward minorities, as well as to women and other historically stigmatized groups, that implicitly communicate or engender hostility" (Lilienfeld, 2017, p. 139). They can take the forms of: blatantly negative statements, negative statements disguised as positive statements—all of which can make people feel invisible or as if they are contaminated (Williams, 2020).

Microaggressions are harmful and amplify bias across organizations. Sometimes, individuals might not even be aware that they commit micro-aggressions. For example, commenting on how well an Asian American co-worker speaks English, presuming that English is not their first language, is a microaggression (Limbong, 2020). Complimenting an African American/Black women employee for being *so articulate* when delivering her speech or not inviting an LGBTQ+ Latinx colleague to a social gathering also are common forms of microaggressions in organizations (Fattoracci & King, 2023). Hence, the presence of intersecting social identity dimensions intensify microaggressions' pain (Dalton & Villagran, 2018)—in terms of physical and emotional health—that ultimately impacts work performance, and overall organizational climate (Williams et al., 2021). For organizations, microaggressions contribute to lower job satisfaction and motivation among employees, resulting in reduced organizational commitment. For victims, microaggressions negatively impact career trajectories (Fattoracci & King, 2023; Washington, 2022). Therefore, organizations must reduce the potential for microaggressions occurring in the first place and offer support to victims.

Conversely, **microaffirmations** are positive small works that organizational members may perform to show one another respect, provide encouragement, foster healthy relationships, and help marginalized people succeed and feel as though they belong (Rowe, 2008). Organizations must encourage microaffirmation in the form of: leading rather than pushing, building a community, listening attentively, giving credit where it is due, providing comfort/support during stressful times, and building on strengths/successes rather than focusing on faults/weaknesses (Pompper, 2020; Scully & Rowe, 2009).

Ways organizations prevent and respond to microaggressions and nurture a culture of microaffirmations can affect their employees' perceptions of fairness at work—and promote organizational justice, overall (Fattoracci & King, 2023). Like leaders taking store of personal privilege, it also is important for organizations to foster a culture for endorsing microaffirmation behaviors and reducing potential for microaggressions. For example, organizations must take stock of commonly used words and phrases that systematically favor dominant groups and can contribute to microaggression behaviors victimizing marginalized groups. In the English language, words such as *blacklist* and *peanut gallery* are rooted in notions that black is negative and white is positive (Andrew & Kaur, 2020; Washington, 2022). In the tech industry, a *blacklist* refers to a directory of specific elements, such as email addresses or IP addresses, that are blocked. A *whitelist*, however, includes elements that are allowed. Simply changing words can help avoid perpetuating microaggressions, as when Google's and Android's open-source projects encouraged developers to instead use the words *blocklist* and *allowlist* instead of *blacklist* and *whitelist* (Andrew & Kaur, 2020). Similarly, *peanut gallery* typically refers to the cheapest seats in a theater and historically is a term associated with BIPOC communities such as less affluent immigrants (Andrew & Kaur, 2020). Organizations that encourage honest and open discussion wherein members may share their perceptions and even create committee group projects for rooting out organizational language contributing to microaggressions are positive active behaviors designed to make DEI goals successful (e.g., Dalton & Villagran, 2018; Fattoracci & King, 2023).

Concluding thoughts

The purpose of this chapter has been to explore ways that intersectionality in social identity dimensions play out in the workplace by highlighting DEI social justice goals and roadblocks in the form of negative outcomes that organizations still work on reversing. Remember that one of this book's goals is to support organizational communicators on their journey toward supporting organizations in meeting their DEI goals, taking them to action steps and not merely offering lip service in the form of lofty vision and mission statements that address a desire to achieve DEI. This chapter offered several concrete means for organizations to advance *social identity intersectionality thinking* after defining several terms associated with social identity dimensions. Truly being inclusive at work can involve a great deal of effort—especially when organizations are mired in the past and resistant to change. Yet, when leaders are willing to engage in the painful responsibility of taking stock of their privilege, the tasks required for infrastructural change can unfold much more smoothly. An inclusive work environment means an organizational culture rooted in mutual trust, engagement, innovation, and ethical behavior (Dweck et al., 2014). Having an organizational culture that promotes organizational justice is not only morally the right thing to do for organizations, but it is a legal requirement for organizations in the U.S. and several other nations. Organizations that fail to follow the law and morally address members' perceptions with real and supportive actions run the risk of tarnishing their reputation in the public sphere. It is an organization's leaders' responsibility to create and maintain an inclusive and equitable work environment for everyone so they can thrive within the workplace. Creating an inclusive environment where everyone feels valued and respected does not happen overnight. It takes continuous listening, learning, and growing.

Next, Chapter 4, "Power differentials in organizations and society" covers power differentials, an important barrier to effective relationship building between organizations and publics.

Key words

Ageism—Ageism is "a process of systematic stereotyping of and discrimination against people because they are old" (Butler, 1975, p. 35).

Business case—This term characterizes many organizations' justification for advocating for DEI on the basis of its benefits to a company bottom line. Numerous researchers have criqitued the term and its rationale as lacking in morality. Rather, need organizations justify advocating for DEI and making it a reality at all when they rarely do so for other organizational values like "innovation, resilience, or integrity" (Georgeac & Rattan, 2022, para. 1)?

Difference—The term is used to examine the different, complex, and overlapping facets that define an individual's social identity (Pompper, 2014).

Equal opportunity—Equal opportunity is "the idea that men and women, people of different races, religions, etc. should all be treated fairly and have the same opportunities, especially relating to employment" (*Cambridge Dictionary*).

Gender—Gender usually denotes the "social, cultural, and historical distinctions between men and women, and is sometimes described as the study of masculinity and femininity" (Curthoys, 2005, p. 140).

Hegemony—Hegemony indicates "the dominance of one group over another, often supported by legitimating norms and ideas" (Britannica, n.d.).

Identity—Identity is "a person's sense of self, established by their unique characteristics, affiliations, and social roles." (Yilmaz, n.d., para. 4).

Microaffirmations—Microaffirmations are small statements and body language gestures that communicate inclusion, caring, and support (Sadighi, n.d.)—through nodding, facial expressions, word choices, tone of voice, and more.

Microaggressions—Microaggressions are defined as "black–white racial interactions [that] are characterized by white put-downs, done in an automatic, preconscious, or unconscious fashion" (Pierce, 1974, p. 515). Both popular use and the academic study of microaggressions have grown rapidly over the years and the definition has been expanded to various groups where there exists stigma and/or a power imbalance (Williams, 2020, p. 3).

Organizational justice—Organizational justice refers to the perception of fair treatment of employees in organizations (Aycan, 2004).

Personal identity—People's self-concept comprises the attitudes, memories, behaviors, and emotions that define them as idiosyncratic individuals, distinct from other individuals (Hornsey, 2008). "The unique ways that people define themselves as individuals (the 'I')" (Leaper, 2011, p. 363).

Privilege—"First, privilege is a special advantage; it is neither common nor universal. Second, it is granted, not earned, or brought into being by one's individual effort or talent. Third, privilege is a right or entitlement that is related to a preferred status or rank. Fourth, privilege is exercised for the benefit of the recipient and to the exclusion or detriment of others. Finally, a privileged status is often outside of the awareness of the person possessing it" (Black & Stone, 2005, p. 244).

Social group—Social group consists of "two or more individuals who share a common social identification of themselves or, which is nearly the same thing, perceive themselves to be members of the same social category" (Turner, 1982, p. 15).

Social identity—Social identity is "the individual's knowledge that he belongs to certain social groups together with some emotional and value significance to him of the group membership" (Tajfel, 1972, p. 31). "The social component of identity is the perception of 'oneness' with others" (Ashforth & Mael, 1989, p. 21).

Tokenism—Tokenism is a surface-level symbolic attempt to offer an appearance of authenticity—especially with regard to recruiting members of underrepresented groups and then failing to support them on to success in organizations.

Discussion questions for deep engagement

1. How would you describe your social identity? Which social identities are most central to you as a person? Why?
2. What assumptions do you think other people at work (or school) make about you based on your social identities?
3. What should be done to apply intersectionality thinking in organizations?
4. In what ways do gender and age intersect with other social identity dimensions in your lived experience?
5. What are some biases about marginalized communities in your workplace or at school that you have experienced or witnessed?
6. What are some examples of microaggressions and microaffirmations that you have experienced or witnessed in your workplace or at school?

Resources

Abrams, D., & Hogg, M. A. (1990a). An introduction to the social identity approach. In D. Abrams & M. A. (Eds.) *Social identity theory: Constructive and critical advances* (pp. 1–9). Harvester-Wheatsheaf.

Abrams, D., & Hogg, M. A. (1990b). *Social identifications: A social psychology of intergroup relations and group processes*. Taylor & Francis.

Amaechi, C. (2020, November 17). Privilege blinds us to plight of others who lack it. *Financial Times*. https://www.ft.com/content/e394fd7b-5bdb-4d96-8375-a10a 24e960c2. Accessed July 10, 2023.

Andrew, S., & Kaur, H. (2020, July 7). Everyday words and phrases that have racist connotations. CNN. https://www.cnn.com/2020/07/06/us/racism-words-phrases-slavery-trnd/index.html. Accessed July 14, 2023.

Aragao, C. (2023, March 1). Gender pay gap in U.S. hasn't changed much in two decades. Pew Research Center. https://www.pewresearch.org/short-reads/2023/03/01/gender-pay-gap-facts/. Accessed July 7, 2023.

Ashforth, B. E., & Mael, F. (1989). Social identity theory and the organization. *Academy of Management Review, 14*(1), 20–39. https://psycnet.apa.org/doi/10.2307/258189.

Asiodu, I. V., Bugg, K., & Palmquist, A. E. L. (2021). Achieving breastfeeding equity and justice in Black communities: Past, present, and future. *Breastfeeding Medicine, 16*(6), 447–451. DOI: https://doi.org/10.1089%2Fbfm.2020.0314.

Aycan, Z. (2004). Industrial/organizational psychology across cultures. In C. D. Spielberger (Ed.), *Encyclopedia of applied psychology* (pp. 271–283). https://doi.org/10.1016/B0-12-657410-3/00690-5.

Baldwin, S. (2006). Organisational justice. Institute for employment Studies. Downloaded November 27, 2023 from https://www.employment-studies.co.uk/system/files/resources/files/mp73.pdf.

Bauer-Wolf, J. (2023). College presidents are still overwhelmingly White men. *Higher Ed Dive*. Downloaded November 26, 2023 from https://www.highereddive.com/news/college-presidents-are-still-overwhelmingly-white-men/647749/#:~:text=Dive%20Brief%3A&text=The%20remaining%2067%25%20of%20survey,down%20from%2083%25%20in%202016.

Beeson, J. (2009). Why you didn't get that promotion. *Harvard Business Review*. Downloaded November 27, 2023 from https://hbr.org/2009/06/why-you-didnt-get-that-promotion.

Bies, R. J., & Moag, J. S. (1986). Interactional justice: Communication criteria of fairness. In R. J. Lewicki, B. H. Sheppard, & B. H. Baseman (Eds.), *Research on negotiation in organizations* (pp. 43–55). JAI Press.

Black, L. L., & Stone, D. (2005). Expanding the definition of privilege: The concept of social privilege. *Journal of Multicultural Counseling and Development, 33*(4), 243–255. https://doi.org/10.1002/j.2161-1912.2005.tb00020.x.

Britannica. (n.d.). Hegemony. https://www.britannica.com/topic/hegemony. Accessed July 24, 2023.

Bush, M. (2021, April 13). Why is diversity and inclusion in the workplace important? Great Place to Work. https://www.greatplacetowork.com/resources/blog/why-is-diversity-inclusion-in-the-workplace-important. Accessed July 12, 2023.

Butler, J. (2008). *Gender trouble: Feminism and the subversion of identity*. Routledge.

Butler, R. N. (1975). *Why survive? Being old in America*. Harper & Row.

Cambridge Dictionary. Equal opportunities. https://dictionary.cambridge.org/us/dictionary/english/equal-opportunities. Accessed July 12, 2023.

Caredda, S. (2022, March 7). Yes, I'm privileged. Medium. https://medium.com/the-intentional-organisation/yes-im-privileged-5473cafba06e. Accessed July 10, 2023.

Carruthers, R. (2022, February 17). Examples of diversity, equity, inclusion, and belonging performance goals: how to set and achieve them. Together. https://www.togetherplatform.com/blog/diversity-and-inclusion-performance-goals-examples. Accessed July 12, 2023.

Carter, S. (2021, December 8). how companies can celebrate the holidays inclusively this season. Worth. https://www.worth.com/how-companies-celebrate-holidays-inclusively-this-season/. Accessed July 12, 2023.

Center for Creative Leadership (2023, February 7). Understand social identity to lead in a changing world. CCL. https://www.ccl.org/articles/leading-effectively-articles/understand-social-identity-to-lead-in-a-changing-world/. Accessed July 5, 2023.

Choi, N. G. (1997). Racial differences in retirement income: The roles of public and private income sources. *Journal of Aging & Social Policy*, 9(3), 21–42. https://doi.org/10.1300/j031v09n03_02.

Chodyniecka, E., De Smet, A., Dowling, B., & Mugayar-Baldocchi, M. (2022, March 28). Money can't buy your employees' loyalty. McKinsey Company. https://www.mckinsey.com/capabilities/people-and-organizational-performance/our-insights/the-organization-blog/money-cant-buy-your-employees-loyalty. Accessed July 13, 2023.

Collins, P. H., & Bilge, S. (2020). *Intersectionality*. Polity.

Cooks-Campbell, A. (2022, September 28). Promotion policy guidelines and best practices. BetterUp. https://www.betterup.com/blog/promotion-policy. Accessed July 13, 2023.

Cox, G., & Lancefield, D. (2021). 5 strategies to infuse D&I into your organization. *Harvard Business Review*. https://hbr.org/2021/05/5-strategies-to-infuse-di-into-your-organization. Accessed July 6, 2023.

Crenshaw, K. W. (1989). Demarginalizing the intersection of race and sex: A Black feminist critique of antidiscrimination doctrine, feminist theory and antiracist politics. *University of Chicago Legal Forum*, 1(8), 139–167. Available at: http://chicagounbound.uchicago.edu/uclf/vol1989/iss1/8.

Curthoys, A. (2005). Gender. In T. Bennett, L. Grossberg, & M. Morris (Eds.), *New keywords: A revised vocabulary of culture and society* (pp. 140–142). Blackwell Publishing.

Dalton, S., & Villagran, M. (2018). Minimizing and addressing microaggressions in the workplace. *College and Research Libraries*, 79(10), 538–564.

Danna, K., & Griffin, G. (1999). Health and well-being in the workplace: A review and synthesis of the literature. *Journal of Management*, 25(3), 357–384. https://doi.org/10.1177/014920639902500305.

Diehl, A., Dzubinski, L. M., & Stephenson, A. L. (2023, June 16). Women in leadership face ageism at every age. *Harvard Business Review*. https://hbr.org/2023/06/women-in-leadership-face-ageism-at-every-age. Accessed July 7, 2023.

Doonan, C. (2022). There's no formula for a good mother: Shame and estranged maternal labour. *Feminist Theory*, 23(4), 512–538. DOI: https://doi.org/10.1177/14647001211042488.

Dray, K. K., Smith, V. R. E., Kostecki, T. P., Sabat, I. E., & Thomson, C. R. (2020). Moving beyond the gender binary: Examining workplace perceptions of non-binary and transgender employees. *Gender, Work, & Organization*, 27(6), 1181–1191. https://doi.org.prox.lib.ncsu.edu/10.1111/gwao.12455.

Drydakis, N., Paraskevopoulou, A., & Bozani, V. (2022). A field study of age discrimination in the workplace: The importance of gender and race. Pay the gap. Discussion Paper Series, IZA Institute of Labor Economics. https://docs.iza.org/dp15567.pdf. Accessed July 7, 2023.

Dweck, C., Murphy, M., Chatman, J., & Kay, L. (2014). Why fostering a growth mindset in organizations matters. Senn-Delaney Leadership Consulting Group. https://www.aesc.org/insights/thought-leadership/assessment-culture/senn-dela ney-heidrick-struggles-company-fostering.

Ely, R. J., & Thomas, D. A. (2020). Getting serious about diversity: Enough already with the business case. *Harvard Business Review*. Downloaded November 24, 2023 from https://hbr.org/2020/11/getting-serious-about-diversity-enough-alrea dy-with-the-business-case?utm_medium=paidsearch&utm_source=google& utm_campaign=domcontent_bussoc&utm_term=Non-Brand&tpcc=dom content_bussoc&gad_source=1&gclid=Cj0KCQjw8J6wBhDXARIsAPo7QA_ GJqROms2J_0ZX7PeB0gFNvgZdZZ6-XjXT0A5xR6Uc-Uy5yoepzgsaAnX LEALw_wcB.

Fattoracci, E. S. M., & King, D. D. (2023). The need for understanding and addressing microaggressions in the workplace. *Perspectives on Psychological Science*, 18(4), 738–742. https://doi.org/10.1177/17456916221133825.

Fry, R. (2022, January 14). Some gender disparities widened in the U.S. workforce during the pandemic. Pew Research Center. https://www.pewresearch.org/short-reads/2022/01/14/some-gender-disparities-widened-in-the-u-s-workforce-during-the-pandemic/. Accessed July 24, 2023.

Fuchs, B., Reitz, M., & Higgins, J. (2018, April 10). Do you have "advantage blindness"? *Harvard Business Review*. https://hbr.org/2018/04/do-you-have-advantage-blindness?registration=success. Accessed July 10, 2023.

Gardiner, J. K. (2002). Introduction. In J. K. Gardiner (Ed.), *Masculinity studies & feminist theory* (pp. 1–29). Columbia University Press.

Georgeac, O., & Rattan, A. (2022). Stop making the business case for diversity. *Harvard Business Review*. Downloaded November 26, 2023 from https://hbr.org/2022/06/stop-making-the-business-case-for-diversity.

Gonzales, E., Lee, Y. J., Marchiondo, L. A. (2021). Exploring the consequences of major lifetime discrimination, neighborhood conditions, chronic work, and everyday discrimination on health and retirement. *Journal of Applied Gerontology*, 40(2), 21–131. https://doi.org/10.1177/0733464819892847.

Gregory, A. (2022, March 2). Covid has intensified gender inequalities, global study finds. *The Guardian*. https://www.theguardian.com/world/2022/mar/02/covid-intensified-existing-gender-inequalities-global-study-finds. Accessed July 24, 2023.

Grondelle, I. W.-V. (2021, November 9). Inclusive promotion in practice—3 case examples. LinkedIn. https://www.linkedin.com/pulse/inclusive-promotion-practice-3-case-examples-woudstra-van-grondelle/?trk=pulse-article. Accessed July 13, 2023.

Gurchiek, K. (2018, March 23). Prayer and meditation rooms can increase inclusion. SHRM. https://www.shrm.org/resourcesandtools/hr-topics/behavioral-compe tencies/global-and-cultural-effectiveness/pages/prayer-meditation-rooms-can-increase-inclusion.aspx. Accessed July 12, 2023.

Haymon, M., & Wang, L. (2020, October 7). Intersectionality in organizations: Why 'Bringing Your Whole Self to Work' is not sufficient. Dalberg. https://dalberg.com/our-ideas/intersectionality-in-organizations-why-bringing-your-whole-self-to-work-is-not-sufficient/. Accessed July 6, 2023.

Helmore, E. (2018, August 10). Nike hit with lawsuit from four women who allege gender discrimination. *The Guardian*. https://www.theguardian.com/busi ness/2018/aug/10/nike-lawsuit-women-gender-discrimination. Accessed July 7, 2023.

Hershey. (n. d.). Fostering diversity, equity, and inclusion. https://www.thehershey company.com/en_us/home/sustainability/sustainability-focus-areas/diversity-equity-inclusion.html. Accessed July 12, 2023.

Hochschild, A. R. (1989). *The second shift*. Penguin Books.

hooks, b. (1984). *Feminist theory: From margin to center*. Boston: South End.

Hornsey, M. J. (2008). Social identity theory and self-categorization theory: A historical review. *Social and Personality Psychology Compass*, 2(1), 204–222. https://doi.org/10.1111/j.1751-9004.2007.00066.x.

HRC. (n.d.). Talking about pronouns in the workplace. Human Rights Campaign Foundation. https://www.thehrcfoundation.org/professional-resources/talking-about-pronouns-in-the-workplace#:~:text=These%20employees%20may%20opt%20to,the%20more%20inclusive%20%E2%80%9CMx.%E2%80%9D. Accessed July 10, 2023.

Irby, C. M. (2020. What to do about our aging workforce—the employers' response. Monthly Labor Review. U.S. Bureau of Labor Statistics. Downloaded November 26, 2023 from https://www.bls.gov/opub/mlr/2020/beyond-bls/what-to-do-about-our-aging-workforce-the-employers-response.htm.

Jackson, A. (2022, July 1). Black women are in 'survival mode' at work—and company diversity efforts 'fall short'. CNBC. https://www.cnbc.com/2022/07/01/company-diversity-efforts-to-support-black-women-fall-short.html. Accessed July 7, 2023.

Kahn, M. (2016, April 19). The best lactation rooms across America. *Elle*. https://www.elle.com/culture/career-politics/g28143/the-best-lactation-rooms-across-america/. Accessed July 12, 2023.

Kiesewetter, J. S. (2021). Best practices for using pronouns in the workplace and everyplace! Spark. https://www.adp.com/spark/articles/2021/06/best-practices-for-using-pronouns-in-the-workplace-and-everyplace.aspx. Accessed July 7, 2023.

Kochhar, R. (2023). The enduring grip of the gender pay gap. Pew Research Center. Downloaded November 26, 2023 from https://shorturl.at/frzW6.

Kramer, A. (2020, January 7). Recognizing workplace challenges faced by Black women leaders. *Forbes*. https://www.forbes.com/sites/andiekramer/2020/01/07/recognizing-workplace-challenges-faced-by-black-women-leaders/?sh=6008fc7d53e3. Accessed July 7, 2023.

Lewis, K. (2023, January 19). Lactation room to support breastfeeding at work. Verywellfamily. https://www.verywellfamily.com/lactation-room-breastfeeding-at-work-3545106. Accessed July 12, 2023.

Lilienfeld, S. O. (2017). Microaggressions: Strong claims, inadequate evidence. *Perspectives on Psychological Science*, 12, 138–169. https://doi.org/10.1177/1745691616659391.

Limbong, A. (2020, June 9). Microaggressions are a big deal: How to talk them out and when to walk away. NPR. https://www.npr.org/2020/06/08/872371063/microaggressions-are-a-big-deal-how-to-talk-them-out-and-when-to-walk-away. Accessed July 13, 2023.

Manzi, C., Paderi, F., Benet-Martínez, V., & Coen, S. (2018). Age-based stereotype threat and negative outcomes in the workplace: Exploring the role of identity integration. *European Journal of Social Psychology*, 49(4), 705–716. https://doi.org/10.1002/ejsp.2533.

Marcus, B. (2021, September 20). Gendered ageism affects women's job security and financial viability. *Forbes*. https://www.forbes.com/sites/bonniemarcus/2021/09/20/gendered-ageism-affects-womens-job-security-and-financial-viability/?sh=3b6673f2bc42. Accessed July 7, 2023.

Martin, J. N., Krizek, R. L., Nakayama, T. K., & Bradford, L. (1999). What do White people want to be called? In T. K. Nakayama and J. N. Martin (Eds.), *Whiteness: The communication of social identity* (pp. 27–50). Sage.

Martinez, L. (2021, August 24). 8 ways to have a fair process for promotions. Great Place to Work. https://www.greatplacetowork.com/resources/blog/how-to-ensure-promotions-go-to-those-who-most-deserve-them. Accessed July 13, 2023.

Mazziotta, J. (2018, October 24). 47 percent of pregnant women have considered quitting for more breastfeeding-friendly jobs. People. https://people.com/health/pregnant-women-considered-quitting-breastfeeding-friendly-jobs/. Accessed July 24, 2023.

McClendon, D. (2022, June 21). How to promote diversity, equity, and inclusion in the workplace. CERIDIAN. https://www.ceridian.com/blog/support-diversity-and-inclusion-in-the-workplace#5acknowledgeholidays. Accessed July 12, 2023.

McNair, S., & Flynn, M. (2006). *Managing an ageing workforce in the manufacturing sector: A report for employers.* The Department for Work and Pensions.

Middlehurst-Schwartz, M. (2021). Las Vegas Raiders' Carl Nassib comes out as first openly gay active NFL player. *USA Today.* Downloaded November 267, 2023 from https://www.usatoday.com/story/sports/nfl/raiders/2021/06/21/carl-nassib-comes-out-first-openly-gay-active-nfl-player/5298365001/.

Moore, P., & Moore, R. L. (2014). *Fundamentals of occupational & environmental health nursing AAOHN core curriculum.* American Association of Occupational Health Nursing.

Myers, A. (2022, May 9). Hershey moves to sixth on DiversityInc's Top 50 Companies list. *Confectionery News.* https://www.confectionerynews.com/Article/2022/05/09/Hershey-moves-to-sixth-on-DiversityInc-s-Top-50-Companies-list?utm_source=copyright&utm_medium=OnSite&utm_campaign=copyright. Accessed July 24, 2022.

Ng, T. W. H., & Feldman, D. C. (2010). The relationships of age with job attitudes: A meta-analysis. *Personnel Psychology, 63,* 677–718. https://doi.org/10.1111/j.1744-6570.2010.01184.x.

Leaper, C. (2011). More similarities than differences in contemporary theories of social development?: A plea for theory bridging. *Advances in Child Development and Behavior, 40,* 337–378. https://doi.org/10.1016/B978-0-12-386491-8.00009-8.

Olson, M. L. (2022). Contributed: Seniors aren't tech averse. We're just not designing for their needs. *Mobihealthnews.* Downloaded November 26, 2023 from https://www.mobihealthnews.com/topics/healthy-aging?page=8.

Pandey, E. (2020, November 17). Corporate America's revolving door for Black employees. AXIOS. https://www.axios.com/2020/11/17/corporate-america-black-employee-turnover-rate. Accessed July 24, 2023.

Phillips, K. W. (2014, October 1). How diversity makes us smarter. *Scientific American.* https://www.scientificamerican.com/article/how-diversity-makes-us-smarter/. Accessed July 7, 2023.

Pierce, C. M. (1974). Psychiatric problems of the Black minority. In S. Arieti (Ed.), *American handbook of psychiatry* (pp. 512–523). Basic Books.

Place, A. (2021, February 24). Yet another hurdle for women at work: Their age. *EBN.* https://www.benefitnews.com/news/age-is-another-hurdle-for-women-at-work. Accessed July 7, 2023.

Pompper, D. (2011). Fifty years later: Mid-career women of color against the glass ceiling in communications organizations. *Journal of Organizational Change Management, 24*(4), 464–486. https://doi.org/10.1108/09534811111144629.

Pompper, D. (2014). *Practical and theoretical implications of successfully doing difference in organizations.* Emerald Books.

Pompper, D. (2020). Public relations' role as diversity advocate: Avoiding microaggressions and nurturing microaffirmations in organizations. *Public Relations Journal, 13*(2), https://prjournal.instituteforpr.org/wp-content/uploads/Pompper-_Diversity_Advocate_EDITED2.12.pdf

Pompper, D., Ertem-Eray, T., Amevor, E., Diop, L., Nadel, S., & Adae, E. K. (2021). Diversity at the big table: A snapshot of Fortune 500 boards of directors. In D. Pompper (Ed.) *Public relations for social responsibility: Affirming DEI commitment with action* (pp. 51–69). Emerald Group Publishing.

Posthuma, R. A., & Campion, M. A. (2009). Age stereotypes in the workplace: Common stereotypes, moderators, and future research directions. *Journal of Management*, 35, 158–188. https://doi.org/10.1177/0149206308318617.

Praslova, L. N. (2022, June 21). An intersectional approach to inclusion at work. *Harvard Business Review*. https://hbr.org/2022/06/an-intersectional-approach-to-inclusion-at-work. Accessed July 12, 2023.

Rock, D., & Grant, H. (2016). Why divese teams are smarter. *Harvard Business Review*. Downloaded November 26, 2023 from https://hbr.org/2016/11/why-diverse-teams-are-smarter.

Rowe, M. (2008). Micro-affirmations and micro-inequities. *Journal of International Ombudsman Association*, 1(1), 45–48.

Sadighi, D. (n.d.) Micro-affirmations: How small actions can yield big results. Employers Council. Downloaded November 28, 2023 from https://www.employerscouncil.org/resources/its-the-little-things-that-count-how-small-actions-can-yield-big-results/.

Scully, M., & Rowe, M. (2009). Bystander training within organizations. *Journal of the International Ombudsman Association*, 2(1), 89–95.

Short, E. (2018, November 28). 5 case studies of companies trying to correct the gender gap. Silicon Republic. https://www.siliconrepublic.com/careers/gender-gap-case-studies. Accessed July 7, 2023.

Stets, J. E., & Burke, P. J. (2000). Identity theory and social identity theory. *Social Psychology Quarterly*, 63(3), 224–237. https://www.jstor.org/stable/2695870.

Tajfel, H. (1972). Social categorization. English manuscript of 'La catégorisation sociale'. In S. Moscovici (Ed.) *Introduction à la psychologic sociale* (pp. 272–302). Larousse.

Tajfel, H., & Turner, J. C. (1986). The social identity theory of intergroup behavior. In S. Worchel & W. G. Austin (Eds.), *Psychology of intergroup relations* (pp. 7–24). Nelson Hall.

Tulshyan, R. (2022). *Inclusion on purpose: An intersectional approach to creating a culture of belonging at work*. The MIT Press.

Turner, J. C. (1982). Towards a cognitive redefinition of the social group. In H. Tajfel (Ed.), *Social identity and intergroup relations*. Cambridge University Press.

U.S. Bureau of Labor Statistics. (2021, November 4). Number of people 75 and older in the labor force is expected to grow 96.5 percent by 2030. https://www.bls.gov/opub/ted/2021/number-of-people-75-and-older-in-the-labor-force-is-expected-to-grow-96-5-percent-by-2030.htm. Accessed July 11, 2023.

U. S. Equal Employment Opportunity Commission (n.d.) Age discrimination. Downloaded November 26, 2023 from https://www.eeoc.gov/age-discrimination.

Van Dam, Q. (2021, May 14). For Black workers, age discrimination strikes twice. *Washington Post*. https://www.washingtonpost.com/business/2021/05/14/age-discrimination-black-workers/. Accessed July 11, 2023.

Van Maanen, J. (1979). Reclaiming qualitative methods for organizational research: A preface. *Administrative Science Quarterly*, 24, 520–526.

Warr, P. (2007). *Work, happiness, and unhappiness*. Routledge.

Washington, E. F. (2022, May 10). Recognizing and responding to microaggressions at work. *Harvard Business Review*. https://hbr.org/2022/05/recognizing-and-responding-to-microaggressions-at-work. Accessed July 13, 2023.

White, M. S., Burns, C., Conlon, H. A. (2018). The impact of an aging population in the workplace. *Workplace Health & Safety*, 66(10), 493–498. https://doi.org/10.1177/2165079917752191.

Wilks, D. C., & Neto, F. (2012). Workplace well-being, gender and age: Examining the 'double jeopardy' effect. *Social Indicators Research*, 114, 875–890. https://doi.org/10.1007/s11205-012-0177-7.

Williams, M. T. (2020). Microaggressions: Clarification, evidence, and impact. *Perspectives on Psychological Science*, 15(1), 3–26. https://doi.org/10.1177/1745691619827499.

Williams, M. T., Skinta, M. D., & Martin-Willett, R. (2021). After Pierce and Sue: A revised racial microaggressions taxonomy. *Perspectives on Psychological Science*, 16(5), 991–1007. https://doi.org/10.1177/1745691621994247.

Wooll, M. (2021, October 15). Gender inequality in the workplace: The fight against bias. *BetterUp*. https://www.betterup.com/blog/gender-inequality-in-the-work-place. Accessed July 7, 2023.

Yilmaz, E. (n.d.). Identity: Definition, types, & examples. *Berkeley Well-Being Institute*. https://www.berkeleywellbeing.com/identity.html. Accessed July 14, 2023.

Part II

Examining organizations and what motivates them

4 Power differentials in organizations and society

Donnalyn Pompper

This chapter offers a close look at an important obstacle, or barrier, to effective relationship building between organizations and publics—with some of the many effects. The obstacle is **power differentials**. Power is a central dynamic in society; one that rationalizes day-to-day interactions and makes sense of institutional arrangements (Leitch & Motion, 2013). Certain people have certain kinds of power while others do not. Organizations and institutions they represent reinforce the uneven power differentials. Importantly, communication is the tool that produces and maintains power. This means that power can be subject to change and renegotiation via good communication skills, too.

Power is perceptual *and* it is real. When a group of people or an organization has all or most of the power and an individual or marginalized group has little to no power, outcomes may be quite negative and thwart attempts to create and sustain organizations authentically embracing DEI. Yet, there is good news. A power relationship between an organization and its publics may be monitored regularly to evaluate relationships. Doing this work can help to ensure equity and fairness to fully understand roles and needs of internal and external audiences. Specific tools that help organizations' communication professionals accomplish DEI goals include environmental scanning, situation analyses, SWOTT analyses, and benchmarking against competitor organizations for additional intel and insights.

Understanding how power works, how it can change, ways power relations between organizations and people/groups interplay, and how to measure/assess it is central to DEI work. To explore just how important recognizing the effects of power can be to making organizations and the institutions they represent truly authentic and embracing of DEI, belonging, and social identity difference, this chapter covers these key areas: 1) power's import across structures and functions; 2) uneven power differential effects; 3) relevance of power in relationship building; 4) barriers, blinders, business case, and social justice case; 5) steps for moving forward; 6) access to power; 7) communication liaison; and 8) concluding thoughts.

DOI: 10.4324/9781003279129-6

Importantly, Edwards (2010) reminded public relations practitioners that actually "being 'authentic' is easier said than done" (p. 192), though. Degrees of authenticity are socially constructed and often contested. This means that no two people may define *authentic* the same way. Among public relations practitioners, however, codes of ethics may offer some shades of agreement about what is considered ethical, or right, as further addressed in Chapter 5, "Social responsibility in corporations and nonprofits."

Power's import across structures and functions

Understanding exactly what's meant by the social construction of power—as it is located within and across organizations—is the best starting point for understanding power's role in helping organizations and the institutions they represent to embrace and sustain authentic DEI. This section addresses four main factors that influence the social construction of power—humans' subjectivity, social location of publics, economic system, and history. But first, here is what's meant by *social construction of power*.

Berger and Luckmann (1966) theorized that power is a social construction, meaning that people communicate in ways that uphold certain kinds of social realities and identities that become dominant as they are applied and reproduced. Here's just one example of how it works. When a clothing retail chain store requires that job applicants take a test to assess personality traits and skill sets, applicants may engage in **self-reflexivity** processes to measure themselves against whom and what they perceive the organization wants employees to be. Sometimes outcomes can be stressful and otherwise negative (Nadesan, 1997). This may be because the personality test instrument is constructed by people who represent groups other than those actually taking the test and the process could reinforce the test makers' perspectives rather than enabling the applicants to express their authentic selves.

Another social constructionist, Michel Foucault (1980) theorized that these processes of emphasizing and perpetuating dominant perspectives makes discourses (written or spoken communication) such as the personality test *appear* commonsensical, natural, and normal—when it is highly subject to interpretation. This means that power operates at systemic, deep, and often unconscious levels—and it is so important for organizations to be cognizant and on guard to make adjustments and avoid negatively impacting both internal and external audiences in ways that cause harm or thwart authentic relationship building. Several people have criticized the form of questions printed on the questionnaire used by the U.S. Census Bureau designed to gather information about U.S. citizens' race, concluding that the questions are unclear and confusing. For example, the census instrument has asked about race since 1790. Even today, the process is anything but straightforward. Roth's (2010) interviews conducted among Puerto Rican-identifying research participants, for instance, revealed that some people believe that one drop of blood from a White parent means their child cannot be Black—and this is confusing to people filling out the census form since it offers no checkboxes for any in-between options. Gupta (2020) reported on Roth's concern:

> There are a lot of other people who don't understand how to complete the U.S. census . . . because it doesn't match their way of understanding race . . . Sometimes they will identify in ways that are the complete opposite of what the U.S. census is trying to capture.
>
> (Para. 6)

For further context of the one-drop rule with regard to race, consider Davis's (n.d.) detailed historical background.

So, the social constructionism perspective suggests that power and its effects are navigated by subjective humans who act as individuals with unique perspectives. On the positive side, this means that power dynamics are always subject to change through renegotiation across groups and that individuals and groups of lesser power may use their own social identity **standpoint** to resist discourses they perceive as negative or harmful. For instance, the 2020 murder of George Floyd in Minneapolis gained significant social media attention and the event and its aftermath rallied disenfranchised groups around online (hashtag) activism to speak out against police brutality and advocate for social change (Pfeffer et al., 2014). Importantly, this movement was multicultural and multiracial, amplifying the importance of solidarity and advocacy for belonging which elevated the movement to one of DEI in action (Miller, 2020).

Another means for considering power differentials in organizations and across society is to consider key publics according to their location, or ways that key publics may be primarily internal or external. Internal publics include employees, managers, and perhaps even suppliers who provide raw materials used to manufacture products (like flour and eggs for baking cakes) or provide services (like water used to operate public services such as sewage waste treatment). External publics may include voters, stockholders, customers, residents, transporters, retailers, reporters, influencers, and more. Each specific group—whether located internally or externally—holds an important space in the business- and service-provision cycle for organizations.

Sometimes, contextualizing each group of publics according to the broad economic system in which an organization operates illuminates social construction of power differentials. For example, under the economic system of capitalism, competition and desire to consistently improve the financial bottom line every quarter drives corporations to operate efficiently so they may generate profits for shareholders. On a global scale, economic divisions separating the Global South areas (including regions in Latin America, the African continent, and developing parts of Asia) that are not considered part of the economically and industrially developed Global North (e.g., Australia, Canada, Europe, Hong Kong, Macau, Israel, Japan, New Zealand, Russia, Singapore, South Korea, United States) means that uneven economic resources, standard of living, and historic exploitation of natural resources in the Global South negatively impacts the quality of life among people who live in the Global South (Mahler, 2018).

Finally, considering an organization's history over time that has shaped its foundation and contemporary systems—especially among corporations—illuminates just how systemic and deeply entrenched some barriers to equitable change can be. For example, Logan (2021) reminded us that in the U.S., corporations since Reconstruction have engaged in processes of racial discrimination and some continue to resist today's DEI efforts (Blackmon, 2009; Crenshaw et al., 1995). So, the contexts of economic system and history combine in undeniably strong ways to reveal entrenched discriminatory practices that thwart DEI efforts no matter how well intentioned corporate leaders may be about dismantling bias causes and effects (Thomas & Plout, 2008).

So, looking through a social construction of power lens to examine power's import across structures and functions enables communicators to see how four main factors interplay with organizations' attention to DEI—humans' subjectivity, social location of publics, economic system, and history. Next, this chapter examines the effects, or what can happen in DEI work when power is distributed and experienced unevenly.

Uneven power differential effects

Power exists everywhere and it impacts every living being and the natural environment. Power involves active processes that shape identities, form values, and offer interpretations of world events. Knowing that power is a social construction helps us to understand how uneven power differentials between organizations and people play out in inequitable ways. These conditions make authentic relationship building and embrace of DEI a challenge. Based on historic systems of oppression, organizations generally have power—as authorities—and individuals and small groups do not. As a result, organizations often fail to consider long- and short-term effects of the organization's actions on publics. This means that powerful authorities' interpretations, knowledge, norms, and values are imposed on everything else.

While one effect of these dynamics is social order maintenance—like state and local police and emergency medical technicians working together during weather emergencies—there can be negative effects, such as people feeling less powerful or less in control of pursuing their own interpretations and choices. For instance, some people may choose to remain in their home and community during forced evacuations (e.g., wildfires, tornadoes), unwilling to sever cultural ties to their surroundings. About 5% of the U.S. population ignores state and local evacuation orders during hurricanes (Forced evacuation, 2017). Yet, the U.S. federal government has the power to enforce public safety with evacuation orders, not entirely unlike it did during World War II following Japan's attack on Pearl Harbor in Hawaii. Japanese Americans (as well as some Germans, Italians, and Aleuts) were forcibly interred in camps. Executive Order 9066 signed by U.S. President Franklin D. Roosevelt impacted 120,000 people during 1942–1945 by relocating them to internment camps and other facilities in Arizona, California, Colorado, Georgia, Idaho, Montana, New Mexico, Oregon, Texas, Utah, Washington, Wyoming (Burton et al., 2002; history.com editors, 2021). While the U.S. Supreme Court upheld constitutionality of internment in 1944, a dissenting justice called this ruling "legalization of racism" (Zahniser, 2023, para. 44). So, events wherein authorities exercise their power often can have DEI implications.

Uneven power differential effects include people and groups speaking truth to power. During the COVID-19 pandemic, Asian Americans and others used social media to rally together to advocate for the #StopAsianHate movement in the U.S. and globally. At least 9,000 anti-Asian incidents were reported since the beginning of the pandemic—including beatings and bullying (Associated Press, 2021). Former U.S. President Donald Trump's 2020 reference to the coronavirus as "Kung flu" and "Chinese virus" inspired the social stigmatization (Ponder et al., 2023).

Civic engagement that includes consulting with key publics and involving them in important decision making could make all the difference in contexts of uneven power differential effects. Bourdieu (2005) introduced reproduction of social inequality theory, arguing that upper classes are better able to amplify their own perspectives and interpretations while simultaneously depicting low-status groups as inferior—such as when authorities make housing policies. For example, housing policies in the U.S. have "systematically limited access to homeownership for persons of color and segregated many into disadvantaged neighborhoods" (Sanders, 2020, para. 1). The environmental justice movement in the U.S.—also known globally as responding to "environmental racism" (Beech, 2020)—was born of the U.S. Civil Rights Movement of the 1960s (Environmental Justice Timeline, n.d.).

The movement persists today with the Environmental Protection Agency (EPA) advocating for "equal access to the decision-making process to have a healthy environment in which to live, learn, and work" (Environmental Justice, n.d.). The National Environmental Justice Advisory Council (NEJAC) serves as a federal advisory committee to the EPA, offering advice and providing a forum for "discussions about integrating environmental justice with other EPA priorities and initiatives" (National Environmental Justice Advisory Council, n.d., para. 1).

Beyond government settings, companies have learned that conversing with employees can offer mutually beneficial solutions to organizations' problems. Waters (2017) examined issues of employee suicides at telecoms provider, France Télécom (rebranded Orange in 2013), in France, and electronics supplier, Foxconn, in China, resolving that the international division of digital labor involves high human costs on lived experiences of work. Talking with employees about their concerns is one direct means for resolving employee concerns. As already noted, some organizations provide prayer and meditation rooms as a strategy for increasing workplace inclusion. Gurchiek (2018) reported that mobile computer manufacturer, Bak USA, created a prayer room for its 100 employees, accommodating 14 cultural groups. The company's vice president said the dedicated space for prayer and meditation provides "that inclusion piece where people felt they could bring their 'full selves' to work" (Gurchiek, 2018, para. 9).

To summarize uneven power differential effects, communicators working with organizations committed to embracing authentic DEI must be willing to recognize that the organizations whom they serve usually have most (if not all) of the power and many key publics possess significantly less power. Consequently, these key publics' voices may be unheard and unheeded. In the case of employer–employee relationships, organizations know that people who work there need a job and, therefore, may be less willing to speak openly about their concerns so as not to put their employment status at risk. In communities with sharp economic divides, taxpayers such as business enterprises and people who live in large houses have more powerful voices in public policymaking decisions than community residents who are unemployed or unhoused.

Relevance of power in relationship building

Understanding how power works across organizations and among their relationships with other organizations, groups, and individuals is highly relevant to examining the extent to which some organizations are more successful in accomplishing DEI goals than others. Organizations, generally, are considered as authority figures in society with high status. For example, we rely on employment, healthcare, and housing officials (e.g., charitable organizations, government officials, doctors, food producers, construction companies, utility providers) to help us feel safe, comfortable, informed, healthy, and well fed. We look up to organizations like this and respect those that satisfy our needs. Such organizations—whether for-profit or nonprofit—possess and are given high degrees of power in society. Organizations' managers and employees may have access to large degrees of expertise, insights, knowledge, and networks that the average person does not. This means that formal organization members possess higher degrees of power than most of the rest of us—and with power comes great responsibility to use power for good.

Ensuring that organizations authentically treasure and act on DEI values that society holds should be the role of every person affiliated with the organization—especially management teams and professional communicators. Organizations' management teams have the capacity to exercise control over others when they set organizational policy to ensure that vision/mission statements declaring a commitment to DEI goals actually becomes real and authentic. The professional communicators—as people who exercise discursive power—produce the words and express the voice of the organization. This authority over speaking on behalf of others is relevant to our DEI discussions because **sensemaking** about DEI and framing an organization's values about DEI may be the responsibility of the organization's communication or human resources staff. This means that organizations' specific understandings are communicated to multiple audiences—and these dynamics are embedded with power given that the messages being communicated are designed to influence or impact others' perceptions and actions in our socially constructed world. People then may choose to accept organizations' messages or resist organizations' power by ignoring or negotiating the embedded meanings.

We can see power at work when power is enacted. Foucault (1980) posited that while exercise of power may be repressive or destructive, it also can be democratic and productive. For example, utility companies that provide services for a community may want to inform residents that conserving energy during high peak hot summer days benefits everyone. When the utility company's website link with story and images fails to represent the actual demographics of people who live in the community being targeted with messaging, the information piece may fail to communicate the benefits of energy conservation because residents may not see someone who "looks like me" and perceive that the message is "not for me." So, solid positive relationship building among organizations and people/groups is supported when representations show and tell stories of people whose culture, ethnicity, physical ability, faith/religion, and other social identity dimensions match those in neighborhoods that utility companies serve.

Even among marginalized communities, or **counterpublics** in the **public sphere**, there are power differentials. Findings of a study comparing Twitter use among #BlackLivesMatter and #BlackTransLivesMatter counterpublics (Dunklin & Jennings, 2022) suggested that some groups have more amplified voices on social media than others—even though Black Twitter, Black Lives Matter, and #BlackLivesMatter all were started by Black queer women. For example, the most marginalized communities—like #BlackTransLivesMatter—"must approach activism and social issues differently than dominant counterpublics" (Dunklin & Jennings, 2022, p. 780). Communicators working on behalf of organizations and groups must recognize and navigate strategies, limitations, and future possibilities for social media activism. In Chapter 7, "Social media as a tool and as a weapon," we explore ways that organizations use social media platforms to connect with audiences and ways that publics and activist groups use social media as a weapon to target organizations. See Sidebar 4.1 offering historical context of the power of public opinion and its relationship in assuring DEI authenticity.

Sidebar 4.1　Public opinion's central role in keeping DEI authentic

Donnalyn Pompper

Public opinion is powerful. It's the collection of individual views or attitudes about a particular issue that becomes stronger as it gains amplification and numbers of people adopting the same view or attitude. The power of public opinion—understanding how it works so as to harness and shape it for organizations' benefit—was the goal of Edward Bernays back in 1923 when he wrote *Crystallizing Public Opinion*. Since then, the relevance of public opinion in our daily lives has grown exponentially. Public opinion is a shape shifter, too, so it is fluid and dynamic.

Even though some publics may be passive—beyond maybe posting about an issue on social media—organizations have learned the value of keeping their finger on the pulse of public opinion. Those committed to real DEI care about public opinion because its power impacts people's lived experiences and organizations know how DEI is connected to their reputation now and for the future. Public opinion forms where interpersonal communication and mass communication intersect (L'Etang, 2008). As intermediaries, social media influencers and other opinion leaders wield significant power, too. The respect that influencers have gained as experts with large and/or key followings is a marker of their power.

Bernays' book pre-dated today's technology, but his lessons about public opinion are more relevant than ever. He was the double nephew of Sigmund Freud, founder of psychoanalysis. An intellectual, Bernays used the study of psychology to strategize political persuasion. For example, Bernays linked corporate sales campaigns with popular social causes so that when the American Tobacco Company asked him to find ways to convince more women in the 1920s to become tobacco smokers, Bernays launched the "Torches of Freedom" campaign for women's rights marchers to hold up their Lucky Strikes cigarettes (Ewen, 2011).

Figure 4.1 Bernays' Torches of Freedom campaign debutante and beau smoking in Easter Parade, 1929.

Having public opinion on one's side is a valuable commodity. Because social media's opinion leaders can be virtually anyone with a following, brands or anyone looking to amplify a perspective highly value opinion leaders with connections and an ability to get followers to take action. Being in possession of knowledge and charisma to influence others is a great power, indeed. Social media would have greatly interested Bernays, had he lived beyond age 103. Bernays reacted to social changes that had taken place in the U.S. the decade before *Crystallizing Public Opinion* was published in 1923. Bernays responded to "social unrest and widespread anti-business activism" (Ewen, 2011, p. 14) with a playbook for organizations about why they must take public opinion seriously.

Today, we know the power of public opinion to shape politics on a national level and to develop grassroots organizing at local levels that can grow internationally. Back in 2007, "little-known" African American U.S. Senator Barack Obama (Aaker & Chang, 2009, para. 1) harnessed the power of social media to use Instagram for sharing behind-the-scenes images of campaign life, and eventually was elected the 44th president of the U.S. Fast forward to 2023, Jacques and colleagues documented the utility of TikTok as a space for #StopAsianHate and for "marginalized groups to raise consciousness on public health issues and injustices" (p. 1) in conjunction with political unrest in the U.S. in the midst of a pandemic. Reporting on public opinion also appeals to media, such as when public polling organization, Gallup, shares findings of public opinion research such as a 71% high in "same-sex marriage support" in the U.S. (McCarthy, 2023). Also, disabilities communities know the power of public opinion when it intersects with social media as they use these platforms to find community (Reuters, 2022) and participate in activism to pressure organizations to comply with Americans with Disabilities rules such as wheelchair accessibility (Rajkumar, 2022). There are many social media opinion leaders who identify disability influencers (Moss, 2022). These few examples offer evidence that the horizontal or bottom-up flow of communication among citizens harnessing the power of public opinion for debate about DEI-related issues and concerns can greatly impact society.

Resources

Aaker, J., & Chang, V. (2009). Obama and the power of social media and technology. *Stanford Business*. https://rb.gy/5mvy7.

Ewen, S. (2011). Introduction. In E. Bernays, *Crystallizing public opinion* (pp. 9–41). Ig Publishing.

Jacques, E. T., Basch, C. H., Fera, J., & Jones, V. II (2023). #StopAsian-Hate: A content analysis of TikTok videos focused on racial discrimination against Asians and Asian Americans during the COVID-19 pandemic. *Dialogues in Health*, 2, 1–4. https://doi.org/10.1016/j.dialog.2022.100089.

L'Etang, J. (2008). *Public relations: Concepts, practice and critique*. Sage.

McCarthy, J. (2023). U.S. same-sex marriage support holds at 71% high. Gallup. Downloaded June 12, 2023 from https://rb.gy/72v1h.

Moss, H. (2022). Disability influencers: The who's who to follow on social media. Direct Employers Association. Downloaded November 23, 2023 from https://directemployers.org/2022/10/20/disability-influencers-the-whos-who-to-follow-on-social-media/.

Rajkumar, S. (2022). The ADA was a victory for the disabled community, but we need more. My life shows why. NPR. Downloaded June 12, 2023 from https://rb.gy/lkxdw.

Reuters (2022). Young adults with disabilities find community on social media. *U.S. News*. Downloaded June 11, 2023 from https://rb.gy/jfgp1.

In the public relations field, communicators long have recognized that relationship building across and among connections/networks with publics results in varied power outcomes. Optimally, interpersonal, interorganizational and organization–public relationships are rooted in mutual control among the parties for maximum stability and positivity (Grunig & Huang, 2000). This means that organizations value and respect multiple voices regardless of degrees of power since this is the organizations' social responsibility (Yang, 2023). For example, British Petroleum (BP) partnered with a vast network of non-governmental organizations (NGOs) in conjunction with environmental cleanup following its 2010 Gulf of Mexico oil spill and subsequent damaged reputation (Diers & Donohue, 2013). In this case, the natural ecosystem had no voice or power of its own, but public outrage about how BP had handled the situation garnered significant attention among five states bordering the region, including low-SES (socio-economic status) communities and other under-served populations (Baldera & Guillory, 2019).

When for-profit organizations strategically use DEI as a tool of commerce, however, degrees of authenticity may be lost. For example, Starbucks' 2015 Race Together campaign has been hailed by many as a failure. Shah (2015) qualified it as "laughing stock of the internet" (para. 1) for several reasons, including misguided expectations that a sensitive subject of race could be fronted by a "white billionaire" (Howard Schultz), baristas expected to engage customers in conversations about race, and unconvinced Starbucks board members who questioned the campaign from the outset. While any financial profit from the campaign has not been reported publicly, Starbucks experienced negative backlash, with its senior vice president of global communications reportedly deactivating his Twitter account in 2015 due to negative campaign response (Starbucks, 2015). Logan (2016) resolved that Starbucks' critics' concerns are "legitimate because corporations are often viewed as being self-serving, profit-obsessed, and unconcerned about the greater social good" (p. 107). Communicators working with organizations may prove exceptionally useful in helping leadership come to terms with messaging strategies and communicating authenticity about DEI issues.

Barriers, blinders, business case, and social justice case

There are two major rationales for DEI in organizations—the business case and the social justice case. The business case means, simply—as addressed previously—that DEI is good for the business bottom line. The more diverse a workforce, the more effective the organization will be (cost saving, talented employees, positive community relations), and the more profitable a DEI strategy can be when promoted properly (e.g., Robinson & Dechant, 1997; Kochan et al., 2003). Textbooks have amplified the business case for DEI perspective for years (O'Leary & Weathington, 2006). Whereas a social justice case ethic means advocating for DEI because it is the morally right, just, and humane thing to do. The social justice case rationale for DEI in organizations is rooted in an ethic of humanity which considers people valuable regardless of any possible economic contribution to an organization (Steimel, 2021).

Barriers and blinders thwarting authentic attention to DEI in organizations happens regardless of which major rationale is considered. Such roadblocks have ideological roots shaping ways we go through life networking with others, forming social groups (Swingewood, 2000), and marginalizing others. For example, conflict over ideological differences during the seizure of some 1.5 billion acres from North America's native peoples from 1776 through present day involved White people believing—ideologically—it was their manifest destiny to go west and take the land, while indigenous peoples were dispossessed of the land and their culture (Haselby, 2015).

Although there are some U.S. laws that protect specific groups of people, and these laws extend to organizations—there persist many blinders and barriers that must be eradicated on the path to ensuring authentic DEI in organizations and society. As popular media have reported, some organized religion groups that consider sexual orientations other than heterosexuality as sinful may attempt to "cure" LGBTQIA+ members and engage in gay conversion therapy (Cruz, 1999) because their ideological orientation is rooted in heterogeneity. On the other hand, U.S. employers know that the Civil Rights Act of 1964 prohibiting sex discrimination also extends to prohibiting sexual orientation and gender identity discrimination, too (Liptak, 2021). Quite simply, workers cannot be fired for being bisexual, gay, or transgender.

Despite such laws, however, some employees and organizations react negatively to dismantling of homophily inside organizations, as discussed in Chapter 2, "Factoring in globalization, (mis)trust, risk, and sociopolitical contexts." Negative outcomes create barriers for BIPOC community members working to achieve their maximum potential in organizations and beyond. In organizations, managers seek to reduce risk so that operations run smoothly without disruption. Maintaining a status quo—keeping things the same consistent with a **social homophily thesis**—can minimize risk. To explain this dynamic, self-categorization theory posits that people define themselves and others according to demographic categories (Monge & Contractor, 2001) and a similarity-attraction hypothesis (Moreno & Flowerday, 2006) suggests that people gravitate toward people they perceive as similar to themselves. Ultimately, the kinds of work environments yielded by adherence to homophily can be unwelcoming to BIPOC community members. This means that inequality and exclusion persist in the workplace (Scott et al., 2013). Human resources and other managers in organizations must take to heart a responsibility for restructuring power relations, developing action plans, and for measuring their outcomes to ensure that DEI goals eradicate homophily effects throughout the organization. In the words of masculinities scholars Brod and Kaufman (1994), the way to end negativity involving social identity dimensions (e.g., ableism, homophobia, transphobia, racism) is to consciously, routinely, and vigorously take note of ways "we and our brothers get hooked into privileges" (p. 3) so that investigating why biases are so resistant to change can yield authentic embrace of DEI. Specifically, recognizing and moving beyond **privilege** must be everyone's goal. Harris (2019) explained that people struggle with understanding and owning privilege for a variety of reasons, including "not knowing or being aware, guilt, unwillingness to accept responsibility for systems they didn't themselves 'create', individual experiences and values around 'merit' and 'working hard', or experiencing oppression due to other aspects of their identities" (para. 3).

Yet, some people consciously choose to resist DEI acceptance in organizations, such as those who criticize affirmative action programs as causing **reverse discrimination**. Dominant majority employees often resist DEI programs, considering them "fluffy and without merit" (Pitts, 2006, p. 252), are cynical about value of DEI training (Dukach, 2022), and feel threatened and manipulated into accepting their new status as victims of reverse discrimination (Cullinan et al., 2023). In the U.S., it is perhaps the federal government which has instituted the largest number of formal DEI and accessibility programs—especially in the federal workplace (Biden, 2021). Misunderstandings often are linked to confusion between affirmative action with DEI management; the former a legal policy for protecting certain groups and the latter organizations' attempts to facilitate acceptance of all individuals in the workplace (Kenton, 2022). Indeed, subjective bias going into awareness-raising workplace DEI programs greatly affects outcomes and degrees of DEI authenticity.

Even among organizations that have worked hard to make DEI a reality find that keeping the commitment authentic requires vigilance, ongoing commitment, and hard work. Dobbin and Kalev (2016) reported that organizations implementing DEI programs to "preempt lawsuits by policing managers' thoughts and actions" find that their DEI training programs for reducing bias on the job, hiring tests and performance ratings to limit bias in recruitment and promotions, and grievance systems for employees to challenge managers constitute "force-feeding" and can perpetuate bias rather than eradicating it (para. 3). Consequently, effects include low BIPOC employee recruitment *and* retention, White males still dominating management, faux pas such as thinking DEI means only hosting an international foods day in the employee cafeteria. As Stovall and Clark (2022) advised, "We can be deliberate, educated, purposeful, and tailor our work to have the greatest impact in the sphere we occupy, but it can fall apart quickly if the practice does not become innate to the way or organization does business" (p. 104). Even celebrations of events such as Black History Month have been criticized as "excessive historicization" that may be ineffective in addressing "the problem of racism [and may be] as oppressive as forgetting" (van de Mieroop, 2016, p. 3).

Steps for moving forward

Organizations have permeable walls—which means society comes to the work environment—and people bring their whole selves to work—meaning everything about people's social identity dimension intersectionalities is part of the work culture and deserves respect. Robbins (2018) explained that bringing one's whole self to work involves

> showing up authentically, leading with humility, and remembering that we're all vulnerable, imperfect human beings doing the best we can. It's also about having the courage to take risks, speak up, ask for help, and connect with others in a genuine way, allowing ourselves to be seen.
>
> (para. 2)

In other words, the future is bright for organizations and communities willing to move forward with respect for all humans and the natural environment. Moreover, Chattopadhyay (2019) explained that responsive, thriving organizations are communities

> no longer defined by fixed workplaces, nine-to-five working hours . . . [they're now] boundary-less and . . . virtual. Operational business models have changed significantly with the advent of enterprises like Uber, Airbnb, Etsy, and Amazon, with no industry being immune to this disruption.
>
> (para. 1)

To begin, the space between organizations' mission and/or vision that includes a promise to embrace DEI—and organizations' authentic embrace of that promise to make DEI a true reality—features a wide power gap that must be narrowed. Pompper and colleagues (2021) examined images of Fortune 500 boards of directors for power inclusivity and discovered that in 2017 only one featured 50–50% gender equity and across all boards there were only 4.1% women of color and 9% men of color—despite The Business Roundtable's commitment to "investing in employees, delivering value to customers, dealing ethically with suppliers and supporting outside communities" (Fitzgerald, 2019). The CEO activism movement offers another view on power sharing as corporations' top managers use their platform to speak out about social issues that may or may not be directly linked to their organization's business (e.g., Adae, 2023; Chatterji & Toffel, 2019). CEO activists in the U.S., Australia, Canada, Europe, and Japan are speaking out against race-based violence, school shootings, and the #MeToo movement (Costigan & Hughes, 2021). For example, Goldman Sachs CEO David Solomon speaks out about gun violence in the U.S. (Egan, 2022). To be sure, there are CEOs who also speak out opposing some BIPOC concerns/issues, too. For example, Chick-fil-A CEO Dan T. Cathy often expresses his religious views about same-sex marriage and reasons why businesses should not operate on Sundays (Zilber, 2023).

Indeed, infrastructures built on foundations of homophily are difficult to change for real on the inside. So, building paths forward is organizational communicators' responsibility, including: involving key publics in decision making, listening, ongoing research, expanding the DEI lens, and providing access to power.

First, involving key publics in organizations' decision making is one means for accomplishing what Larson and colleagues (2022) theorized as "critical inclusion" (p. 63) by breaching the uneven power relations attached to organizations' decision making. Companies and nonprofits often have the voice to do (or not do) things that affect communities. Enabling BIPOC community groups most directly impacted by an organization's issue or situation to have the opportunity to share their voices as part of problem solving is essential. For example, when investigating the interplay of culture, ethnicity, and race on organizational crisis issues, Liu and Pompper (2012) interviewed BIPOC community members who recommended organizations form partnerships with BIPOC communities for "more organic, normative, inclusive, and community spirited" relationships (p. 127). Consulting with key publics and involving them in key decision making in conjunction with civic engagement could make all the difference. See Sidebar 4.2 to learn more about ways communities outside of organizations can use their power to shape public opinion about organizations in a context of identity, representation, and film education.

Sidebar 4.2 A case study in identity, representation, and film education

Rulon Wood, Ph.D.

Historically, Hollywood writers have marginalized LGBTQIA + characters in movies and on television. When included, queer characters appear in a two-dimensional fashion, which can reinforce negative stereotypes and lead to stigmatization. For example, in the film *Clueless*, Christian, the main character's best friend, is depicted in a stereotypical fashion. He loves shopping, fashion, art, and musicals. Although these tendencies in isolation are not necessarily negative, they do tend to be tropes that indicate queerness. Similarly, the character named All in *Zoolander 2* represents an attempt to depict a non-binary character; however, rather than written in a well-developed, three-dimensional fashion, the filmmakers poke fun of All with crass jokes that focus on their genitalia.

One way to facilitate change is through a more nuanced representation of gender and sexuality in film representations so that students and other audience members may experience people and situations with whom they can identify. Film educators can lead this charge through carefully designed collaborations and discussions among faculty, students, and audiences.

I have had the opportunity to work with students on a film program's year-long sequence that culminates in their creating a television pilot or a feature film through a program titled the Narrative Television Arts Initiative (NTVI). Students in the program enroll in four classes: 1) Writer's Room, 2) Pre-Production, 3) Production, and 4) Post-Production. Once complete, the students and faculty premiere the film at the local movie theater. Often, the premiere is followed by a lively discussion with local audiences.

Principal photography for the most recent NTVI production, titled *Out*, was completed during summer 2023. The film follows the main character, Audrey, who has just told her family that she is gay. The family does not accept her lifestyle, and Audrey must find a new home. Her girlfriend's (Sienna) more progressive family invites Audrey to live with them. However, while completing an internship in New York, Sienna, who is exploring her sexuality, cheats on Audrey with a man. The changing dynamics of the living situation force Audrey to decide whether to stay with her partner's family or venture out independently.

Out, as with previous NTVI productions, provided an excellent learning opportunity for students, faculty, and the public to discuss the power dynamics of the entertainment industry through the depiction of LGBTQIA + characters, both historically and within our film. Together, faculty and students learned much from the NTVI production process and we all are more knowledgeable for the experience.

Selecting a script

Faculty colleagues met after the fall semester to select a script for production, using two criteria. First, students must be able to create the film for under $30,000. The meager budget can pose a real challenge because it must cover the cost of locations, actors, costumes, gear rental, and food during a 10–15-day shoot. Second, the script should promote the voices and stories from individuals who have typically been silenced.

This past season, four possible scripts were ready for production: 1) a comedy about four young teens working at a local swimming pool the year before graduation; 2) a mystery in which several biblical stories are retold in a modern context with a feminist critique; 3) a horror story about a haunted mirror that can steal a person's soul; and 4) a drama about the deteriorating relationship of a gay couple within a conservative community. *Out* was the most logical choice with its small cast, limited locations, and a socially progressive message. In addition, *Out* had particular relevance in a conservative state, where gay youth frequently are rejected by their families.

Selecting the director/directors

Once a script has been selected, faculty must choose a director or, in some cases, co-directors. During previous seasons, faculty learned how seemingly minor decisions can have enormous ramifications. During the 2021 production cycle, students produced a film titled *The Chinese Tourist*, about a Chinese student who grappled with racism, cultural difference, pressures to succeed, and oppressive patriarchy.

Two experienced student filmmakers were selected to direct *The Chinese Tourist*, but problems occurred, and faculty discovered them far too late in the production process. Both directors had strong faculty support and experience. Both directors were Asian American, which, as pointed out by some faculty, would add authenticity to the film. Yet, everyone had overlooked additional important social identity dimensions. A hostile learning environment developed when some members of the production team complained that the directors had been selected based solely upon their race and the directors felt undermined on set. One day, one of the student directors walked off the set and refused to be associated with the production. After the film premiere, a discussion on local issues such as immigration and racism followed as the filmmakers and audience discussed ways to make our community more inclusive.

Having learned from this experience the year before, faculty developed a more democratic crew selection process. All individuals who wished to direct were required to give a short presentation to the students and faculty. Each student was encouraged to: 1) describe his/her/their approach to the project, 2) explain how he/she/they felt they possessed lived experience that would assist in telling the story, and 3) provide a detailed explanation of a visual approach to the story. In the end, all of the students created excellent presentations. The two selected directors demonstrated a passion for the project. One student director, who also identifies as queer, like the main character in the script, had been forced to leave her home when she had come out in real life.

Unlike *The Chinese Tourist*, the directors of *Out* did not experience hostility on set. The harmonious set likely occurred for two reasons. First, the selection process was more democratic, allowing all students a voice. Second, because students were more informed on issues related to identity, they seemed to realize how important it was to provide a forum for new directors/voices.

Revising the script before production

The *Out* production process also promoted ample opportunity for students involved to continue to discuss issues of representation. Faculty encourage students to re-read the script by focusing on issues of race, class, and gender. Class members typically have strong opinions during this production stage, and all suggestions are welcome. Final changes, however, must be agreed upon by the producers, writers, and directors.

For *Out*, the most discussions revolved around the character of Sienna, the girlfriend who cheats on her partner while away on an internship. Several students felt that Sienna should have sex with another woman rather than a man. This small, but vocal group of students, believed that the inclusion of a bisexual character marginalized homosexuality. The writer, on the other hand, who identifies as gay, felt that a bisexual character would add some dramatic tension and encourage the audience to consider a wider range of gender and sexuality. Discussions about the Sienna character as either homosexual or bisexual created an opportunity to consider equity, not only in film, but as an ideological construct in society. Sometimes, gay characters are not readily welcomed into the gay community. Some individuals see them as neither gay nor straight. As such, they face discrimination on several fronts. Ultimately, as the goal of NTVI is to represent many voices and experiences, the team decided to stick with the writer's choice of a bisexual character as a means of promoting inclusivity.

Figure 4.2 Rulon Wood.

Casting the film

Historically, actors from marginalized groups have been ignored in Hollywood or, if cast at all, they play minor roles. Before casting *Out*, faculty and students considered the power dynamics. Class discussions involved reviewing popular films with LGBTQIA + characters to determine why certain actors were selected for specific roles. Students discussed why some actors are selected when they have *star power*, which can improve the marketability of a film. With *Out*, the goal was somewhat different. The students hoped to cast individuals who are underrepresented in traditional Hollywood films.

Logistically, casting was reasonably simple due to the limited number of roles. One character, however, proved somewhat challenging, especially in light of class discussion. The writer described Audrey's sidekick (Carter) as a wise-cracking, young, gay male who pushes the boundaries of those around him. Similar characters can be seen in films such as *Clueless*, where Justin Walker plays the character of Christian. Or, more recently, Sean Hayes as Jack in *Will and Grace*. These characters possess a sharp wit, overt sexuality, and a sense of humor about life.

As the students cast for the role of Carter, many local actors read for the part. Most played it as one might expect—somewhat campy, with a high level of theatricality. One actor, however, interpreted the role more seriously and inspired discussion among the directors and writer. The writer felt that a more traditional reading would be more comedic, whereas the directors felt that playing *against type* would be a stronger choice.

After numerous discussions, the team offered the role to the actor who portrayed the character with a more serious tone. With an overall goal to represent the world in a more nuanced fashion, decisions over the comedic appeal of the actor were less important than providing audiences with a diverse range of character types. Clearly, discussions around casting became an essential component of the learning experience. Casting directors affect the finished film, but, more importantly, they also influence how audiences view the world.

Premiering the film

Exhibiting a student film such as *Out* is an important and often overlooked opportunity to interrogate questions of identity and power. Screenings have been well attended, with students, faculty, and the public filling every seat on the floor and balcony. It's also an opportunity for students, faculty, and the public to engage in discussions about LGBTQIA + issues of gender and sexuality and social identity intersectionalities. Equally important, we hope the production will provide a model for film education and have a broader impact on the entertainment industry.

Second, beyond physically involving BIPOC communities in decision making, organizations also must truly listen to people's concerns and vision. In recent years, scholarly attention has emphasized the importance of listening as an active communication component (e.g., Macnamara, 2015a; O'Neil et al., 2022; Place, 2023). Martin (2023) interviewed researchers who studied community reaction to police shooting of a Fort Worth woman in her home: "Good public relations is about building relationships, listening, dialoguing, engaging . . . We thought it would be a unique contribution to look at listening and city government and Black communities" (para. 8). Ensuring key audience participation relies on organizational listening to marginalized communities, which is tangential to democratic governance and involves interpersonal relationship building, cross-cultural competency, and sensitivity for maximum engagement. All too often, the most listened to audiences are "White and usually tied to wealth, business, or political power and privilege" (O'Neil et al., 2022, p. 811). Rather, Macnamara (2015b) concluded that there is a "crisis of listening" (p. 7) in contemporary societies as he urged organizations to build an "architecture of listening" in conjunction with reporting findings of an international study of government, corporate,

Figure 4.3 Julie O'Neil, Jacqueline Lambiase, and Ashley E. English study ways to improve communication between city government officials and Fort Worth residents.

non-government, and nonprofit organizations' attention to organizational listening. He urged organizations to change communication practices that currently involve an average of 80% speaking and only 20% listening (Macnamara, 2015b).

See Sidebar 4.3 to learn more about how to work on the inside to influence positive change for eradicating gender binary dualisms in spaces such as locker rooms.

Sidebar 4.3 When locker rooms can be tricky spaces

Donnalyn Pompper

In recent years, athletic fields, bathrooms, diaper changing/ nursing rooms, and locker rooms have been problematized by concerns about privacy/safety undergirded by gender gaps, stereotypes, and power struggles. Trans people have witnessed discrimination, abuse, and violence in conjunction with bathroom usage (e.g., Blumell et al., 2019) and athletic space access (Oliveira et al., 2022). It all adds up to some people feeling like they do not belong. People who oppose gender identity inclusivity in public accommodation nondiscrimination laws raise concerns about safety and privacy violations and advocate for laws protecting people from transgender people using public accommodations such as locker rooms. Proponents of such legislation posit that laws are needed to protect transgender people themselves in conjunction with these aforementioned (and unfounded) safety and privacy concerns (Hasenbush et al., 2019). For decades, female journalists have encountered sexual harassment in male-dominated newsroom workplaces, as well as adjunct workspaces of locker rooms (Hardin & Shain, 2005). Locker rooms are places where people shower and change their clothes, making these spaces unique in comparison to other types of public and workspaces.

Gendered division of labor

Further complicating usage of gendered public spaces such as locker rooms are gender-defined childcare tasks, where/when they may be performed, and by whom. In public facilities and organizations outside the home, all genders have experienced challenges in nursing/diaper changing, and other tasks associated with child caregiving since there are gender gaps in ways women and men are perceived as caregivers for children (Churchill et al., 2023). Traditionally, women have been presumed to be more nurturing and predominantly responsible for the upbringing of children; a complex set of dynamics that discriminates against some LGBTQ+ individuals and couples and associates the social aspects of pregnancy and childcare with a woman's body (Fontana & Schoenbaum, 2019). The gendered division of labor that considers women as caregivers and men as breadwinners is socially constructed and out of step with the way people live today (Basulto, 2013; Ianzito, 2017). For women, balancing work and family is defined by gender since the home has been characterized as a private space where women's labor is *a given* and is unpaid. During the second half of the 20th century when more middle-class Caucasian/White women than ever joined the paid workforce outside the home (Women in the labor force, 2021), negotiating paid with unpaid work has contributed negatively to women's gender role stress/conflict (Pompper, 2017). Of course, BIPOC women and women of lower SES have worked outside the home for a very long time (Banks, 2019). During the COVID-19 pandemic, research findings suggest that women assumed greater amounts of domestic space care than men (Hayes & Lee, 2022).

Title IX weighs in

In the context of a public education setting, Title IX of the Education Amendments of 1972 prohibits discrimination based on sex in education programs and other activities that receive federal financial support (Sex discrimination, n.d.). Federal law under Title IX specifically allows schools to "provide separate toilet, locker room, and shower facilities on the basis of sex" (Title IX, n.d.).

Yet, just *which* locker rooms small children under the care of adults should/can use is not always a clear-cut issue. Adults may want to take small children to the locker room where the adults feel most comfortable rather than the locker room that matches their child's gender identification. Organizations' ability to communicate locker-room options and rules is not always simple, either.

Listening carefully and taking action

Here's a real-life example. The director of the aquatic spaces of the Recreation Center at a large public university in the Pacific Northwest recently displayed an 8.5 x 11 paper sign on a wall separating the women's locker room and the men's locker room that read: "Children 5 yrs and under may go into the opposite gender locker room with a responsible adult. All use change rooms are available outside the main locker rooms." When students studying in a Gender, Media & Diversity class in the university's School of Journalism discussed ways that the words "opposite gender" on that sign reinforced a gender binary (as if there are only two genders), students recommended to the director that they offer more inclusive language by changing the sign to: "Children 5 yrs and under may go into any locker room with a responsible adult. All use change rooms are available outside the main locker rooms." The director carefully listened to the students' concern and agreed that *any gender* offers greater inclusivity and wider gender fluidity than *opposite gender*—and changed the signage within 24 hours.

Indeed, binary dualisms often creep into our thought processes and communication materials, ultimately risking organizations' ability to modify infrastructures and advance social change. Listening carefully to constituents' perceptions and concerns and following up with real change offers a positive path forward to making DEI and belonging a reality.

Resources

Banks, N. (2019). Black women's labor market history reveals deep-seated race and gender discrimination. Economic Policy Institute. Downloaded November 11, 2023 from https://www.epi.org/blog/black-womens-labor-market-history-reveals-deep-seated-race-and-gender-discrimination/.

Basulto, D. (2013, June 25).When women are the breadwinners and men are the caregivers, how will innovation change? *The Washington Post.* Downloaded November 11, 2023 from https://www.washingtonpost.com/news/innovations/wp/2013/06/25/when-women-are-the-breadwinners-and-men-are-the-caregivers-how-will-innovation-change/.

Blumell, L., E., Huemmer, J., & Sternadori, M. (2019). Protecting the ladies: Benevolent sexism, heteronormativity, and partisanship in online discussions of gender-neutral bathrooms. *Mass Communication and Society*, 22, 365–388. DOI: https://doi.org/10.1080/15205436.2018.1547833.

Churchill, B., Kornrich, S., & Ruppanner, L. (2023). Children of the revolution: The continued unevenness of the gender revolution in housework, childcare and work time across birth cohorts. *Social Science Research*, 111, 102868. DOI: https://doi.org/10.1016/j.ssresearch.2023.102868.

Fontana, D., & Schoenbaum, N, (2019). Unsexing pregnancy. *Columbia Law Review*, 119(2), 309–368.

Hardin, M., & Shain, S. (2005). Female sports journalists: Are we there yet? No. *Newspaper Research Journal*, 26(4), 22–35. DOI: 10.1177/073953290502600403.

Hasenbush, A., Flores, A. R., & Herman, J. L. (2019). Gender identity nondiscrimination laws in public accommodations: A review of evidence regarding safety and privacy in public restrooms, locker rooms, and changing rooms. *Sexuality Research and Social Policy*, 16, 70–83. https://doi.org/10.1007/s13178-018-0335-z.

Hayes, A. R., & Lee, D. (2022). Women, work, and families during the COVID-19 pandemic: Examining the effects of COVID policies and looking to the future. *Journal of Social Issues*, 79, 1088–1105. DOI: https://doi.org/10.1111/josi.12510.

Ianzito, C. (2017). The hidden male caregiver. AARP. Downloaded November 11, 2023 from https://www.aarp.org/caregiving/life-balance/info-2017/hidden-male-caregiver.html.

Oliveira, J., Frontini, R., Jacinto, Mi, & Antunes, R. (2022). Barriers and motives for physical activity and sports practice among trans people: A systematic review. *Sustainability*, 14, 2–11. DOI: https://doi.org/10.3390/su14095295.

Pompper, D. (2017). *Rhetoric of femininity: Female body image, media, and gender role stress/conflict*. Lexington Books.

Sex discrimination: Overview of the law (n.d.) U.S. Department of Education. Downloaded November 11, 2022 from https://shorturl.at/uyKZ4.

Title IX (n.d.) Civil Rights Division, U.S. Department of Justice. Downloaded November 11, 2023 from https://www.justice.gov/crt/title-ix.

Women in the labor force (2021). BLS Reports. U.S. Bureau of Labor Statistics Downloaded November 11, 2023 from https://www.bls.gov/opub/reports/womens-databook/2022/home.htm.

Third, organizations must beware of challenges associated with getting bogged down in defining *diversity*. It's one of those words that means different things to different people at different points in time. *Diversity* may be best defined by considering the concept of social identity, which has been theorized by many (e.g., Mcleod, 2023; Tajfel & Turner, 1986). Ways that people are unique according to the intersecting dimensions that make us who we are (e.g., age, social class, culture, ethnicity, faith/spirituality, gender, physical/psychological ability, sexual orientation) constitutes our social identity. Yet, each dimension must be considered flexibly, always capable of shifting and crosscutting boundaries and interests. Cox (2001) offered a widely accepted definition of diversity used across the communication discipline that's grounded in an organization context: "the variation of social and cultural identities among people existing together in a defined employment or market setting" (p. 3) wherein "social and cultural identity refers to personal affiliations with groups that research has shown to have significant influence on people's major life experiences" (p. 4).

Workforce diversity research and social identity theory are inextricably linked. Some researchers suggest that there must be as much diversity within an organization as there is outside it for the organization to be optimally effective (Weick, 1995), especially now that organizations operate in and rely on global outreach. One group of social identity researchers earmarked diversity as a "business paradigm for differences" (Zanoni et al., 2010, p. 12). Often, the goal of studying workforce diversity is to reveal "composition of work units in terms of the cultural or demographic characteristics that are salient and symbolically meaningful in the relationships among group members" (DiTomaso et al., 2007, p. 473). This does not mean that the goal of making diversity real need necessarily be tied to profit generation, however.

Today, a moral goal designed to foster equal opportunity and to maximize human potential at work (Noon, 2007) has replaced a business case cost–benefit analysis goal approach because research assessing how diversity might impact an organization's productivity and financial bottom line has yielded inconclusive results, anyway. Cecchinato (2023) explored the main topics driving discussions on diversity, inclusion, and productivity, concluding that there are far too many variables attached to the discussion that must be isolated and measured to conclusively draw links. For example, just how to measure *productivity* and how to measure *inclusion* offers serious challenges. Also, assessing each individual employees' belief system about others seems to be an impossible task. Indeed, defining diversity inclusively as DEI is inclusive and promotes attention to inclusivity, as well.

Fourth, another way to monitor power tensions in the service of ensuring DEI is an authentic goal involves conducting ongoing research to assess people's perceptions about organizations' DEI commitment and people's comfort level as employees and members of other key audiences (Cecchinato, 2023; Pompper, 2013). Specifically, using a combination of qualitative research methods such as focus groups and in-depth interviews—along with the quantitative survey method for generalizability—may offer a solid start to assessing an organization's DEI goals and then regularly monitoring conditions. Using formal research methods to better understand how social identity dimensions shape our consciousness and relationships with people has great utility among DEI-committed organizations. Dialogue across and within organizations and groups demands an ability to collect and analyze data for purposes of relationship building. Organizations that understand audiences and embrace a responsibility *toward* those audiences for the greater good of *all* rely on findings gained from ethically using research tools. Organizations' communication teams are uniquely positioned to facilitate research processes given that communication is strategic (Zerfass et al., 2018) and an essential part of organizations. As a backdrop for policymakers and others concerned about human rights and ethically negotiating power structures, organizations and communities with a commitment to research and DEI are supported by the U.N. Declaration on the Rights of Indigenous Peoples (UNDRIP) (n.d.) Making commitment to DEI an authentic organizational goal requires research to ensure that the promise is real (and kept over time). The commitment must go beyond the lip service of action-bereft mission statements emblazoned on web pages because it is linked to social responsibility and sustainability, the focus of Chapter 5, "Social responsibility in corporations and nonprofits."

Fifth, thinking about ways each social identity dimension can interplay with power demands that we take the broadest view on a DEI lens to avoid any tendency to default to any one dimension, such as race. Such a promise goes far in ensuring that employees who identify as trans, practice a faith/ spirituality that extends beyond what's considered mainstream wherever an organization is physically located, or consider *family* beyond immediate connections may rest assured that organizations with whom they have a commitment returns the privilege.

A broad perspective on power and social identity dimension interplay among organizations' communicators must include a promise to avoid falling into the same pitfalls as academic social identity researchers who have noted an abundance of research on ethnicity/race and gender, but far less attention to most of the other social identity dimensions. For example, employees who define their social identity according to social identity dimensions not readily apparent experience unique challenges that may involve anxiety. They may face a choice in whether or not to reveal at work (to hide what they consider to be a potential stigma) or to pass (conceal or closet). Dynamics associated with the choice may result in generating positive feelings of authenticity, creating opportunities for consciousness raising, education, social changes and coalition building (Martin, 2022)—or conclude in negative outcomes such as repressing one's true self. A 2019 Glassdoor report offered findings suggesting that 47% of LGTBQ+ research participants worried that coming out could hurt their career and that 61% have witnessed identity-based workplace discrimination along dimensions of LGBTQ+, age, or race (Hess, 2019). On the other hand, employers that offer support groups are positively viewed by employees (Wax et al., 2017). According to one source, there are over 500,000 support groups in the United States serving people dealing with a variety of concerns and needs (Creating, n.d.). Indeed, any given organization has a substantial impact on individual disclosure decisions (Wax et al., 2017). Enabling employees to be authentic contributes positively to the workplace because employees who self-describe according to stigmatized social identity dimension(s) otherwise would spend significant resources in managing their social identities.

Finally, providing access to power must be central to authentic DEI in organizations. As noted earlier, many for-profit and nonprofit organizations occupy high status, authoritative positions in our collective social mind. Organizations and celebrities have the resources—money and access to media—that many private individuals do not. In addition to using their power in the daily routines of running the organization, managers of organizations also lobby politicians and lawmakers to influence decisions that will benefit the organization in the future. This occurs at all local, national, and international levels.

But what about individuals unaffiliated with a particular organization who seek power to influence social change? As regular people, many of us lack the money, time, and access to decision makers that organizations do. Some minority voices may use public relations as a means to share their ideas across the public sphere. By gaining the ear of what Edwards (2012) called a *cultural intermediary*, people who lack power may have their voices elevated when the public relations practitioner shares people's concerns with organizations. Employees and other key publics may make their perceptions known to influencers, managers, and others with power to affect social change when those with power make themselves available via social media and in person. For example, the concept of management by walking (or wandering) around (MBWA) since 1982 when former Hewlett Packard co-founder Tom Peters (Peters & Waterman, 2006) introduced it to acknowledge that some people generally feel intimidated by those who possess power (especially those who may seem distant or unapproachable), so encountering a powerful figure in the cafeteria or a meditation space may offer a more comfortable context for sharing ideas and concerns. MBWA can lead to higher morale and greater levels of participation—yet it must be authentic and not be perceived by anyone as a chore or disingenuous lip service (Mind, n.d.). X (formerly Twitter) owner Elon Musk learned from negative publicity that mocking an employee with a disability (Duffy, 2023).

Communications liaison

As noted earlier, even though applying DEI to communications work is "relatively new as a discipline" (Stovall & Clark, 2022, p. 193), an organization's communicator can play a central role in negotiating power downsides (e.g., clarifying details, clearing up misunderstandings, supporting minorities when their voices are unheard/silenced) and in making DEI a reality across organizations from the inside out. Often, it is the public relations consultant who gains acceptance into an organization's dominant coalition, or "organizational corridors of power," who performs a strategic role managing organizational relationships (Dozier & Broom, 2006; L'Etang, 2008, p. 162). Enabling management teams to clearly think through their societal role, impact, and social responsibility to manage DEI across internal and external relationships is central to making DEI a reality. The importance of good communication skills needed to accomplish this work cannot be understated—and anticipating all the good that may come from this precision-sharp focus and commitment is exciting, indeed!

Concluding thoughts

The purpose of this chapter is to closely examine impediments to effective relationship building between organizations and publics and some of the many long-reaching effects; namely, power differentials. We began by exploring the role of power's import across structures and functions with attention to the social construction of power, examining effects of uneven power differentials, noting the relevance of power in relationship building, uncovering barriers attached to business case thinking and instead advocating for social justice case thinking, and then wrapping up by advancing specific steps for moving forward with a communication liaison at the helm. Upon this foundation, here are some thought-provoking ideas about power and DEI interplay with encouragement to support belonging with attention to marginalized voices from within, or inside, organizations.

The strategic communicator working within organizations has tremendous normative potential as a powerful **insider-activist** social change agent. This new millennium is the time for "the activist within" to tap into their intellectual domain (Adae, 2023; Bader, 2014; Dozier & Lauzen, 2000, p. 4) by pondering consequences of business in society; a postmodernist perspective of insider-activists to ensure that viewpoints and conditions of "the Other" are respectfully and wholly represented "without asking anything in return" (Holtzhausen, 2014, p. xv). This worldview is explored in greater depth in Chapter 5, "Social responsibility in corporations and nonprofits." Stovall and Clark (2022) warned that companies that prefer *not* to invest in honoring and protecting employees (and all key audiences) with attention to DEI for social justice change must be prepared to "pay for DEI on the backend" in the form of legal expenses associated with harassment and discrimination lawsuits (p. 195).

Perhaps the most positive stories about for-profit corporations' authentic willingness to remake organizations in order to reduce or eradicate power differentials are those able to admit their shortcomings and commit to working hard to make their organization better. For example, organizations like Patagonia (n.d., para. 1–2), a U.S.-based retailer of outerwear, host DEI conversations with employees and friends:

> We can, and should, be doing a lot more to actively engage with individuals and communities who are historically underrepresented in the outdoor community, the environmental movement and our own company. While Patagonia has a history of championing gender equality, we also realize our own shortcomings when it comes to being more inclusive. We are working deliberately to create meaningful change by conversing with and listening to the communities we do not represent adequately. We know we'll make mistakes, and probably upset some people along the way, but our 40-plus years of building the best products while caring for the earth has taught us that doing the right thing takes time and practice.

Next, in Chapter 5, "Social responsibility in corporations and nonprofits," the focus on power sharpens to closely examine how organizations' authentic embrace of DEI for social justice is a *social responsibility*.

Key words

Counterpublics—Oppressed people, with their dissenting and often marginalized voices, form counterpublics in reaction to dominant discourses (Warner, 2005).

Insider activist—People working on the inside of organizations who may be influential in advocating for and implementing policy changes and commitments, such as those related to DEI programs (Buchter, 2020).

Power differential—There exists a power inequality separating people in authority positions from people in subordinate positions, making people in the subordinate positions vulnerable to the actions of people in authority positions (Barstow, 2015).

Privilege—This is enjoyed by an individual or group beyond what's available to others, often translating to some special advantage, benefit, or favor. As explained in Chapter 1, "DEI and social identity intersectionality in organizational communication," some people are born into socio-economic privilege in the form of wealth, and some are born with the privilege of male gender, which even some DEI allies and advocates might be unwilling to lose (McIntosh, 1989). White people, as a privileged group, "take their identity as the norm and the standard by which other groups are measured," making their identity invisible and unconscious (Martin et al., 199, p. 28).

Public sphere—Habermas (1974) characterized öffentlichkeit as "a realm of our social life in which something approaching public opinion can be formed [and into which] access is guaranteed to all citizens" (p. 49). While media support spaces for public discussions in the public sphere, the concept of public sphere remains mostly theoretical given that a wholly equitable society has not yet been achieved.

Reverse discrimination—In the wake of the Civil Rights Act of 1964 with affirmative action programs in the U.S., some majority White people perceive that they have become a minority group and sue organizations (especially in business and education) for discriminating against them (Martin et al., 1999). This pattern has become increasingly apparent since passage of legislation informed by the 2021 American Rescue Plan Act to support farmers and restauranteurs of color in conjunction with the global pandemic (Tomkin, 2021).

Self-reflexivity—This is a process wherein people think about how their own social identity dimensions and their intersectionalities impact what they say and do. In organizations, communicators and others who use formal research tools critically consider themselves and the role they play in shaping meaning "around the binaries, contradictions, and paradoxes that form our own lives" (Lincoln & Guba, 2003, p. 283).

Sensemaking—The process of using communication to bring clarity to events, issues, and situations that involves people working to understand things which may be confusing, ambiguous, and sometimes contentious. Given complexity of the DEI concept and organizations' programs designed to ensure it, the formal communicator (e.g., marketing communications, public relations, strategic communications) or human resources personnel may play a significant role in inspiring fruitful conversations about DEI in organizations (Weick, 1995).

Social homophily thesis—A social homophily thesis underpins preservation of the status quo in order to facilitate ease in communication and reduce management costs (Appold et al., 1998). Often, this term is used to describe a predominantly Caucasian/White and heterosexist workplace which is preserved in organizations based on an assumption that sameness maintains harmony and avoids conflict. Critique of the social homophily thesis in organizations reveals several negative outcomes for social identities shaped by difference—such as *othering, tokenism, pigeonholing,* and other *microaggressions.*

Standpoint—Social theorists explain that each human possesses a standpoint that is multifaceted and changeable, as shaped by their perspectives rooted in social and political experiences. Wood (1993) recommended use of standpoint epistemology—examining reality through the eyes of marginalized lives. This approach is inherently critical and has the added benefit of revealing systemic causes for perceptions of inequality, exclusion, and homogeneity in organizations.

Discussion questions for deep engagement

1. How many power differentials are at play in your life? Name at least three.
2. How would you describe your social identity standpoint? Offer as many details as you can.
3. How might you explain to someone who's not in your class that "power is a social construction?"
4. What kind of counterpublics do you encounter as part of your social media scanning? What issues/concerns/points do they amplify?
5. What barriers and blinders to authentic DEI have you witnessed at your school, employer, or place where you've done volunteer work (now or in the past)?

Resources

Adae, E. K. (2023). CEOs on a mission. Emerald Publishing.

Appold, S. J., Siengthai, S., & Kasarda, J. D. (1998). The employment of women managers and professionals in an emerging economy: Gender inequality as an organizational practice. *Administrative Science Quarterly*, 43, 538–565. DOI: https://doi.org/10.2307/2393675.

Associated Press (2021). More than 9,000 anti-Asian incidents have been reported since the pandemic began. NPR. Accessed May 11, 2023 from https://www.npr.org/2021/08/12/1027236499/anti-asian-hate-crimes-assaults-pandemic-incidents-aapi.

Bader, C. (2014). *The evolution of a corporate idealist: When girl meets oil.* Bibliomotion.

Baldera, A. & Guillory, R. (2019). Remembering the 9th anniversary of the Deepwater Horizon oil disaster. Ocean Conservancy. Downloaded May 31, 2023 from https://rb.gy/zd8yz

Barstow, C. (2015). The power differential and why it matters so much in therapy. Good Therapy. Downloaded June 10, 2023 from https://rb.gy/05omg.

Beech, P. (2020). What is environmental racism and how can we fight it? World Economic Forum. Downloaded May 31, 2023 from https://www.weforum.org/agenda/2020/07/what-is-environmental-racism-pollution-covid-systemic/.

Berger, P. L., & Luckmann, T. (1966). *The social construction of reality.* Anchor Books Doubleday.

Biden, J. R. (2021). Executive order on diversity, equity, inclusion, and accessibility in the federal workforce. The White House. Downloaded June 2, 2023 from https://rb.gy/tnwxi.

Blackmon, D. A. (2009). *Slavery by another name: The re-enslavement of Black Americans from the Civil War to World War II.* Anchor.

Bourdieu, P. (2005). *The social structures of the economy.* Polity Press.

Brod, H., & Kaufman, M. (1994). Introduction. In H. Brod and M. Kaufman (Eds.), *Theorizing masculinities* (pp. 1–9). Sage.

Buchter, L. (2020). Escaping the ellipsis of diversity: Insider activists' use of implementation resources to influence organization policy. *Administrative Science Quarterly*, 66(2), 521–565. DOI: https://doi.org/10.1177/0001839220963633

Burton, J., Farrell, M., Lord, F., & Lord, R. (2002). *Confinement and ethnicity: An overview of World War II Japanese American relocation sites.* University of Washington Press.

Cecchinato, G. (2023). Why we need to study the links between diversity and productivity. London School of Economics. Downloaded June 8, 2023 from https://rb.gy/5ge8g.

Chatterji, A. K., & Toffel, M. W. (2019, February 22). The right and wrong way to do CEO activism. *Wall Street Journal.* Downloaded June 2, 2023 from https://rb.gy/jeb4j.

Chattopadhyay, S. (2019). Organizations as communities. Networkweaver. Downloaded June 2, 2023 from https://rb.gy/pc6zx.

Costigan, A., & Hughes, V. (2021). CEO activism: Trend brief. Catalyst. Downloaded June 2, 2023 from https://rb.gy/nm4yy.

Cox, T. (2001). *Creating the multicultural organization: A strategy for capturing the power of diversity.* Jossey-Bass.

Creating and facilitating peer support groups (n.d.) Community Tool Box. Downloaded June 8, 2023 from https://rb.gy/e5f78.

Crenshaw, K. W., N. Gotanda, G. Peller, & K. Thomas (Eds.) (1995). *Critical race theory: The key writings that formed the movement.* The New Press.

Cruz, D. (1999). Controlling desires: Sexual orientation conversion and the limits of knowledge and law. *Southern California Law Review*, 72(5), 1297–400.

Cullinan, M., Maison, K., Parks, M. M., Krall, M. A., Krebs, E., Mann, B., & Jensen, R. E. (2023). Seedlings in the corporate forest: Communicating benevolent sexism in Dow Chemical's first internal affirmative-action campaign. *Management Communication Quarterly*, 37(1), 171–196. DOI: 10.1177/08933189221115748.

Davis, F. J. (n.d.) Who is Black? One nation's definition. *Frontline.* Downloaded November 23, 2023 from https://www.pbs.org/wgbh/pages/frontline/shows/jefferson/mixed/onedrop.html.

Diers, A. R., & Donohue, J. (2013). Synchronizing crisis responses after a transgression: An analysis of BP's enacted crisis response to the Deepwater Horizon crisis in 2010. *Journal of Communication Management*, 17(3), 252–269. DOI: https://doi.org/10.1108/JCOM-04-2012-0030.

DiTomaso, N., Post, C., & Parks-Yancy, R. (2007). Workforce diversity and inequality: Power, status, and numbers. *Annual Review of Sociology*, 33, 473–501.

Dobbin, F., & Kalev, A. (2016). Why diversity programs fail. *Harvard Business Review.* Downloaded November 11, 2023 from https://hbr.org/2016/07/why-diversity-programs-fail.

Dozier, D., & Broom, G. (2006). The centrality of practitioner roles to public relations theory. In C. Botan and V. Hazleton (Eds.), *Public relations theory II* (pp. 137–170). Lawrence Erlbaum Associates.

Dozier, D. M., & Lauzen, M. M. (2000). Liberating the intellectual domain from the practice: Public relations, activism, and the role of the scholar. *Journal of Public Relations Research*, 12(1), 3–22. DOI: https://doi.org/10.1207/S1532754XJPRR1201_2.

Duffy, C. (2023). Elon Musk publicly mocks Twitter worker with disability who is unsure whether he's been laid off. CNN. Downloaded June 9, 2023 from https://rb.gy/2wwcq.

Dukach, D. (2022). DEI gets real. *Harvard Business Review*. Downloaded June 2, 2023 from https://hbr.org/2022/01/dei-gets-real.

Edwards, L. (2010). Authenticity in organisational context: Fragmentation, contradiction and loss of control. *Journal of Communication Management*, 14(3), 192–205. DOI: https://doi.org/10.1108/13632541011064481.

Edwards, L. (2012). Exploring the role of public relations as a cultural intermediary. *Cultural Sociology*, 6(4), 438–454. DOI: https://doi.org/10.1177/1749975512445428.

Egan, M. (2022). First on CNN: Goldman Sachs CEO speaks out on gun violence. CNN. Downloaded June 2, 2023 from https://www.cnn.com/2022/05/26/business/goldman-sachs-ceo-gun-violence/index.html.

Environmental Justice (n.d.) United States Environmental Protection Agency. Downloaded May 31, 2023 from https://www.epa.gov/environmental justice.

Environmental Justice Timeline (n.d.) United States Environmental Protection Agency. Downloaded May 31, 2023 from https://www.epa.gov/environmental justice/environmental-justice-timeline.

Fitzgerald, M. (2019). The CEOs of nearly 200 companies just said shareholder value is no longer their main objective. Downloaded August 21, 2019 from https://rb.gy/7ofws.

Forced evacuation (2017). American Bar Association. Accessed May 11, 2023 from https://www.abalegalfactcheck.com/articles/forced-evac.html.

Foucault, M. (1980). *Power/knowledge*. Tavistock.

Grunig, J. E., & Huang, Y.-H. (2000). From organizational effectiveness to relationship indicators: Antecedents of relationships, public relations strategies, and relationship outcomes. In J. A. Ledingham and S. D. Bruning (Eds.), *Public relations as relationship management: A relational approach to the study and practice of public relations* (pp. 23–53). Lawrence Erlbaum.

Gupta, S. (2020). To fight discrimination, the U.S. census needs a different race question. *Science News*. Accessed May 10, 2023 from https://www.sciencenews.org/article/census-2020-race-ethnicity-questions.

Gurchiek, K. (2018). Prayer and meditation rooms can increase inclusion. Society for Human Resource Management. Downloaded May 31, 2023 from https://rb.gy/bhhz1.

Habermas, J. (1974). *Theory and practice* (trans. J. Vlental). Heinemann.

Harris, B. J. (2019). Unpacking the conversations that matter: Moving beyond the veil of privilege. The Inclusion Solution. Downloaded June 2, 2023 from https://rb.gy/qh0vl.

Haselby, S. (2015). The invasion of America. Aeon. Downloaded June 1, 2023 from https://rb.gy/kt91x.

Hess, A. J. (2019). 53% of LGBTQ employees have faced or witnessed verbal discrimination at work. CNBC.com. Downloaded June 8, 2023 from https://rb.gy/hpnqo.

history.com editors (2021). Japanese internment camps. Accessed May 11, 2023 from https://www.history.com/topics/world-war-ii/japanese-american-relocation.

Holtzhausen, D. R. (2014). *Public relations as activism: Postmodern approaches to theory and practice*. Routledge.

Kenton, W. (2022). What is affirmative action? Definition, how it works, and example. Investopedia. Downloaded June 2, 2023 from https://rb.gy/gax8h.

Kochan, T., Bezrukova, K., Ely, R., Jackson, S., Joshi, A., Jehn, K., Leonard, J., Levine, D., & Thomas, D. (2003). The effects of diversity on business performance: Report of the diversity research network. *Human Resource Management*, 42(1), 3–21. DOI: https://doi.org/10.1002/hrm.10061.

Larson, E. W., Linabary, J. R., & Long, Z. (2022). Communicating inclusion: A review and research agenda on inclusion research in organizational communication. *Annals of the International Communication Association*, 46(2), 63–90, DOI: 10.1080/23808985.2022.2069045.

Leitch, S., & Motion, J. (2013). Power, discourse. In R. L. Heath (Ed.), *Encyclopedia of public relations*, 2nd ed. (pp. 671–673). Sage.

L'Etang, J. (2008). Writing PR history: Issues, methods and politics. *Journal of Communication Management*, 12(4), 319–335. https://www.emerald.com/insight/content/doi/10.1108/13632540810919783/full/html.

Lincoln, Y. S., & Guba, E. G. (2003). Paradigmatic controversies, contradictions, and emerging confluences. In N. K. Denzin and Y. S. Lincoln. Sage (Eds.), *The landscape of qualitative research: Theories and issues* (pp. 191–215). Sage.

Liptak, A. (2021, Oct. 14). Civil rights law protects gay and transgender workers, Supreme Court rules. *New York Times*. Downloaded June 1, 2023 from https://rb.gy/3576s.

Liu, B. F., & Pompper, D. (2012). The 'crisis with no name': Defining the interplay of culture, ethnicity, and race on organizational issues and media outcomes. *Journal of Applied Communication Research*, 40(2), 127–146. https://doi.org/10.1080/00909882.2012.654499.

Logan, N. (2016). The Starbucks race together initiative: Analyzing a public relations campaign with critical race theory. *Public Relations Inquiry*, 5(1), 93–113. DOI: 10.1177/2046147X15626969.

Logan, N. (2021). Breaking down barriers of the past and moving toward authentic DEI adoption. In D. Pompper (Ed.), *Public relations for social responsibility: Affirming DEI commitment with action* (pp. 3–17). Emerald.

Macnamara, J. (2015a). *Organizational listening: The missing essential in public communication*. Peter Lang.

Macnamara, J. (2015b). Creating an 'architecture of listening' in organizations. University of Technology, Sidney. Downloaded June 7, 2023 from chrome-extension://efaidnbmnnnibpcajpcglclefindmkaj/https://www.uts.edu.au/sites/default/files/fass-organizational-listening-report.pdf.

Mahler, A. G. (2018). From the tricontinental to the Global South: Race, radicalism, and transnational solidarity. Duke University Press.

Martin, J. A. (2022). Coming out at work is hard. It could also change your life. *Indeed/Lead*. Downloaded June 8, 2023 from https://rb.gy/071qp.

Martin, J. N., Krizek, R. L., Nakayama, T. K., & Bradford, L. (1999). What do White people wanted to be called. In T. K. Nakayama and J. N. Martin (Eds.), *Whiteness: The communication of social identity* (pp. 27–50). Sage.

Martin, L. (2023). Learning to listen. *TCU Magazine*. Downloaded June 7, 2023 from https://rb.gy/hvzd0.

McIntosh, P. (1989). White privilege: Unpacking the invisible knapsack. *Peace and Freedom*, July/August, 10–12. Wellesley College Center for Research on Women.

Mcleod, S. (2023). Social identity theory. Definition, history, examples, & facts. Simply Psychology. Downloaded June 8, 2023 from https://rb.gy/glxum.

McPherson, M., Smith-Lovin, L., & Cook, J. M. (2001). Birds of a feather: Homophily in social networks. *Annual Review of Sociology*, 27, 415–444. DOI: https://doi.org/10.1146/annurev.soc.27.1.415

Miller, L. (2020, June 7). George Floyd protests have created a multicultural movement that's making history. *Los Angeles Times.* Downloaded November 23, 2023 from https://www.latimes.com/california/story/2020-06-07/george-floyd-protests-unite-black-activists-new-allies.

Mind tools content team (n.d.) Management by wandering around (MBWA). Mind Tools. Downloaded June 9, 2013 from https://rb.gy/0w1wk.

Monge, P. R., & Contractor, N. S. (2001). Emergence of communication networks. In F. M. Jablin and L. L. Putnam (Eds.), *The new handbook of organizational communication: Advances in theory, research, and methods* (pp. 440–502). Sage.

Moreno, R., & Flowerday, T. (2006). Students' choice of animated pedagogical agents in science learning: A test of the similarity-attraction hypothesis on gender and ethnicity. *Contemporary Educational Psychology*, 31(2), 186–2007. DOI: https://doi.org/10.1016/j.cedpsych.2005.05.002.

Nadesan, M. (1997). Constructing paper dolls: The discourse of personality testing in organizational practice. *Communication Theory*, 7(3), 189–218. DOI: https://doi.org/10.1111/j.1468-2885.1997.tb00150.x.

National Environmental Justice Advisory Council (n.d.) U.S. Environmental Protection Agency. Downloaded May 31, 2023 from https://www.epa.gov/environmentaljustice/national-environmental-justice-advisory-council.

Noon, M. M. (2007). The fatal flaws of diversity and the business case for ethnic minorities. *Work Employment Society*, 21, 773–784.

O'Leary, B. J., & Weathington, B. L. (2006). Beyond the business case for diversity in organizations. *Employee Responsibilities and Rights Journal*, 18(4), 283–292. DOI: https://doi.org/10.1007/s10672-006-9024-9.

O'Neil, J., English, A. E., & Lambiase, J. (2022). After the killing of Atatiana Jefferson: Black stakeholder experiences within a municipal listening structure. *Journalism & Mass Communication Quarterly*, 99(3), 802–825. DOI: https://doi.org/10.1177/10776990221105588.

Patagonia (n.d.) A gathering for diversity, equity and inclusion with Teresa Baker. Patagonia. Downloaded June 9, 2023 from https://rb.gy/qusjl.

Peters, T. J., and Waterman, R. H., Jr. (2006). *In search of excellence: Lessons from America's best-run companies.* Harper Business.

Pfeffer, J., Zorbach, T., & Carley, K. M. (2014). Understanding online firestorms: Negative word-of-mouth dynamics in social media networks. *Journal of Marketing Communications*, 20(1–2), 117–128. DOI: http://dx.doi.org/10.1080/13527266.2013.797778.

Pitts, D. W. (2006). Modeling the impact of diversity management. *Review of Public Personnel Administration*, 26, 245–268. DOI: https://doi.org/10.1177/0734371X05278491.

Place, K. R. (2023). Organizational listening for diversity, equity, and inclusion. *Organizational listening for strategic communication: Building theory and practice* (pp. 181–198). Routledge.

Pompper, D. (2013). Volunteerism and corporate social responsibility: Definitions, measurement, roles, & commitment. In L. Lewis, L. Gossett and M. Kramer (Eds.), *Volunteering and communication: Studies from multiple contexts* (pp. 273–295). Peter Lang Publishers.

Pompper, D. (2023). *Discovering answers: Research methods for public relations.* Kendall/Hunt Publishing.

Pompper, D., Ertem-Eray, T., Amevor, E., Diop, L., Nadel, S., & Adae, E. K. (2021). Diversity at the big table: A snapshot of Fortune 500 boards of directors. In

D. Pompper (Ed.), *Public relations for social responsibility: Affirming DEI commitment with action* (pp. 51–69). Emerald Group Publishing.

Ponder, M. L., Uddin, J., & Sun, W. (2023). Asian American's lived experiences with and perceptions of social stigma during COVID-19. *Howard Journal of Communications*, 34(2), 151–169. DOI: 10.1080/10646175.2022.2106168.

Robbins, M. (2018). How to bring your whole self to work. *Greater Good Magazine*. Downloaded June 2, 2023 from https://rb.gy/c0m67

Robinson, G., & Dechant, K. (1997). Building a business case for diversity. *Academy of Management Perspectives*, 11(3), 21–31. DOI: https://doi.org/10.5465/ame.1997.9709231661.

Roth, W. D. (2010). Racial mismatch: The divergence between form and function in data for monitoring racial discrimination of Hispanics. *Social Science Quarterly*, 91(5), 1288–1311. DOI: https://doi.org/10.1111/j.1540-6237.2010.00732.x.

Sanders, A. (2020). Housing: Often overlooked but a critical pillar for older adults. Downloaded May 31, 2023 from https://generations.asaging.org/housing-older-adults-health-inequities-policy.

Scott, K. L., Restubog, S. L. D., Zagenczyk, T. J. (2013). A social exchange-based model of the antecedents of workplace exclusion. *Journal of Applied Psychology*, 98(1), 37–48. DOI: 10.1037/a0030135.

Shah, K. (2015). Why Starbucks' race together campaign failed. Eater. Downloaded May 31, 2023 from https://rb.gy/ahrl6.

Starbucks 'race together' campaign brews backlash. Reuters. Downloaded May 31, 2023 from https://rb.gy/xfiwo.

Steimel, S. J. (2021). Beyond the business case for diversity and inclusion: Approaches to promoting organizational diversity. *Communication Teacher*, 35(3), 197–201. DOI: 10.1080/17404622.2021.1923771.

Swingewood, A. (2000). *A short history of sociological thought*. Palgrave Macmillan.

Stovall, J. M., & Clark, K. (2022). *The conscious communicator: The fine art of not saying stupid sh*t, adding depth to your organization's communications*. Publish Your Purpose.

Tajfel, H., & Turner, J. (1986). The social identity theory of inter-group behavior. In W. G. Austin & S. Worchel (Eds.), *Psychology of Intergroup Relations* (2nd ed.) (pp. 7–24). Nelson-Hall Publishers.

Thomas, K. M., & Plout, V. C. (2008). The many faces of diversity resistance in the workplace. In K. M. Thomas (Ed.), *Diversity resistance in organizations* (pp. 1–22). Lawrence Erlbaum.

Tomkin, A. R. (2021). The case for selective discrimination. *Nonprofit Quarterly*. Downloaded June 10, 2023 from https://rb.gy/mq8b1.

United Nations (n.d.) United Nations declaration on the rights of indigenous peoples. Downloaded December 30, 2022 from https://rb.gy/ipgegv.

van de Mieroop, K. (2016). On the advantage and disadvantage of Black History Month for life: The creation of the post-racial era. *History and Theory*, 55(1), 3–24. DOI: https://doi.org/10.1111/hith.10784.

Warner, M. (2005). *Publics and counterpublics*. Zone Books.

Waters, S. (2017). Workplace suicide and states of denial: The France Télécom and Foxconn cases compared. *tripleC*, 15(1), 191–213. DOI: http://dx.doi.org/10.31269/vol15iss1pp191-213.

Wax, A., Coletti, K. K., & Ogaz, J. W. (2017). The benefit of full disclosure: A meta-analysis of the implications of coming out at work. *Organizational Psychology Review*, 8(1), 3–30. DOI: https://doi.org/10.1177/2041386617734582.

Weick, K. (1995). *Sensemaking in organizations.* Sage.

Wood, J. T. (1993). Gender and moral voice: Moving from woman's nature to standpoint epistemology. *Women's Studies in Communication,* 15, 1–24. DOI: https://doi.org/10.1080/07491409.1992.11089757.

Yang, A. (2023). Stakeholder networks and corporate social responsibility. In D. Pompper, K. R. Place, and C. K. Weaver (Eds.), *The Routledge companion to public relations* (pp. 253–264). Routledge.

Zahniser, J. D. (2023). Japanese internment camps: America's great mistake. Historynet. Accessed May 11, 2023 from https://www.historynet.com/japanese-internment-camps-wwii/.

Zanoni, P., Janssens, M., Benschop, Y., & Nkomo, S. (2010). Unpacking diversity, grasping inequality: Rethinking difference through critical perspectives. *Organization,* 17(1), 9–29.

Zerfass, A., Verčič, D., Nothhaft, H., & Werder, K. P. (2018). Strategic communication: Defining the field and its contribution to research and practice. *International Journal of Strategic Communication,* 12(4), 487–505. DOI: https://doi.org/10.1080/1553118X.2018.1493485.

Zilber, A. (2023). Chick-fil-A CEO Dan Cathy's shoe shine story causes viral storm as old clip resurfaces. New York Post. Downloaded March 30, 2024 from https://nypost.com/2023/05/31/former-chick-fil-a-ceo-dan-cathy-shined-black-mans-shoes/.

5 Social responsibility in corporations and nonprofits

Donnalyn Pompper

Both for-profit and nonprofit organizations have a social responsibility to value and respect multiple voices (e.g., Yang, 2023). Believing that all living things have rights, conservation-philosopher Henry David Thoreau helped to launch the environmental movement in the U.S. (Weiner, 2010), saying, "Every creature is better alive than dead, men and moose and pine-trees, and he who understands it aright will rather preserve its life than destroy it." Whether an organization's purpose is profit centric or nonprofit service provision, ensuring that commitment to DEI is authentic and actively engaged must be prioritized to affect real social justice.

Some for-profit organizations take the *S* in *social* of the **environmental, social, governance (ESG)** acronym so seriously that they work to achieve the status of a **certified B corporation (B corp)**. This means that in addition to turning a profit, some corporations are committed to revising their business model so that it may meet high standards of verified performance, accountability, and transparency on factors such as employee benefits, charitable giving, supply-chain practices, and input materials. Each of these factors has DEI implications felt by people who work *in* or *with* organizations and are impacted by the organizations' operations. B corporation certification applies to an entire organization across its operations and distribution and the designation is conferred by B Lab, a nonprofit corporation that certifies B corporations (Bell, 2023).

This chapter builds upon Chapter 4, "Power differentials in organization and society," underscoring why and how attention to DEI is every organization's social responsibility with these subsections: the 1970s ecology movement, shifting from **corporate social responsibility and sustainability (CSR/S)** to ESG, environmental justice without greenwashing or stereotyping in economic disparity, decolonizing and other wicked problems, social networks and indigenous ways of knowing, and resisting not in my back yard (NIMBY) and moving forward, and concluding thoughts.

DOI: 10.4324/9781003279129-7

The 1970s ecology movement

In particular, people born in the 21st century may wonder what does "the environmental decade" in the 1970s (Devall, 1980, p. 307) have to do with today's organizations' attention to DEI? Philosophically, there are many parallels connecting environmental issues both inside and outside organizations—to respecting target audiences and enabling people to achieve their maximum potential. Fostering healthy work environments and producing brands and services that do not harm society (or the planet) now or in the future is a significant responsibility. Because often organizations need to be reminded of their social commitment, grassroots activism has become synonymous with the U.S.'s democratic impulse. Collective action designed to remedy an acute problem at a local level makes grassroots activism effective—even if it's just one person pressuring elected officials, government representatives, or organizations to change for the better (Rivard, 2023).

In the U.S., the **ecology** movement was partly inspired by the 1962 exposé, *Silent Spring* (Carson, 2022[1962]), urging for greater regulation

Figure 5.1 The pioneering work of marine biologist and nature writer Rachel Carson was commemorated on a U.S. postage stamp.

of pesticides. The ecology movement also benefitted from development of groups such as the Sierra Club, Nature Conservancy, and the National Audubon Society. These nonprofits are charged with preserving and protecting nature. Animal deaths (e.g., bald eagles, swans, owls) to the point of near extinction (Ebersole, 2020) and toxins harming humans in widely publicized incidents such as the 1978 evacuation of the Love Canal neighborhood in upstate New York and the earlier 1969 Santa Barbara oil spill raised public consciousness about human-made environmental disasters, thanks to the work of activists like **Lois Gibbs**. Other legacies of the 1970s ecology movement include the first time Earth Day was celebrated, creation of the Environmental Protection Agency, and passage of the Clean Air Act to provide governmental oversight and policymaking. Raising consciousness about the contamination of air, land, and water by industrialization and urbanization's forces associated with many for-profit organizations is an ongoing effort, requiring several decades to formally address. This is because what Devall (1980) called the "dominant social paradigm," or economic growth and progress, is fundamental to "ever increasing demands of humans" (p. 300)—and these demands are not without negative environmental degradation impact.

Today, organizations refer to ESG commitments to ensure that no groups of people are singled out to bear the brunt of environmental degradation caused by organizations' operations. Critics charge, however, that this desire is not guaranteed.

Shifting from CSR/S to ESG

To some people, it seems that organizations everywhere are amplifying their commitment to the planet. There are others who maintain a "blind faith" that technology will save us from climate change effects (Soromenho-Marques & Ribeiro, 2022). In the CSR/S space, this trend of the last decades has metamorphosed into current assessing of organizations' ESG non-financial impacts. Some investors keep score so they may build portfolios supporting organizations committed to ESG issues related to the economy, public health, and social justice. The *S* for *social* is directly linked to DEI concerns because it corresponds with labor standards, wages and benefits, workplace and board diversity, racial justice, pay equity, human rights, talent management, community relations, and more (Bergman et al., 2020). All of these issues/concerns impact various social groups uniquely, with some being more vulnerable than others—depending on historical roots of bias and discrimination, intersecting social identity dimensions, and degrees of formal regulation. For example, transgender people experience high rates of stigma and violence at work which threatens their safety and existence (Baboolal et al., 2023), workers with disability historically have faced workplace discrimination despite the Americans with Disabilities Act of 1990 (ADA)—with women facing lower full-time employment rates than both men with disabilities and women without disabilities (Gitnux, 2023). This means organizations' accountability to social justice must be regularly monitored. DEI advocates applaud organizations' *voluntary* ESG commitment, as well as consumers' and investors' emphasis on the importance of ESG disclosures with metrics in publicly available reports and rankings.

Back in the mid-1990s, corporations responded to the dot.com collapse and sought to reverse ethics lapses like Worldcom and Enron failures, which robbed stockholders of billions (Verschoor, 2005) with attention to CSR/S—and promoting their efforts and plans so that audiences would consider them to be acting responsibly in light of these high-profile ethics crises. Over time, many observers began calling the CSR trend "a smokescreen for masking poor accountability and camouflage for exorbitant profit making while carrying on with business as usual" (Pompper, 2015, p. 1).

On the other hand, the *sustainability* component of CSR/S refers to reactions to perhaps unintended consequences of natural resource consumption and commerce (Millar et al., 2012). Combined, the CSR/S trend was designed for corporations to be held accountable to more than just profits—as inspired by the Earth Charter Initiative—drawn in 2000 following the United Nations World Commission on Environment and Development in 1987 and the United Nations Global Compact in 1999. Turning worldwide attention to corporations' impact on the planet meant going beyond Rachel Carson's important critique of pesticide companies in the 1960s and expanding scrutiny to financial firms, food companies, petrochemical companies, and more (O'Higgins, 2005). Considering planet impact also meant long-term thinking *and* doing beyond simply trying to capture trendy headlines.

Yet, the most persistent critique of the CSR/S trend has been that it was doomed to fail—according to business thinkers and human rights activists—because it lacked authenticity (e.g., Frankental, 2001), overlooked social contract thinking (e.g., Morrison, 2014), and was voluntary and inconsistent with corporations' profit-centric motives (e.g., Banerjee, 2003; Gond, 2017). These same critiques also haunt the newer ESG trend because corporations have little (or no) incentive to save the planet or to support DEI programs benefiting the people who live on the planet. See Sidebar 5.1 to discover a case study about ways public utilities blend ESG and DEI that include an invitation to embrace modern taken-for-granted luxuries like toilets and faucets with running water.

Sidebar 5.1   The communications connection: ESG & public utilities

Tricia Garrison

Have you hugged your toilet today? How about the faucet in the bathroom sink? Well, in my opinion, if you're lucky enough to live with these modern luxuries, you totally should. Your plumbing doesn't discriminate, so long as it's working. So what is the connection between your plumbing, the public utility sewer service connected to it, and ESG? This sidebar explores that connection, and how communications practitioners help.

Figure 5.2 Tricia Garrison.

Chances are if you're reading this, you are an undergraduate student living in a place that has access to clean drinking water, a functional toilet, and power, anytime you like, day or night. Charging your phone happens pretty easily (if you remember to do it), and doing laundry might be a bore, but it's a given that the washing machine will work with clean water magically pouring in, and dirty water magically disappearing.

So what? Well, if you are fortunate enough to have access to these services, you might be taking them for granted. What if you weren't able to shower today? Or tomorrow? What if you couldn't flush "it" away after a night of wolfing down one burrito too many? What if you did not have access to a toilet at all, within a reasonable walking distance?

Doesn't everyone get to use the services of public utilities in the same way? And just what is a *public utility*, anyway? According to *Market Business News*,

> a public utility often forms part of a natural monopoly . . . that exists because a specific market's economies of scale make it the most cost-effective way to provide consumers with the best quality and price. For example, if several companies operated in the supply of tap water, each one with its own infrastructure, the additional costs of having more than one water pipeline would not benefit the consumer, and would raise prices considerably.
>
> (What is a public utility?, n.d., para. 2)

Examples of public utilities include water, electricity, natural gas, waste disposal, and sewage treatment.

The *S* in ESG

A growing number of families in the U.S. struggle to pay for, and receive, these basic services (Brooks, 2022). Internationally, the numbers are far higher, and many places are without clean water, proper sanitation, or power. For example, 663 million people on our planet lack access to safe drinking water (Clean water changes everything, n.d.) In the context of ESG and the world of public utilities, let's look at the *S* in ESG, as in the *social* implications of the work of public utilities, and the role of the communications practitioner.

As economic disparity gaps continue to widen between haves and have nots in too many communities, unfortunately more are challenged to have enough money to cover their basic needs. Socio-economic status (SES) is something people may not think about. Poverty, unfortunately, is a social identifier that can be invisible. The social identity of customers is an important standpoint to consider while regarding public utilities as critical services that are a *need to have* rather than simply a *nice to have*. From the utility standpoint, with aging infrastructure (pipes, roads, buildings deteriorating) and inflation (costs going up), it is a constant challenge to keep equipment maintained and functioning around the clock. Managing to secure the necessary financing to cover it all is another part of the picture. Costs are rising for these vital services. And vulnerable populations can be hit hardest. This social issue needs our collective attention.

In the U.S., nearly 40 million people live in poverty and according to the U.S. Water Alliance, "more than 2 million Americans live without basic access to safe drinking water and sanitation" (Closing the water access gap in the United States policy brief, n.d., para. 1). With these harsh statistics, do public utilities bear a greater social, ethical, and/or moral responsibility toward those in greater need? How then does the *S* in ESG fit into this dynamic? And how can communications practitioners help guide their public utilities toward greater social sensitivity, and inclusivity with their communities?

Being trusted to be stewards of public natural resources, as well as financial resources, public utilities *do* have a responsibility to the communities they serve. While many private corporations tie ESG benchmarks to profitability, a public wastewater utility is a nonprofit with a zero-sum game. This means they pay for what's needed with no one earning a profit. With a public sewage treatment utility, the community members (that means everyone, in all their beautiful diversity) are the shareholders.

Communications practitioners are uniquely positioned to encourage their leadership to think beyond their utility fence, to drive their actions and intentions and think more about DEI while working with the communities they serve. So, how does this happen, and where does it begin?

Don't go it alone: #StrongerTogether

For starters, communications practitioners needn't go it alone. Indeed, a powerful proverb holds that *if you want to go fast, go alone; if you want to go far, go together.* Many organizations, including public utilities, are reaching out to their communities seeking counsel to help guide ESG initiatives for the organization—and to prioritize what should happen first. From a grassroots perspective at community levels, communications practitioners can reach out to their colleagues to gain valuable insight into what the staff thinks. This can be a great starting point for the journey. Honest staff feedback can point out deficiencies across an organization where strengths lie and help identify allies who are interested in helping move ESG efforts forward.

Do the research, listen to the community, tell the story

Communications practitioners can add their unique skillsets in storytelling, setting goals, and writing objectives, tactics, and key performance indicators (KPIs) to help keep the team focused, motivated, and moving forward. The communications practitioner can serve as a catalyst, or a spark, to ignite these efforts, if the initiatives are not already underway.

The communications practitioner can leverage the power of data and story, like an in-house journalist, to show their colleagues why it's important. But why bother with *that*? Without the internal team having an understanding of why ESG matters, there will be no buy-in among other employees and managers in an organization. With no buy-in, progress toward ESG goals can be tough. By building this understanding, communications practitioners can help build a coalition of ESG champions. Launch the coalition-building process with research. How many in your community live below the poverty line? What does DEI in your community look like? How does that stack up with your current staff, and your current leadership team? Is the organization being truly inclusive of the community it serves?

Where to next? Identify, prioritize, and look to the future

Selecting vendors that reflect populations within communities being served is one way public utilities may demonstrate a commitment to inclusivity. Obviously, public utilities require specific equipment, services, and material goods. However, through the vendor search and selection process, more inclusivity can be achieved, and communications practitioners can inspire this.

For example, reviewing an organization's established rules, policies, and procedures to ensure these are respectful and applied thoughtfully is just one way the communications practitioner can play a chief role in public utility settings. Are policies gender inclusive? For example, does the organization's dress-code policy dictate that women must dress a certain way, or wear makeup, while not addressing what men should wear, or how they should look? Are the policies sensitive to different religious practices, or those who don't practice at all? Are hiring managers trained on their implicit biases? Or do they default to hiring *someone who is like them*? An open and willing human resources (HR) leader who embraces ESG can be an incredible resource for communications practitioners to partner with. Together, these ESG allies can work together to identify meaningful and relevant goals for the utility, to galvanize C-suite attention and buy-in, to implement change, and to drive organizational ESG (or DEI) goals forward.

Public information, marketing, and creative content is another area where communications practitioners may play an important role to ensure inclusivity in organizations. Public service announcements (PSAs) and marketing pieces can be produced to be culturally appropriate and inclusive of the various languages spoken in communities. Communications practitioners also may identify opportunities where utilities can improve accessibility options within the various places and spaces that the utility intersects with their audiences.

Cost matters: who's hardest hit?

Public utilities play a unique and important role in communities because they can provide essential services to sustain life itself. Public utilities are nonprofit organizations. They are a shared community resource with a shared community cost. Many of them seek to protect public health and the precious environmental resources with which they have been trusted—all while continuously planning for the future so their critical services can continue uninterrupted. On the other hand, for-profit corporations seek to increase profit margins for their shareholders.

Public utilities strive for equitable charges, in that you pay according to your usage of the system. But how does this impact the most vulnerable populations in the community? Many public utilities have begun to realize that the *S* in ESG means stepping in to help people avoid shut offs of their utility services. Partnering with community organizations on affordability measures is something that communications practitioners can persuade the C-suite to consider.

Staff: the #1 ambassadors

Considering the *S* in ESG starts from within an organization. Public utilities have what are sometimes called the hands-on staff—those in the field doing highly technical jobs, working with their hands. They also have administrative staff, who tend to spend more time in front of computers, video calls, in offices and in conference rooms for meetings. Communications practitioners often are based in an office building—or even work remotely. However, they must hold themselves accountable to get out in the facility and field to engage with (and be inclusive of) all staff within their organization to experience multiple points of view. It's critical to engage shift workers, front-line workers, and office staff from all rungs of the organizational ladder. Truly great things can happen when the staff feel included.

In order to provide sound counsel to senior leadership—as ambassadors—the communications practitioners must engage with their internal teams. A *committee* is a great way to convene employees, and the communications practitioner would be wise to join this effort! If one doesn't exist, they can start it. Like anything, ESG initiatives won't go far if the staff isn't on board. That all starts with answering the question: *why are we doing this?* And it's a story the communications practitioner can illustrate.

Look forward

As technicians, operators, engineers, scientists, and the hands-on staff continue to operate utilities, the communications practitioner can influence senior leadership to be more intentional about the social aspects of its operations, and to synthesize these efforts into organizational strategy.

Communications practitioners at public utilities can serve a critical role in helping senior leadership identify and articulate ESG goals, help implement initiatives to achieve these goals, and ensure that they're checking themselves against each stated goal. Public service is a noble profession, and communications practitioners stand poised to help organizations be more inclusive of the communities they serve, whilst they steward their community's precious natural and financial resources. Our communities deserve no less.

Resources

Brooks, K. J. (2022). Americans struggle to pay utilities as energy prices surge. CBS News. Downloaded August 21, 2023 from https://shorturl.at/ghZ67.
Clean water changes everything. (n.d.) Water is basic. Downloaded August 21, 2023 from https://www.usaid.gov/water-sanitation-and-hygiene-partner ships-and-learning-sustainability-washpals#:~:text=Globally%2C%20 663%20million%20people%20lack,from%20diarrheal%20disease%20 each%20year.
Closing the water access gap in the United States policy brief (n.d.) US Water Alliance. Downloaded August 21, 2023 from https://www. inthepublicinterest.org/wp-content/uploads/ITPI_Water_Feb2021.pdf.
Creamer, J., Shrider, E. A., & Chen, F. (2022). Poverty in the United States: 2021. The United States Census Bureau. Downloaded August 21, 2023 from https://www.census.gov/library/publications/2022/demo/p60-277.html
What is a public utility? (n.d.) *Market Business News*. Downloaded August 21, 2023 from https://marketbusinessnews.com/financial-glossary/public-utility-definition-meaning/

Nearly two decades into the next century following the launch of the ecology movement and publication of Rachel Carson's incendiary warning in *Silent Spring*, a nonprofit group of 181 corporate CEOs—the Business Roundtable—had signed a statement on the purpose of a corporation (aka the BRT Statement). The declaration expanded corporations' definition of primary shareholders beyond stockholders to include customers, workers, suppliers, and communities as "a modern standard for corporate responsibility" (Business Roundtable, 2019, para. 2). The BRT Statement commits to delivering value to customers, investing in employees, dealing fairly and ethically with suppliers, supporting communities, and generating long-term value for shareholders (Business Roundtable, 2019). Yet, as with the earlier CSR/S trend, there is no international consensus or regulatory control regarding ESG disclosures. There are, however, some global frameworks and indices to aid corporations in reporting their ESG-related compliance as information for investors, such as the Global Recording Initiative standards, the Sustainability Accounting Standards Board (SASB) standards, the United Nations Principles for Responsible Investment, and the United Nations Sustainable Development Goals (Bergman et al., 2020). Moreover, the power of public opinion—as addressed in Chapter 4, "Power differentials in organizations and society"—cannot be understated as a means for pressuring organizations to do the right thing. As Bergman and colleagues (2020, para 11) noted, public opinion is a tool for pressuring organizations:

> As more companies provide ESG disclosures and commitments, and given the speed of social media responses and the news cycle, observations about a company's ESG actions or inactions are often published and sometimes go viral. Companies that are out of step with public opinion and market demands may face punishing reputational consequences.

Additionally, public opinion remains vitally important to monitor organizations' delivery on promises made with regard to their mission statements and/or vision statements and other documents that outline DEI goals and initiatives. Some specific means for tracking organizations' DEI commitment include: organizations appointing internal teams tasked with monitoring its ESG goals/actions, making public all DEI commitments, including measurable outcomes (specific timeframes and quantities), and strengthening relationships between organizations and key audiences to ensure that no facet of DEI is overlooked.

Next, this chapter explores some specific pitfalls to achieving real DEI outcomes for social justice to offer a realistic picture of just how challenging the task can be.

Environmental justice without greenwashing or stereotyping in economic disparity

Today's environmental justice movement in the U.S. has roots in the ecology and environmental movements, as well as the racial justice movement of the 1990s when civil rights activists pressured policymakers to level the playing field for BIPOC community members and especially those of lower socio-economic status (SES) who bore a disproportionate burden of environmental risks (Cutter, 1995). For example, locating waste dumps and pollution-producing factories in neighborhoods where people lacking in financial resources live means that these communities' future generations are born into disadvantaged living conditions. When the environmental, social equality, and civil rights movements merged into the politically potent force of environmental justice, advocates became empowered to influence public policy at multiple levels and to call out organizations whom they perceived as inauthentically engaged with DEI goals as part of an ESG commitment.

Because for-profit and nonprofit organizations reporting on their ESG commitment remains a *voluntary* act—since there are no universal laws, policies, or rules that make reporting on ESG *mandatory* (nor should there be, some argue)—communities remain beholden to organizations for making morally correct decisions and being truthful about their actions (and inactions). This section addresses only a handful of significant hurdles organizations face in committing to ESG—greenwashing, stereotyping, and environmental justice in an economic disparity context—and organizations that seem to be succeeding in blending DEI with ESG.

First, **greenwashing** is a process of "conveying a false impression or misleading information about how a company's products are environmentally sound" (Hayes, 2023, para. 1) and can take the form of emphasizing sustainable aspects of a product/service as a ploy to mask an organization's involvement in environmentally damaging activities, as well as attempts to capitalize on public demand for environmentally sound products/services with those that may or may not be environmentally conscious or friendly. For example, organizations' press releases and advertisements can contribute to greenwashing when they amplify **cause marketing** campaigns to boost organizational image whether or not the organization's ESG work is authentic (e.g., Yoon et al., 2006). Hayes (2023) explained that the *greenwashing* term emerged in the 1960s when the hotel industry asked guests to reuse towels to "save the environment," but the hotels simply earned more by cutting costs with lower laundry expenses (para. 4). Perhaps more harmful greenwashing has emerged from "the world's biggest carbon emitters," such as conventional energy companies, that simply rename, rebrand, and repackage the same old way of doing business while conveying "the idea that they're more natural, wholesome, or free of chemicals than competing brands" (Hayes, 2023, para. 5).

Perhaps greenwashing's staying power of nearly seven decades is due to its linkages with profit-centric motives that drive a **free-market economy**. More pointedly, Johansen (2015) calls the use of marketing and advertising tools that blatantly promote greenwashing "eco-hustle." Going green is good for business when consumers are willing to pay more for eco-friendly products (Gibbens, 2022). Yet, when **consumer watchdog** groups, activists, and others discover that organizations are stretching the truth or blatantly lying, the tide of public opinion quickly turns against the brand and organizations that generate the products or services. Organizations' communications teams can avoid producing messages that serve as a publicity arm for greenwashing tactics by ensuring that the organization's ESG-focused activities are authentically supporting DEI goals and not simply spreading misinformation about being sustainable, biodegradable, or environmentally conscious.

Second, **stereotyping** in organizations persists in the U.S. free-market economy as yet another hurdle to realizing actual DEI inside organizations to match the population beyond organizations' physical boundaries. This means many organizations seem unable to achieve goals attached to the *S* in *social* of the ESG acronym. When organizations espouse equity in labor standards, wages and benefits, workplace and board diversity, racial justice, pay equity, human rights, talent management, community relations, and more (Bergman et al., 2020), they must ensure that workplace bias and discrimination are eradicated. As revealed in Chapter 2, "Factoring in globalization, (mis)trust, risk, and sociopolitical contexts," a stereotype is a "fixed, over-generalized belief about a particular group or class of people" (Mcleod, 2023, para. 1). Stereotypes negatively impact relationships among organization members and can lead to potential legal implications. The U.S. Equal Opportunity Commission (EEOC) detailed nearly 70,000 charges of workplace discrimination in 2020 (EEOC, 2022). The EEOC enforces federal laws making it "illegal to discriminate against people in work situations, including hiring, firing, promotions, harassment, training, wages, and benefits—according to (race, color, religion, sex (including pregnancy and related conditions, gender identity, and sexual orientation), national origin, age (40 or older), disability or genetic information" (EEOC, n.d., para. 1).

Stereotypes are very powerful and there seems to be little means of escaping them. According to cultivation theorists, humans' worldviews are shaped by mass-mediated images (Gerbner, 1969)—including the Internet (Perrin, 2015)—which reinforce implicitly developed and strongly held beliefs about characteristics of members of particular social categories (Greenwald & Banaji, 1995) which can be incomplete and misleading when applied to individuals (Miller, 2015). For example, stereotyping an Asian American as being a **model minority** because they are *smart* and *hardworking* "flattens the diverse experiences of Asian Americans in to a singular, narrow narrative . . . paints a misleading picture about the community that doesn't align with current statistics" (Hanzhang Jin, 2021, para. 4). Moreover, this stereotype can contribute to people's internal stressors when they feel pressured to meet this expectation, forcing themselves to work even harder (Woo, 2000).

In some organizations, stereotyping has long endured and developed into glass ceilings that have prevented some groups—such as women and BIPOC community members—from achieving their maximum potential as managers and top executive levels. Researchers and journalists write extensively about the **glass ceiling**—the invisible barricade that blocks upward career advancement for women and people of color (e.g., Lockert, 2022) and the importance of leadership in embracing DEI initiatives (e.g., Castillo, 2018). In 2021, women CEOs still made up only 8.2% of Fortune 500 companies (Ascend et al., 2021) and the number of women and BIPOC community members leading for-profit and nonprofit boards of directors remains consistently low (e.g., Castillo, 2018). Many agree that "progress is still too slow and not reflective of the nation" (Ascend et al., 2021, p. 3).

Across organizations' levels and hierarchies, employees still endure bias related to work–life balance and internal policies that discriminate along intersecting social identity dimensions including gender, sexual orientation, and more. Employees experience pressure, stress, and burnout when they experience a lack of boundaries separating paid and non-paid work (Thomas, 2022)—with women socialized to handle most of the domestic chores at home based on gendered beliefs and accountability practices serving as a root cause of gendered behavior in the household (Thébaud et al., 2019). Since the COVID-19 pandemic, technology has made meetings and working from home even easier, further exacerbating the dotted-line separation of work and home life (Barroso, 2021; Schneider, 2023). Organizations' leaders could offset some of these negative outcomes by providing team members with "a definition of work–life balance that is relevant to the current business environment" (Thomas, 2022, para. 6). For example, creating policies for attracting and keeping talent, embracing values for separating work and home life by suggesting things like not responding to work email while at home during non-emergency situations, and offering other guidelines for employee behavior across organizational levels. Other examples of gender bias in the workplace include resistance from male-identifying employees who seek parental leave benefits that female-identifying employees receive—yet are met with stereotypes as displaying weakness or lacking work commitment (Cox, 2021). Moreover, LGBTQ parents also experience challenges when they seek parental leave policies at work (Niewiarowski, 2023).

Third, the 2010 *Citizens United v. Federal Election Commission* ruling by the U.S. Supreme Court will continue to further entrench economic disparity with its unequal power dimensions, enabling corporations to use significant amounts of money and influence to bend political agendas in their favor. The Supreme Court's 5–4 free speech protection vote means that the First Amendment of the U.S. Constitution protects independent expenditures for political campaigns by corporations, nonprofits, labor unions, and other associations. Given this landmark case, critics worry that the rich and powerful may support political candidates who offer

quid pro quo in exchange for favorable treatment for the organization once the candidate is elected: "It allows activists to take up the mantle for political causes by implementing in the boardroom what they cannot do through the ballot box" (e.g., Perils, 2023, para. 6). For example, choosing tax breaks and a booming stock market rather than dissolving corporate political action committees (PACs) which "can be used to obscure the extent of influence" (Polman, 2021, para. 7) with leadership that includes embracing actionable DEI initiatives is unethical and thwarts authentic DEI in organizations.

The "summer of racial reckoning" hosted global social protest of U.S. murders of George Floyd, Breonna Taylor, and Ahmaud Arbury (Chang et al., 2020) and organizations' leaders have taken notice. Yet, achieving DEI in society and its organizations remains a slow process. Over 30 years ago, Valian (1989) asked "why so slow?" and answers have proven unsatisfying for women and other marginalized social identity groups. Former CEO of the British/Dutch consumer goods company Unilever Paulus Polman and many others urge for reversal of the *Citizens United* decision because it puts too much power into the hands of the wealthy powerful few which may be used to influence Washington policymakers. Polman (2021) urged leaders to follow Unilever, IBM, and Charles Schwab, who created rules about never forming PACs or spending money on political donations in an effort to "stamp money out of politics" (para. 9).

Next, taking a look at organizations that have found success in blending DEI goals with the ESG (*S* in *social*) trend illustrates how barriers such as temptation to acquiesce to greenwashing techniques and stereotyping can be overcome in both for-profit and nonprofit organizations. For example, Rosenberg's (2009) case study of Interface Carpet's commitment to becoming an environmentally sustainable business, as launched by then-CEO Ray Anderson, explains how the U.S.-based carpet tile manufacturing company has become "a poster child for sustainable business practices" by eliminating waste and saving energy (p. 427). Today, Interface's CEO Laurel Hurd explained in the company's 2021 ESG report ways that the company has established a DEI framework with actions such as: forming a Global DEI Task Force and Steering Committee; launching a global culture and DEI survey; boosting activity in community engagement; and complying with a comprehensive code of business conduct and ethics covering employees, directors, and suppliers (Interface, 2021). Interface's Executive Director of DEI explained (Interface, 2021, p. 24):

> Our purpose includes efforts to achieve our sustainability objectives, but also cultivating an inclusive culture built around trust, openness, representation, and belonging. We recognize that there is not a one-size-fits-all

approach to DEI, which is why we are seeking input and engagement from all our employees to determine the way forward and identify the most important areas of focus. We're building the foundation to create a culture where every employee can thrive.

In another for-profit instance, XPO Logistics, a global freight transportation services company, received a top score of 90 out of 100 on the 2022 Disability Equality Index for the second year, making it recognized for disability inclusion as a best place to work (Millett, 2022). The index is a benchmarking tool that helps companies improve workplace inclusivity and is a joint initiative of the American Association of People with Disabilities (AAPD) and the global Disability:IN network. The company's chief diversity officer, LaQuenta Jacobs, explained that workplace culture "is as important as title and compensation. Today's job seeker and employee is not simply looking for a job, but a culture that provides meaningful connection (Stovall & Clark, 2022, p. iv).

Among nonprofits ranked highly for providing advocacy programs, support services, and awareness-raising initiatives aiding both for-profit and nonprofit organizations are those that assess impact on increasing social cohesion. These nonprofits offer transparency ratings that make DEI come alive. Examples include the American Civil Liberties Union, the National Immigration Law Center, and the Advancement Project (Lopez, n.d.) The National Council of Nonprofits denounces racism, intolerance, and exclusion when advising nonprofits to: explore terms and definitions for deep conversations, understand implicit/unconscious biases, weave DEI values through programs and policies and back them up with action, and shift from transactional DEI work to transformational work (Why diversity, equity, and inclusion matter for nonprofits, n.d.)

To summarize, considering ESG's S in *social* in terms of authentic DEI commitment is not exactly a new idea. Historically, some of the wealthiest people of America's Gilded Age (the elites' thin veneer of wealth masked broader social issues for many of the lower and middle classes) discovered how rewarding it could be to give back to the community despite the means by which they had made their fortunes by exploiting workers and fostering unsafe work conditions (Sollinger, 2015). For example, industrialist Andrew Carnegie founded the Carnegie Museum of Natural History, Carnegie Mellon University, the Carnegie Science Center, the Carnegie Library of Pittsburgh, and more—even though he was known to break up unions, give his workers only one holiday, and shut down operations when his workers organized the Homestead Strike of 1892. Also, automobile magnate Henry Ford gave away "roughly one-third of his income to those in need . . . directly to the people who needed it," built hospitals, housed World War I refugees, and more, yet was a Hitler-awarded anti-Semite (Barlow, 2021, paras. 8–9). Explaining why industrialists to this day are accused of exploiting people and the planet—Jeff Bezos of Amazon, for example (Khan, 2017)—but then act charitably in other arenas is a paradox.

Decolonizing and other wicked problems

Organizations' communicators working to achieve ESG goals face increasingly complicated social issues and problems such as global warming, pandemics, polarization—amidst globalization. As addressed in Chapter 2, "Factoring in globalization, (mis)trust, risk, and sociopolitical contexts," globalization refers to ways that people across large physical distances become more connected—with numerous effects. Exactly how to practice responsible persuasion while communicating across uncertainty and complexity involves considering personal, professional, organizational, and societal accountability. The term **VUCA** characterizes **wicked problem** conditions that are volatile, uncertain, complex, and ambiguous. The United States Army War College invented VUCA as a decision-making concept in response to late-1980s' changing geopolitical dynamics (Horney et al., 2010). The social planning concept for complex, interdependent, unpredictable, open-ended wicked problems (Rittel & Webber, 1973) is even older. Indeed, VUCA conditions and wicked problems set the scene for organizations' DEI work today.

Enduring traces of colonization is one such wicked problem. People with privilege rarely realize how the history of colonization continues to affect life today (e.g., Ross, 2019). In the nonprofit arena, one significant context for the lack of progress in achieving DEI in organizations is colonization's roots which demand a "need to redefine ourselves as a society based on exploring what it means to be in relationship with one another and addressing tensions of reconciling past wrongs of colonization" (Castillo, 2018, para. 2). While conducting interviews for a study of ways culture, ethnicity, and race interplay with organizational crises, Liu and Pompper (2012) discovered that many social identity groups never forget how organizations have disrespected them in the past, making the handling of organizational reputation in the face of crises even more thorny when organizations fail to learn from history (e.g., discriminating against specific groups of people) and repeat the same mistakes going forward. See Sidebar 5.2 for a case study raising concerns about a need to remember the past as one means for respecting the S in ESG—specifically by exploring the wicked problem of colonization through a lens of how it negatively has impacted indigenous communities when the Six Grandfathers became Mount Rushmore in the present-day Black Hills of South Dakota.

Sidebar 5.2   Considering the Six Grandfathers

Donnalyn Pompper

Amplified across this book's pages is an emphasized need to remember the past as one means for respecting the *S* in ESG. In the U.S., organizations mustn't forget the wicked problem of colonization and how it negatively has impacted indigenous communities. Honoring nature as it was treasured by the Lakota Sioux in present day Black Hills of South Dakota before it was remade into Mount Rushmore is one highly visible reminder that "one of the United States' great iconic images . . . one of the top tourist attractions in the country" (Pletcher, 2023, para. 4) is rooted in a past of "desecrate[d] sacred land" (Pletcher, 2023, para. 4, 11).

The natural mountain site is granite and the six entities honored at Tȟuŋkášila Šákpe were the supernatural deities—North, South, East, West, Above (sky), and Below (Earth)—who are "responsible for Lakota creation," or the Six Grandfathers (Morton, 2020, para. 2). In 1930, the area was named for wealthy New York investor Charles Rushmore after construction was underway to reshape the faces into U.S. presidents George Washington, Thomas Jefferson, Theodore Roosevelt, and Abraham Lincoln (Pletcher, 2023).

Figure 5.3 The Tȟuŋkášila Šákpe featured the Six Grandfathers supernatural deities—North, South, East, West, Above (sky), and Below (Earth)—who are responsible for Lakota creation in the present-day Black Hills of South Dakota before it was remade into Mount Rushmore.

Because the area remains "an important spiritual site for the Lakota," some tribal members have demanded that the carvings be removed because it is "a great sign of disrespect," while others support enabling nature's erosion elements to take their course (Morton, 2020, para. 3, 23). Indigenous communities have objected to each of the U.S. presidents' forced assimilation and/or violence against indigenous people who resisted (Rose, 2018).

For organizations like the U.S. National Park Service, which has managed the tourist attraction since 1933 (Pletcher, 2023), this history means enabling people to come "face to face with a rich heritage we all share" at this (ironically) "shrine to democracy" (Way, 2016, para. 2, 1) and that includes accepting the responsibility for not forgetting this past. As addressed in Chapter 5, "Social responsibility in corporations and nonprofits," there is much uncertainty in social life across conditions that are VUCA. For example, in 1971 protestors associated with the American Indian Movement occupied Mount Rushmore demanding that the U.S. honor the 1868 Fort Laramie Treaty (Morton, 2020). This is a painful and highly complex issue that deserves careful and respectful attention. In cases such as this, Adi and Stoeckle (2023) advise communicators to confront wicked times by using approaches that are anything but "tame" (p. 303). Rather, nonprofits and for-profits alike must practice responsible persuasion (Ehninger, 1974) that considers personal, professional, organizational, and societal accountability and responsibility.

With regard to indigenous community injustices, including members in organizations' decision-making processes offers an important step in a new direction. For example, Rose (2018) reported that a new Mount Rushmore superintendent offered radical new ideas for inspiring a healing process across communities and concerns. Such a move echoes Holtzhausen's (2012) insider-activism approach wherein organizations' internal communicators assume an activist role in persuading leadership to authentically attend to difficult problems and forge relationships with groups and individuals who may be considered adversarial to organizations.

Resources

Adi, A., & Stoeckle, T. (2023). Public relations as responsible persuasion: Activism and social change (pp. 302–314). In D. Pompper, K. Place, and C. K. Weaver (Eds.) *The Routledge public relations companion*. Routledge.

Ehninger, D. (1974). *Influence, belief, and argument: An introduction to responsible persuasion*. Scott, Foreman.

Holtzhausen, D. R. (2012). *Public relations as activism: Postmodern approaches to theory & practice.* Routledge.

Morton, M. C. (2020). Mount Rushmore's Six Grandfathers and four presidents. *EOS Science News.* Downloaded August 30, 2023 from https://shorturl.at/akl48.

Pletcher, K. (2023). Mount Rushmore national memorial. *Britannica.* Downloaded August 30, 2023 from https://shorturl.at/bxOVZ.

Rose, C. (2018). Native history: Construction of Mount Rushmore begins. *1CT.* Downloaded August 30, 2023 from https://ictnews.org/archive/native-history-construction-of-mount-rushmore-begins.

Way, R. (2016). The real history of Mount Rushmore. *Star Tribune.* Downloaded August 30, 2023 from https://eos.org/features/mount-rushmores-six-grandfathers-and-four-presidents.

Considering colonization's traces—such as language and images we use to represent people and issues—is the responsibility of an organization's communicator. Hall (1992) explained how representation plays a role in the way people think about the world, their place in it, and power relations among people and groups. As explored in Chapter 4, "Power differentials in organizations and society," people in power influence *what* gets represented and *how* it gets represented—so that representations always are connected with society's power dynamics. The coloniality of power (Quijano, 1998) is the ongoing reproduction of inequalities and hierarchies based on gender, geopolitics, and race. No one likes being represented by words or images that they consider disrespectful or discriminatory. Among Jewish people, the "cross with bent arms" (Ramirez, 2022, para. 1) is a symbol representing evil, genocide, and hate as a swastika—but to Dharmic cultures, it is an ancient sign of peace and prosperity. Finding a noose at work can constitute a hostile workplace, given the painful past of slavery in the U.S. (Goldman, 2023). Yet, some symbols are reappropriated for group solidarity. For example, LGBTQ rights groups use a pink triangle to represent the gay community even though the symbol was used to target and persecute homosexuality in Nazi Germany (Editors, 2021).

As Wynter (2003) explained, the idea of race became a justification for repressing racialized groups' identities as part of a pattern of domination of those without power by those with the power. Furthermore, Reiter (2018) argued that this arrangement supported capitalist expansion ventures by way of subduing and controlling large populations so that they could be exploited and moved to the margins. In addition to using race to classify and divide people, so, too, has gender been used to systematically regard women and feminized bodies as inferior (Lugones, 2011). In sum, colonization's effects include ways certain groups of people historically experience **marginalization** and **othering.**

Today, many organizations recognize the value of **decolonization** as one tool for addressing this wicked problem and its ongoing negative effects. Perhaps one measure of proof of decolonization is the growing number of new countries that have joined the United Nations, which has nearly quadrupled since it was founded in 1945. Muschik (2022) also noted the 20th century's growth in number of international organizations and the role they play in decolonizing nations around the world. Among nonprofit organizations today, decolonizing work involves education, analysis of power structures, and scrutiny of hiring practices. In Spokane, Washington, a consultant who is a member of the Iñupiat Alaskan Native group, explained:

> The focus on nonprofits is because in a capitalist society, capitalism is in and of itself a racist construct . . . Nonprofits were birthed out of creating tax breaks for the rich. But in our society, they work as a safety net for those with the least.
>
> (Thomas, 2021, para. 5)

About decolonizing nonprofits' boards of directors, the consultant added: "You might have a board that may or may not be related to the work that's happening, or being impacted by it, or have actual subject matter expertise in the work" (Thomas, 2021, para. 20). Work at Greenpeace to support Latinx/Latine people and other communities of color who are most impacted by the climate crisis means recognizing that over 70% of Latinx/Latine people in the US are concerned about the environment, as one volunteer explained:

> We came to Greenpeace from many different places, with the hope of making the movement stronger, more inclusive, and more resilient. We are here to fight against environmental racism and for environmental justice, to decolonize environmentalism, and uncouple it from Western traditions.
>
> (Stackl, 2022, para. 5)

To authentically achieve goals attached to the *S* in *social* of the ESG acronym, organizations' communicators might consider applying **standpoint epistemology.** Doing so by considering issues and opportunities from perspectives of people who often feel that they do not belong, or are ignored or considered irrelevant can help. In other words, *walking around in other people's shoes* has many benefits—and using standard research tools like focus groups, interviews, and surveys to collect intel and data supports ESG goal achievement. To begin, standpoint theorists—such as feminist standpoint theorists—are committed to describing a common standpoint women occupy while simultaneously recognizing differences among women (e.g. O'Brien Hallstein, 2009). For example, Buzzanell (2003) used standpoint theory to explore ways women with disabilities make meaning about maternity and maternity leave at work based on childbirth and adoption experiences, as they experience degrees of employer support. Similar studies involve exploring the role of spirituality and religion in the workplace (e.g., Benefiel et al., 2014) which takes on deeper meaning as employees increasingly feel depressed or demoralized at work due to organizational changes and ways they feel about organizations that accommodate their particular meditation or belief system or style (e.g., Petchsawang & Duchon, 2012).

Social networks and indigenous ways of knowing

Seeking out *cooperative others* within organizations and beyond organizations' physical walls offers a useful strategy for building **social networks** necessary in developing and achieving goals attached to the *S* in *social* of the ESG acronym. Organizational communication workers know that because a social network is a community of people who listen, share information, exchange messages, and cooperate while working on mutually beneficial activities, these processes facilitate two-way communication exchanges to build understanding and trust. Thus, embedded social relations incentivize cooperation (e.g., Granovetter, 1985). For example, at least seven outdoor gear and apparel companies develop strong relationships with consumers—not only to market their products—but to improve access to the outdoors for all people regardless of socioeconomic status, to recover the environment, to clean up the planet by making donations to conservation-focused nonprofits, to build clean water systems in developing areas around the globe where textiles are manufactured, to create sustainable paths out of poverty, and to provide grants for improving park trails and impoverished inner-city areas in the U.S. (Chen, 2019).

In recent years' attention to ESG, there has been a resurgence of placing value on indigenous ways of knowing that have accumulated over vast periods of time—as a means for understanding people at fundamental levels and for addressing social challenges and problems. Often, these valuable insights are gained from tribes, first peoples/nations, aboriginals, ethnic groups, adivasi, janajati—while using the word *indigenous* carefully because some groups find it has negative connotations (Masaquiza, n.d.) Rather, the United Nations Permanent Forum on Indigenous Issues recommends identifying, rather than defining, these communities while working to respect them as "holders of unique languages, knowledge systems and beliefs" given that they possess "invaluable knowledge of practices for the sustainable management of natural resources" and to support efforts to protect their rights, identities, ways of life, and right to traditional lands, territories, and natural resources (Masaquiza, n.d., paras. 5–6). Amnesty International (Indigenous, n.d.) estimates that there are 476 million indigenous people across 90 countries in the world, or 5% of the world's population—with 70% living in Asia and making up 15% of the world's "extreme poor." Facing marginalization and discrimination, these communities are "vulnerable to violence and abuse," such as being uprooted from their land given that it constitutes 80% of Earth's biodiversity and is rich in natural resources, such as oil, gas, timber, and minerals (Indigenous, n.d.) This means that organizations working for and among these industries should be especially vigilant in respecting the intersecting social identity dimensions of people who live in these areas.

One means for accomplishing such tasks is for communication workers to build relationships and to learn traditional value systems considered vitally important among communities with unique ties to their land. As hooks (1994) posited, "our solidarity must be affirmed by shared belief in a spirit of intellectual openness that celebrates diversity, welcomes dissent, and rejoices in collective dedication to truth" (p. 33). Connecting DEI goals to ESG, Adae (2023) explored Afrocentric philosophies of sustainability across the continent of Africa—especially balance, harmony, justice, law, morality, and order—as traditional African worldviews, beliefs, customs, and usages measure up against contemporary organization's sustainability goals by exploring concepts of Bilchiinsi (Mohammed, 2022), Ma'atic philosophy (Asante & Dove, 2021), as well as Caritas, Negritude, Ujamaa, Consciencism, Bantu philosophy, Ubuntu, the spirit of Harambee, Akan philosophy, Yorba epistemology, and Sankofa philosophy (Pompper & Adae, 2023).

Bringing together traditional, indigenous ways of knowing—and considering these as fundamental to organizations' work in authentically addressing the *S* in *social* of the ESG acronym—involves a commitment to making all people feel that they belong. It also involves real relationship building via social networks. Acknowledging that most humans understand the concept of *the good life* and the richness of how everyone defines it is a resource worth tapping into. For example, Hove (2022) suggested that doing this can reveal ethical values within and across cultures; a more fruitful endeavor than trying an impossible task of developing some universal, global code of ethics. Also, the rate and quality of humans cooperating with one another depends on respect and people's willingness to embrace the fact that social networks are dynamic and change over time (Fehl et al., 2011). In addition to discussing the good life and striving for cooperation, a background context worth acknowledging is that greedy corporations have been driven to plunder riches in the shortest time possible over the course of centuries (e.g., Kirby, 2016; Kunnie, 2013; Pacific, 2021; Sautman & Hairong, 2007), making exploitation of people and natural resources a way of life even though it has scarred the planet.

Resisting NIMBY and moving forward

For-profit corporations with their entrenched systemic processes and infrastructures—are not the only entities who find change difficult. As individuals, humans can, too. Yet, positive change is exactly what's needed for the authentic embrace of DEI in order to make the *S* in *social* of the ESG acronym real, robust, organic, and ongoing. For example, while many humans like the idea of recycling, some do not want the recycling processes playing out in their community and would prefer that the collection, sorting, cleaning, and storage take place in some other area. This is called not in my backyard (NIMBY) syndrome. This acronym emerged in the 1980s to characterize high levels of self-interest among neighbors who support strict land-use regulations and oppose nearby construction and development of low-income housing, cell towers, wind turbines, drug treatment facilities, high-speed rails, retail warehouses, and more (e.g., Axel-Lute, 2021). At the heart of people's concerns are potential for crime, congestion, decreased property values, overcrowding of schools, and overall diminished quality of life.

The role of proximity among people comes into play when building cooperation and trust—both within organizations and across social networks that now know no geographic boundaries, thanks to social media. Whether communicating online or face to face, organizations seek to avoid conflict that could interrupt operations. Yet, sometimes the *potential* for conflict cannot be allowed to offset the benefits of working on relationships designed to foster cooperation and trust. In their test of the NIMBY syndrome as it relates to energy projects, Konisky and his colleagues (2020) found that the more favorably people view the environmental conditions in their community, the greater the likelihood that they will support proposed energy developments. So, perhaps the role of organizations' communicators might include positively impacting public opinion about the value of DEI in everything the organization does—to persuade key audiences and groups across social networks about the value of DEI.

Organizations working together via interorganizational collaborations can generate solutions to societal problems that go far beyond what is possible at individual organizational levels. For example, organizations working together to solve water contamination challenges involve horizontal structures of problem solving, as well as joint exploration and explanation of the situation and its multiple dimensions (Heath & Isbell, 2021; Morris et al., 2013) not unlike manufacturers working with their suppliers to ensure safe work conditions for employees. Thus, both DEI and ESG goals are addressed for the benefit of all when organizations' communicators lead these discussions and counsel top management about ways to see beyond their back fence.

Concluding thoughts

When organizations see peers and competitors attending to the *S* in *social* of the ESG acronym as it relates to striving for and achieving meaningful DEI goals, perhaps this will inspire them to try similar approaches in *their own* organization. This is social comparison theory at work! Social comparison theory, as introduced by Leon Festinger (1954), suggests that people possess an innate drive to base their own personal and social worth by assessing how they compare to others. There certainly is a historical precedent in the 1960s ecology movement and the later shift from CSR/S to ESG today so that advocating for environmental justice need not involve greenwashing or stereotyping in economic disparity for outcomes to be authentic and mutually beneficial for all involved. Challenges are real, but not insurmountable, especially as for-profit and nonprofit organizations encounter decolonizing effects and other VUCA wicked problem conditions. Some useful strategies include tapping social networks and indigenous ways of knowing, as well as resisting NIMBY while moving forward.

By proxy, organizational communicators such as public relations practitioners have the power to navigate organizations' leaders and decision makers toward social justice thinking to make sure the *S* in *social* of the ESG acronym includes authentic, measurable attention to DEI—to ensure real belonging. In addition to working directly with key audiences, communicators themselves can use social media channels to organize and spread positive messages, write op-eds to advocate for DEI, and overall create collective action to address challenges posed by the lack of DEI in organizations and society, in general. Public relations practitioners also possess the skills required for engaging with research projects—data collection and analysis—for discovering answers to burning questions linked to what they do not know, but must discover to be faithful to audiences *and* their organizations. As encouraged in Chapter 4, "Power differentials in organizations and society," communicators may rely on using combinations of formal research methods to monitor organizations' attention to DEI goals. Using formal research methods to better understand how social identity dimensions shape belonging offers an important step to real relationship building (Pompper, 2023).

Next, Chapter 6, "Universality thinking about publics and its pitfalls" addresses challenges of considering key audiences as one size fits all when making decisions and establishing policy about DEI that affects everyone touched by organizations. Organizations must prioritize belonging and continually make new connections via inclusive communication campaigns.

Key words

Cause marketing—Often, cause marketing is a strategy that for-profit and nonprofit organizations working together employ to increase profits/donations while also performing a social good; all communicated via advertising and/or public relations campaigns.

Certified B corporation—This is a certification achieved by for-profit organizations, as designated by B Lab, which reviews the organization's business model and degrees of achievement in meeting high standards of verified performance, accountability, and transparency on factors such as employee benefits, charitable giving, supply chain practices, and input materials.

Consumer watchdog—At the federal level in the U.S., three governmental agencies provide protection to consumers: the Food and Drug Administration, the National Highway Traffic Safety Administration, and the Consumer Product Safety Commission. Other high-profile individuals working to improve safety for consumers include Ralph Nader, who achieved high-profile status when he wrote the exposé *Unsafe at Any Speed* about the automotive industry's safety record, effectively carving a path for the National Traffic and Motor Vehicle Safety Act in 1966.

CSR/S—This acronym stands for *corporate social responsibility* and *sustainability*.

Decolonization—This is the process of eliminating effects of colonization on institutions, spheres of activity, and society by considering the roots of cultural beliefs about issues and processes being considered in need of change.

Ecology—While ecology is a branch of biology for examining relationships among organisms and their physical environments, the ecology movement grew in the 1960s in conjunction with the acknowledgement that our planet's clean air, land, and water were in crises.

Environmental justice—This social movement expanded racial justice to incorporate a challenge to fair treatment and meaningful involvement of all people regardless of ethnicity or income level with respect to the development, implementation, and enforcement of laws, regulations, and policies associated with the environment.

ESG—This acronym represents *environmental, social, governance* issues/ concerns and the ways organizations attend to each with measurable performance metrics comparable to ways financial metrics are used to assess an organization's performance.

Free-market economy—This economic system is characterized by an environment of services and goods prices being set by supply and demand, as articulated by sellers and buyers—largely without external authority (e.g., government) intervention.

Glass ceiling—This metaphor is applied to organizations that marginalize people according to their social identity dimensions and their intersectionalities, such as BIPOC women who encounter invisible barriers toward achieving top management positions in organizations.

Greenwashing—When misleading advertising, marketing, or public relations campaigns deceive people into thinking that an organization's products, services, goals, or policies are environmentally friendly; often masking campaigns designed simply to generate sales.

Lois Gibbs—She is an American environmental activist widely known for organizing the Love Canal Homeowners Association in New York during an environmental crisis in the late 1970s and later founded a nonprofit group to train and support environmental activist group members.

Marginalization—When people or groups, especially in organizations, are pushed to the periphery of the center where power is located and treated as unimportant or invisible.

Model minority—This is a myth that certain demographic groups (according to social identity dimensions such as ethnicity, gender, religion) with members who are perceived by dominant groups as achieving high degrees of socioeconomic success relative to the general population average; a perception that renders that community as a reference point to other outgroups. The process creates unnecessary stress and anxiety across multiple groups.

NIMBY—*Not in my back yard* has been a popular retort for acknowledging social problems but being unwilling to have one's neighborhood house a solution to those problems; often residents' collective opposition to developments in their local area with strict land-use regulations.

Othering—In organizations, this is a conscious effort to negate certain people's individual and collective humanity, making them feel unworthy of respect.

Quid pro quo—Latin expression meaning "something given or received for something else."

Standpoint epistemology—Standpoint theorists generally support the idea that each person's viewpoint is rooted in some subjective perspective created by their intersecting social identity dimensions. Not all group members occupy the same standpoint. Using this idea can help to avoid essentializing while simultaneously building solidarity among group members. Shared standpoints based on experiences with discrimination can bind individuals together in opposition, resistance, and transformation.

Social networks—This is a social structure composed of social actors (e.g., individuals, organizations) who are linked and interact with one another. Analyzing structures of social networks can be revealing about whole organizations and communities.

Stereotyping—This is a widely held, oversimplified, and overgeneralized view or representation of particular groups of people, such as females being considered more nurturing than males.

VUCA—Qualities of volatility, uncertainty, complexity, and ambiguity were applied to end of the Cold War realities to better understand forward-moving paths for leaders and organizations.

Wicked problems—Usually high-profile challenges that are difficult or impossible to easily resolve because their challenges include incomplete and contradictory information, as well as changing requirements. One example is decolonization.

Discussion questions for deep engagement

1. How would you explain to someone who is not in your class how ESG and DEI are related?
2. How would you argue that authentic support of DEI in organizations is possible (or not) without greenwashing in a free-market economy?
3. In what ways have you (or someone you know) experienced coloniality of power at work or school?
4. What are some indigenous ways of knowing that are shared among your family or wider cultural community?
5. In your opinion, how does the NIMBY syndrome thwart authentic embrace of DEI in communities?

Resources

Adae, E. K. (2023). *CEOs on a mission*. Emerald Publishing.

Asante, M. K., & Dove, N. (2021). *Being human being: Transforming the race discourse*. Universal Write Publications.

Ascend, C200, Catalyst, Women Business Collaborative (2021). Women CEOs in America: *Changing the face of business leadership*. Downloaded June 24, 2023 from chrome-extension://efaidnbmnnnibpcajpcglclefindmkaj/https://www. wbcollaborative.org/wp-content/uploads/2021/10/Women-CEOS-in-America_ 2021_1013-2.pdf.

Axel-Lute, M. (2021). What is NIMBYism and how do affordable housing developers respond to it? Shelterforce. Downloaded June 28, 2023 from https://rb.gy/bt01s.

Baboolal, D., Greenberg, S., Obeid, M., & Zucker, J. (2023). Being transgender at work. McKinsey & Company. Downloaded June 23, 2023 from https://rb.gy/4n519.

Banerjee, S. B. (2003). Who sustains whose development? Sustainable development and the reinvention of nature. *Organization Studies*, 24(1), 143–180. DOI: https://doi.org/10.1177/0170840603024001341.

Barlow, M. (2021). Henry Ford: Entrepreneurship, leadership and philanthropy. *Grey Journal*. Downloaded June 24, 2023 from https://rb.gy/ccdgr.

Barroso, A. (2021). For American couples, gender gaps in sharing household responsibilities persist amid pandemic. Pew Research Center. Downloaded June 24, 2023 from https://rb.gy/9fhqh.

Bell, M. (2023). What is a certified B corporation? Harvard Business Services, Inc. Downloaded June 26, 2023 from https://rb.gy/0csab.

Benefiel, M., Fry, L. W., & Geigle, D. (2014). Spirituality and religion in the workplace: History, theory, and research. *Psychology of Religion and Spirituality*, 6(3), 175–187. DOI: 10.1037/a0036597.

Bergman, M. S., Deckelbaum, A. J., Karp, B. S., and Paul, Weiss, Rifkind, Wharton & Garrison LLP. (2020). Introduction to ESG. Harvard Law School Forum on Corporate Governance. Downloaded June 22, 2023 from https://rb.gy/7kdd5.

Business Roundtable (2019). Business Roundtable redefines the purpose of a corporation to promote 'an economy that serves all Americans.' Business Roundtable. Downloaded June 22, 2023 from https://rb.gy/wrnoa

Buzzanell, P. M. (2003). A feminist standpoint analysis of maternity and maternity leave for women with disabilities. *Women and Language*, 26(2), 53–65. DOI: https://doi.org/10.1177/08948453211037398.

Carson, R. (2022[1962]). *Silent spring*. Mariner Books Classics.

Castillo, E. A. (2018). Why are we still struggling with diversity, equity, and inclusion in nonprofit governance? *Nonprofit Quarterly*. Downloaded June 24, 2023 from https://rb.gy/p5vol.

Chang, A., Martin, R., & Marrapodi, E. (2020). Summer of racial reckoning. NPR. Downloaded June 24, 2023 from https://rb.gy/q9rzy.

Chen, C. (2019). Seven socially responsible outdoor companies that give back to the environment. Insider Reviews. Downloaded June 26, 2023 from https://rb.gy/1oqgi.

Cox, J. (2021). Paternity leave, which comes with multiple benefits, is more widely offered than ever before. So why aren't more men taking it? CNN. Downloaded June 24, 2023 from https://rb.gy/6ntgl.

Cutter, S. L. (1995). Race, class and environmental justice. *Progress in Human Geography*, 19(1), 111–122. DOI: 10.1177/030913259501900111.

Devall, B. (1980). The deep ecology movement. *Natural Resources Journal*, 20(2), 299–322. DOI: https://doi.org/10.1353/een.2001.0004.

Ebersole, R. (2020). This brutal pesticide crates a 'circle of death'. So why is it making a comeback? *Audubon Magazine*. Downloaded June 23, 2023 from https://rb.gy/zniy9.

Editors of Give Me History (2021). Top 15 symbols of rebellion with meanings. Give Me History. Downloaded June 25, 2023 from https://rb.gy/e89qj.

Fehl, K., van der Post, D. J., & Semmann, D. (2011). Co-evolution of behaviour and social network structure promotes human cooperation. *Ecology Letters*, 14(6), 546–551. DOI: https://doi.org/10.1111/j.1461-0248.2011.01615.x.

Festinger, L. (1954). A theory of social comparison processes. *Human Relations*, 7, 117–140. DOI: https://doi.org/10.1177/001872675400700202.

Frankental, P. (2001). Corporate social responsibility: A PR invention? *Corporate Communications*, 6(1), 18–23. DOI: http://dx.doi.org/10.1108/13563280110 381170.

Gerbner, G. (1969). Toward 'cultural indicators': The analysis of mass mediated public message systems. In G. Gerbner, O. Holsti, K. Krippendorff, W. J. Paisley, & P. J. Stone (Eds.), *The analysis of communication content: Developments in scientific theories and computer techniques* (pp. 123–132). John Wiley & Sons.

Gibbens, S. (2022). Is your favorite 'green' product as eco-friendly as it claims to be? *National Geographic*. Downloaded June 23, 2023 from https://rb.gy/a4rmt.

Gitnux (2023). The latest disability discrimination in the workplace statistics 2023 you shouldn't ignore. Gitnux Blog. Downloaded June 23, 2023 from https://rb.gy/d2mgf.

Goldman, D. (2023). ExxonMobil sued after a Black employee allegedly discovered a noose at work. It was the fifth at the same facility. CNN. Downloaded June 25, 2023 from https://rb.gy/5pelb.

Gond, J-P. (2017). Reconsidering the critical corporate social responsibility perspective through French pragmatic sociology: Subverting corporate do-gooding for the common good. In G. Baars and A. Spicer (Eds.), *The corporation: A critical multi-disciplinary handbook* (pp. 360–371). Cambridge University Press.

Granovetter, M. S. (1985). Economic action and social structure: The problem of embeddedness. *American Journal of Sociology*, 91(3), 481–510. DOI: https://psycnet.apa.org/doi/10.1086/228311.

Greenwald, A. G., & Banaji, M. R. (1995). Implicit social cognition: Attitudes, self-esteem, and stereotypes. *Psychological Review*, 102, 4–27. DOI:10.1037/0033–295X.102.1.4.

Hall, S. (1992). Race, culture, and communications: Looking backward and forward at cultural studies. *Rethinking Marxism*, 5(1), 10–18. DOI: https://doi.org/10.1080/08935699208657998.

Hanzhang Jin, C. (2021). Six charts that dismantle the trope of Asian Americans as a model minority. NPR. Downloaded June 23, 2023 from https://rb.gy/se7w7.

Hayes, A. (2023). What is greenwashing? How it works, examples, and statistics. Investopedia. Downloaded June 23, 2023 from https://rb.gy/8vefu.

Heath, R. G., & Isbell, M. G. (2021). Theorizing principled collaboration. *Communication Theory*, 31(4), 654–674. DOI: 10.1093/ct/qtz039.

hooks, b. (1994). Teaching to transgress: Education as a practice of freedom. Routledge.

Horney, N., Pasmore, B., & O'Shea, T. (2010). Leadership agility. A business imperative for a VUCA world. *People & Strategy*, 33(4), 32–38. DOI: https://doi, org/10.1080/1461670X.2015.1017597.

Hove, T. (2022). Global media ethic, the good life, and justice. *Communication Theory*, 33(1), 53–60. DOI: https://doi.org/10.1093/ct/qtac016.

Indigenous peoples. (n.d.) *Amnesty International*. Downloaded June 26, 2023 from https://rb.gy/4cjeb.

Interface 2021 Environmental, Social, and Governance (ESG) Report (2021). *Design with purpose*. Downloaded June 24, 2023 from chrome-extension://efaidnbmnnnibpcajpcglclefindmkaj/https://s22.q4cdn.com/139673446/files/doc_presentations/2022/08/Interface-2021-ESG-Report-FINAL.pdf.

Johansen, B. E. (2015). *Eco-hustle! Global warming, greenwashing, and sustainability*. Praeger.

Khan, L. M. (2017). Amazon's antitrust paradox. *The Yale Law Journal*, 126(3), 564–907. DOI: https://scholarship.law.columbia.edu/faculty_scholarship/2808.

Kirby, A. (2016). Plunder of Earth's natural resources up 200% in 40 years. *The Ecologist*. Downloaded June 28, 2023 from https://rb.gy/0j0ir.

Konisky, D. M., Ansolabehere, S., & Carley, S. (2020). Proximity, NIMBYism, and public support for energy infrastructure. *Public Opinion Quarterly*, 84(2), 391–418. DOI: 10.1093/poq/nfaa025.

Kunnie, J. E. (2013). Restoring Africa's heartland: Earth, women, culture, and community. *Journal of Black Studies*, 44(4), 426–448. DOI: https://doi.org/10.1177/0021934713489880.

Liu, B. F., & Pompper, D. (2012). The 'crisis with no name': Defining the interplay of culture, ethnicity, and race on organizational issues and media outcomes. *Journal of Applied Communication Research*, 40(2), 127–146. https://doi.org/10.1080/00909882.2012.654499

Lockert, M. (2022). Understanding what the glass ceiling is and how it affects women in the workplace. Personal Finance. Downloaded June 24, 2023 from https://www.businessinsider.in/personal-finance/news/understanding-what-the-glass-ceiling-is-and-how-it-affects-women-in-the-workplace/articleshow/90145163.cms.

Lopez, O. (n.d.) Nine best charities for diversity and inclusion (complete 2023 list). Impactful Ninja. Downloaded June 24, 2023 from https://rb.gy/if5eu

Lugones, M. (2011). Methodological notes toward a decolonial feminism. In A. M. Isasi-Diaz and E. Mendieta (Eds.), *Decolonizing epistemologies: Latina/o theology and philosophy* (pp. 68–86). Fordham University Press.

Masaquiza, M. (n.d.) Indigenous peoples, indigenous voices fact sheet. United Nations Permanent Forum on Indigenous Issues. Downloaded June 28, 2023 from chrome-extension://efaidnbmnnnibpcajpcglclefindmkaj/https://www.un.org/esa/socdev/unpfii/documents/5session_factsheet1.pdf.

Mcleod, S. (2023). Stereotypes in psychology: Definition and examples. *Simply Psychology*. Downloaded June 23, 2023 from https://rb.gy/czp16.

Millar, C., Hind, P., Magala, S. (2012). Sustainability and the need for change: Organisational change and transformational vision. *Journal of Organizational Change Management*, 25(4), 489–500. DOI: https://doi.org/10.1108/0953481 1211239272.

Miller, K. (2015). *Organizational communication: Approaches and processes* (7th ed.). Stamford, CT: Cengage.

Millett, C. (2022). XPO excels at disability inclusion for the second year running. *MotorTransport*. Downloaded June 24, 2023 from https://rb.gy/6k7o9.

Mohammed, W. F. (2022). Bilchiinsi philosophy: Decolonizing methodologies in media studies. *The Review of Communication*, 22(1), 7–24. DOI: 10.1080/15358593.2021.2024870.

Morris, J. C., Gibson, W. A., Leavitt, W. M., & Jones, S. C. (2013). *The case for grassroots collaboration: Social capital and ecosystem restoration at the local level*. Lexington Books.

Morrison, J. (2014). The end of CSR? *Corporate Citizenship*. Downloaded June 22, 2023 from https://rb.gy/getxn.

Muschik, E.-M. (2022). Special issue introduction: Towards a global history of international organizations and decolonization. *Journal of Global History*, 17(2), 173–190. DOI: 10.1017/S1740022822000043.

Niewiarowski, E. (2023). Employers should offer same-sex couples same parental leave rights as others, workers say. *Pink News*. Downloaded June 24, 2023 from https://rb.gy/402la.

O'Brien Hallstein, D. L. (2009). A postmodern caring: Feminist standpoint theories, revisioned caring, and communication ethics. *Western Journal of Communication*, 63, 32–56. DOI: https://doi.org/10.1080/10570319909374627.

O'Higgins, E. (2005). Ireland: Bridging the Atlantic. In A. Habisch and J. Jonker (Eds.), *Corporate social responsibility* (pp. 67–76). Springer Verlag.

Pacific plunder (2021). *The Guardian*. Downloaded June 28, 2023 from https://rb.gy/hc7bm.

Perils of ESG (2023). American Cornerstone Institute. Downloaded June 23, 2023 from https://rb.gy/h1qj5.

Perrin, A. (2015). Social media usage: 2005–2015. The Pew Research Center. Downloaded June 23, 2023 from https://rb.gy/sfb60.

Petchsawang, P., & Duchon, D.(2012). Workplace spirituality, meditation, and work performance. *Journal of Management, Spirituality & Religion*, 9, 189–208. DOI: 10.1080/14766086.2012.688623.

Polman, P. (2021). Three actions CEOs must take to uphold U.S. democracy. *Harvard Business Review*. Downloaded June 24, 2023 from https://rb.gy/vm74s.

Pompper, D. (2015). *Corporate social responsibility, sustainability, and public relations: Negotiating multiple complex challenges*. Routledge.

Pompper, D. (2023). *Discovering answers: Research methods for public relations*. Kendall/Hunt Publishing Company.

Pompper, D., & Adae, E. K. (2023). Public relations and sustainability across the African Continent: Using Afro-centric philosophies to remember what's been 'forgotten or lost' (pp. 276–288). In D. Pompper, K. Place, and C. K. Weaver (Eds.) *The Routledge public relations companion*. Routledge.

Quijano, A. (1998). Colonialidad del poder, cultura y conocimiento en America Latina en *Ecuador Debate*, 44, 227–238.

Ramirez, M. (2022). Is the swastika a symbol of hate or peaceful icon? Faith groups try to save reviled emblem. *USA Today*. Downloaded June 25, 2023 from https://rb.gy/zcpmp.

Reiter, B. (2018). Recognition, reparations and political autonomy of Black and native communities in the Americas. In K. Dixon and O. A. Johnson III (Eds.) *Comparative racial politics in Latin America* (pp. 44–63). Routledge.

Rittel, H. W. J., & Webber, M. M. (1973). Dilemmas in a general theory of planning. *Policy Sciences*, 4(2), 155–169. DOI: https://doi.org/10.1007/BF01405730.

Rivard, N. (2023, Summer). Saving wild: The power of grassroots activism. *Friends of Animals*, 8–11.

Rosenberg, B. (2009). Interface Carpet and Fabric Company's sustainability efforts: What the company does, the crucial role of employees, and the limits of this approach. *Journal of Public Health Policy*, 30(4), 427–438. DOI: 10.1057/jphp.2009.41.

Ross, E. (2019). The past is still present: Why colonialism deserves better coverage. *The Correspondent*. Downloaded November 24, 2023 from https://thecorrespondent.com/32/the-past-is-still-present-why-colonialism-deserves-better-coverage.

Sautman, B., & Hairong, Y. (2007). Friends and interests: China's distinctive links with Africa. *African Studies Review*, 50(3), 75–114. DOI: https://doi.org/10.1353/arw.2008.0014.

Schneider, R. (2023). Men's attire: A gentlemen's guide for how to look good on Zoom. Attorney at work. Downloaded June 24, 2023 from https://shorturl.at/emrGI.

Sollinger, M. (2015). What robber barons gave us—after they took from us. *The World*. Downloaded June 24, 2023 from https://rb.gy/4867i.

Soromenho-Marques, V., & Ribeiro, S. (2022). The paradox of 1945 and the blind faith that technology will save us. *London School of Economics* blog. Downloaded November 24, 2023 from https://blogs.lse.ac.uk/businessreview/2022/06/08/the-paradox-of-1945-and-the-blind-faith-that-technology-will-save-us/.

Stackl, V. (2022). Latinx environmentalism: Justice, decolonization, y un mundo verde! *Greenpeace.* Downloaded June 25, 2023 from https://rb.gy/n3oeh.

Stovall, J. M., & Clark, K. (2022). *The conscious communicator: The fine art of not saying stupid sh*t, adding depth to your organization's communications.* Publish Your Purpose.

Thébaud, S., Kornrich, S., & Ruppanner, L. (2019). Good housekeeping, great expectations: Gender and housework norms. *Sociological Methods & Research,* 50(3), 1186–1214. DOI: https://doi.org/10.1177/0049124119852395.

Thomas, M. (2022). What does work–life balance even mean? *Forbes.* Downloaded June 24, 2023 from https://rb.gy/gwtl0.

Thomas, V. (2021). Decolonizing nonprofits. *Journal of Business.* Downloaded June 25, 2023 from https://rb.gy/eody7.

U.S. Equal Employment Opportunity Commission. (2022). EEOC releases fiscal year 2020 enforcement and litigation data. Downloaded June 24, 2023 from https://rb.gy/vf00p.

U.S. Equal Employment Opportunity Commission. (n.d.) Overview. Downloaded June 24, 2023 from https://www.eeoc.gov/overview.

Valian, V. (1989). *Why so slow? The advancement of women.* Cambridge, MA: The MIT Press.

Verschoor, C. C. (2005). Organizational DNA should contain ethics component. *Strategic Finance,* 86(8), 19–21. DOI: https://doi.org/10.1007/s10551-006-9040-6.

Weiner, G. (2010). *Social issues in literature: The environment in Henry David Thoreau's Walden.* Greenhaven Press.

Why diversity, equity, and inclusion matter for nonprofits. (n.d.) *National Council of Nonprofits.* Downloaded June 24, 2023 from https://rb.gy/igd3g.

Woo, D. (2000). *Glass ceilings and Asian Americans: The new face of workplace barriers.* Altamira Press.

Wynter, S. (2003). Unsettling the coloniality of being/power/truth/freedom: Towards the human, after man, its overrepresentation—An argument. *The New Centennial Review,* 3(3), 257–337. DOI: https://doi.org/10.1353/ncr.2004.0015.

Yang, A. (2023). Stakeholder networks and corporate social responsibility. In D. Pompper, K. R. Place, and C. K. Weaver (Eds.), *The Routledge companion to public relations* (pp. 253–264). Routledge.

Yoon, Y., Gürhan-Canli, Z., & Schwarz, N. (2006). The effect of corporate social responsibility (CSR) activities on companies with bad reputation. *Journal of Consumer Psychology,* 16, 377–390. DOI: https://doi.org/10.1509/jm.14.0389.

6 Universality thinking about publics and its pitfalls

Tugce Ertem-Eray

Recognizing that every organization has an audience, constituents, or publics represents one of the most important considerations when an organization seeks to communicate. **Publics** are groups of individuals with shared interests lumped together because they impact an organization—or are impacted by the organization—or both in certain ways (Kelleher, 2018). Thinking about people as all being the same, no matter what, though, boils down to universality thinking. When it comes to recognizing that organizations must respect all human beings, then universality thinking seems OK. Yet, considering publics from a one-size-fits-all point of view when communicating messages that impact people (and they *all* do!), then considering all people to be all the same all the time represents a serious shortcoming (Holland, 2019).

From a business case perspective, organizations traditionally separate key publics into categories such as *consumers*, *viewers*, *voters*, and more—yet, they may fail to address nuances of difference within these clusters. This means missed opportunities to fully respect and appreciate people within each cluster according to their intersecting social identity dimensions. Even seemingly specific categories such as *women*, *men*, *BIPOC community* are too universal to be of maximum utility in respecting DEI when creating messages and communication materials. Moreover, such a one-size-fits-all point of view thwarts organizations' ability to clearly see important individuals or groups of people who are *not* being included based on ways the organization is thinking about those categories of people. For example, when a consumer packaged goods manufacturer seeks to target messages to household grocery shoppers, it should not assume that the person is always a woman—for a variety of reasons—including online shopping trends (Fokina, 2023), children's influences on purchase decisions (Richardson, 2022), and same-sex couple households (Tumin, 2022), to name only a few dynamics. Likewise, when an organization changes its start or close time, it should carefully consider how this shift would impact a wide variety of publics, such as the surrounding community. Because

DOI: 10.4324/9781003279129-8

Figure 6.1 Grocery shopping can be a family event, as defined by cultural practices.

globalization trends are inspiring greater multiculturalism among populations, amidst many other social trends, organizations must consider vast dynamics that include underrepresented individuals and connect via more inclusive communication campaigns (Holland, 2019).

The U.S. population is more diverse now than a short time ago in 2010, so organizations must consider a growing diverse set of external publics, too (Jensen et al., 2021; Nikolova, 2023). Relatedly, organizations must consistently resist binary dualism thinking that contributes to homophily and lack of DEI, as mentioned in Chapter 3, "How intersectionality in social identity works . . . at work." Publics consist of individual people who have unique viewpoints shaped by their social identity intersectionalities and their own personal characteristics that shape their personality, motivations, and behaviors. It is important to know who people are and what their perceptions are. Thus, organizations should be as diverse on the inside as the population is on the outside of organizational walls. Organizations must show an awareness and appreciation of diverse communities for maximum engagement and successful communication campaigns (Becker Digital, 2022). This is not only the right thing to do, morally, but it makes good business and volunteer sense, too. Qualities such as loyalty, trust, and reputation are more important than ever (Benjamin, 2023). Therefore, this chapter focuses on advancing social identity intersectionality thinking for maximum DEI outcomes by avoiding a universal thinking about external publics.

This chapter builds upon the concept of social identity introduced in Chapter 1, "DEI and social identity intersectionality in organizational communication" by applying theory for a deeper understanding of how difference in social categories plays out in organizations seeking to identify and understand external publics—people impacted by organizations beyond employees. Because we covered internal publics in Chapter 3, "How intersectionality in social identity works . . . at work," this chapter shifts the conversation to considering important external publics—people who are outside the organization (Kelleher, 2018). Organizations must live and breathe the concept of social identity intersectionalities in order to understand, explain, and predict behaviors among diverse external publics as part of ongoing communication practices. Social identity intersectionality thinking must become standard for considering how to best manage and operate an organization.

This chapter covers these key areas: 1) considering publics beyond homophily thinking; 2) intersecting social identity dimensions and external publics; 3) searching for solutions: advancing intersectionality thinking for DEI; and 4) concluding thoughts.

Considering publics beyond homophily thinking

Publics, as a term, often is used as synonymous with **audiences** among communication practitioners (Rawlins, 2006) and marketers who often refer to **market segments** (Hallahan, 2000). Some communication practitioners continue to use the word *stakeholders* synonymously with *publics* and *audiences*, yet the *stakeholder* term is considered offensive in some communities given its etymological roots illustrating "the person who drove a stake into the land to demarcate the land s/he was occupying/stealing from indigenous territories" (Switching from stakeholder, n.d., para. 3). Organizations' leadership teams promote homophily thinking when they surround themselves with other people who look and think like them, inadvertently obscuring realities of publics beyond an organization's physical walls whose perceptions and behaviors can greatly impact the organization. The early work of U.S. philosopher John Dewey's (1927) is considered fundamental to understanding the current meaning of publics (Sommerfeldt & Iannacone, 2023) because Dewey examined ways publics evolve in stages. Dewey argued that a public forms once a group of individuals face a similar situation, eventually recognize problems, and then work together to resolve them. For example, some segments of the public are aware of climate change, but may not recognize it as a problem and only after significant media attention or some triggering event, may consider climate change as worthy of their attention for behavior change (Shapiro, 2023). Dewey's conceptualization was expanded when considering ways that groups of people come together about issues so that publics can form around specific issues (Sommerfeldt & Iannacone, 2023). Ponder how one company considered nuances of difference across consumer audiences who eat chocolate treats by reading about this case study in Sidebar 6.1.

Sidebar 6.1 The Golden Goobilee, Cadbury Creme Egg's 50th birthday

Tugce Ertem-Eray

Instead of thinking about publics as a one-size-fits-all exercise when creating a communication campaign, organizations must consider multiple intersecting social identity dimensions of their external publics. These dimensions may include ways they intersect according to age, (dis)ability, ethnicity/race, gender, faith/religion, sexual orientation, and social class. Focusing on people's unique qualities, orientations, and lived experiences can help organizations create more inclusive and respectful communication campaigns. One example of a successful communication campaign that involved attention to external publics' social identity intersectionalities is Cadbury's Golden Goobilee (as in *jubilee*) campaign focusing on the different types of Creme Egg eaters (PML Group, n.d.). Cadbury's campaign underscores just how important it is to represent diverse external publics in communication campaigns (Yates, 2021).

Cadbury, a British multinational confectionery company, launched this campaign in partnership with creative agency, Elvis. The campaign's main publics were a very broad expanse of age demographics—people aged 16–34 years (Jardine, 2021). The campaign showed the many different ways one can eat a Cadbury Creme Egg. They were called all *eggshibitionists* (Sparks, 2021).

As part of the campaign, customers had a chance to find limited edition Golden Creme Eggs in stores across the country (PML Group, n.d.). Starting in January 2021, the company hid Golden Creme Eggs in supermarkets, corner shops, and convenience stores. The prizes for finding one of these elusive eggs included cash prizes of up to €5,000 (Lewis, 2021).

Cadbury represented diverse external publics in the campaign images by showing a same-sex couple kissing while simultaneously noshing on a Creme Egg, passing it between their mouths as the narrator's voiceover says: "Sharers? We are down with that" (Jardine, 2021). Yet, this scene created a backlash on social media against the company when more than 90,000 people signed a petition (Citizengo, 2021) and called for the Advertising Standards Agency, the self-regulatory organization of the advertising industry in the U.K., to ban the commercial. The Christian community saw the commercial as offensive and accused it of selling sex to children (Citizengo, 2021). In a statement emailed to *Ad Age*, a global media brand that publishes news, analysis, and data on marketing and media, Cadbury said:

> Cadbury has always been a progressive brand that spreads a message of inclusion, whether it is through its products or brand campaigns. We are proud of our Golden Goobilee advert which celebrates the many ways that everyone can enjoy a Cadbury Creme Egg. To illustrate this and showcase the joy our products bring, a clip of a real life couple sharing a Cadbury Creme Egg was included in the advert.
>
> (Jardine, 2021, para. 7)

In addition, the Advertising Standards Authority mentioned that the ad did not break any advertising rules, so it would not be investigating (Baska, 2021). Ultimately, the British LGBT Awards (2021) nominated the campaign for successfully promoting the LGBTQ+ community. The competition jury called the Cadbury campaign colorful and creative so that the company's direction was seen as "a great step in the right direction to better representation of LGBT+ people in ads" (British LGBT Awards, 2021, para. 2).

Communicating among diverse external publics requires organizations to think deeper and recognize the multiple social identity dimensions of their external publics. There is no one-size-fits-all solution. Cadbury created an inclusive ad to reflect its broad external publics in the U.K. that included representing a diverse group of people, including the LGBTQIA community. The campaign shows progress in representing diverse external publics and reflecting society (Unstereotypealliance, 2021).

Resources

Baska, M. (2021, March 6). Backlash to Creme Egg advert made real-life queer Cadbury couple question their religious beliefs. Pink News. https://www.thepinknews.com/2021/03/06/cadbury-creme-egg-ad-gay-couple-callum-sterling-dale-k-backlash-religion/. Accessed August 11, 2023.

British LGBT Awards. (2021). Network rail—Top 10 brand or marketing campaigns 2021. https://britishlgbtawards.com/network-rail-top-10-brand-or-marketing-campaigns-2021/. Accessed August 11, 2023.

Cadbury. (n.d.). Our story. https://www.cadbury.co.uk/about/history/our-story/. Accessed August 11, 2023.

CitizenGo. (2021, February 15). Remove 'gay Creme Eggs' advert. https://citizengo.org/en-gb/fm/200615-remove-gay-creme-eggs-advert. Accessed August 11, 2023.

Jardine, A. (2021, January 12). Cadbury defends ad featuring gay couple sharing Creme Egg, after a Twitter storm. *Ad Age*. https://adage.com/article/creativity-news/cadbury-defends-ad-featuring-gay-couple-sharing-creme-egg-after-twitter-storm/2305231#:~:text=By%20Alexandra%20Jardine.,Published%20on%20January%2012%2C%202021.&text=Mondelez%2Downed%20Cadbury%20has%20defended,homophobic%20trolling%20on%20social%20media. Accessed 11, 2023.

Lewis, A. (2021, March 22). Golden Cadbury Creme Eggs have been hidden in shops around The UK. *Delish*. https://www.delish.com/uk/food-news/a34640801/golden-creme-eggs-cadbury/. Accessed 11, 2023.

PML Group. (n.d.). Cadbury Creme Egg celebrates 50th birthday with Golden Goobilee campaign. https://pmlgroup.ie/content/cadbury-creme-egg-celebrates-50th-with-golden-goobilee-campaign/. Accessed August 11, 2023.

Sparks, H. (2021, February 19). Cadbury under fire for same-sex kiss in new Creme Egg commercial. *New York Post*. https://nypost.com/2021/02/19/petition-targets-same-sex-kiss-in-new-cadbury-egg-commercial/. Accessed 11, 2023.

Unstereotypealliance. (2021, August 31). Mondelēz: The Cadbury Creme Egg campaign that sparked a conversation about LGBTIQ+ inclusion. https://www.unstereotypealliance.org/en/resources/member-spotlight/mondelez-international-cadbury-creme-egg Accessed August 11, 2023.

Yates, C. (2021, December 7). Regardless of how woke a brand is, portraying intersectionality is tricky. *The Drum*. https://www.thedrum.com/opinion/2021/12/07/regardless-how-woke-brand-portraying-intersectionality-tricky. Accessed August 11, 2023.

YouTube. (2021, January 7). Cadbury – It's the Creme Egg Golden Goobilee (Mondelēz UK, 2021). https://www.youtube.com/watch?v=t6fdOwluWPI. Accessed 11, 2023.

For-profit and nonprofit organizations need to understand people they touch, what motivates people, and most importantly how diverse are social identity intersectionalities among their external publics—beyond only considering **organizational goals.** Publics are not just masses of individuals who could be influenced or manipulated by organizations and communication professionals to achieve organizational goals (Botan, 2023; Rakow, 2018). Limited one-way dialog is less effective than respectful and mutual dialog linking organizations and publics (Sommerfeldt & Heath, 2023). One way for organizations to do this is to examine publics according to their demographic and psychographic qualities that can relate with their social identity intersectionalities. Social media platforms have played an important role in this shift in thinking about publics beyond merely a quest to accomplish organizational goals, which is the focus of Chapter 7, "Social media as a tool and a weapon." Because publics interact with one another via social media in conjunction with issues, events, and concerns, they are actively involved in thinking about how they see organizations (Botan, 2023). These processes offer a stark reminder to communication practitioners that the globe consists of networks involving simultaneous, multiple, discourse-based publics.

Here, we argue that organizations must do their homework, or research, to gain real insights about people. People forming publics are shaped by their intersecting social identity dimensions and unique lived experiences (Weber, 2001). Consequently, people's complex identities guide their understandings, perceptions, and decisions (Vardeman-Winter et al., 2013a). Moreover, given global, cultural, and technological trends impacting and involving consumers, communication practitioners need new approaches for identifying and communicating among external publics since these groups no longer constitute traditional monolithic categorizations (e.g., Vardeman et al., 2013b). Diversifying the people who work in organizations can go a long way in avoiding homophily so that policies, decisions, and communication materials respectfully consider *external* audiences and avoid mistakes, faux pas and embarrassments that large organizations have experienced in recent years. For example, some soft drink manufacturers have failed in China because they did not pay attention to cultural differences. One company named their product using a Chinese phrase that translated to *bite the wax tadpole*—and another company created a slogan that translated to *our soft drink brings your ancestors back to life*—so neither campaign succeeded (Examples, 2020). Some organizations regularly advertise brands' celebration of unity and diversity (e.g., Heath & Joyner, 2021; Yates, 2021), yet using a one-size-fits-all strategy for communication campaigns without recognizing that publics include people representing multiple social identity intersectionalities do so at their own peril (Sommerfeldt & Iannacone, 2023).

Intersecting social identity dimensions and external publics

An organization's key external audiences, or publics, offer a gateway to demonstrating an organization's DEI commitment via relationships with: activist groups, consumers/customers, communities, government, media, stockholders, suppliers, and more. Applying social identity theory can help communicators understand what people who live and work external to an organization's operations perceive about an organization and how they relate to it based on ways their social identity dimensions intersect and interplay. When organizations reduce their external publics simply to demographic descriptors—such as *general public* or *consumers*—they can overlook the nuances of lived experiences and social identity dimensions that affect how publics select, receive, react to, and processes organizational messages (Vardeman-Winter & Tindall, 2010a; Vardeman et al., 2023). Rather than considering such large demographic descriptors, organizations are better situated for successful communication when they consider publics in terms of their social identity dimension intersectionalities.

Unfortunately, there tends to be a gap between the identities of those who create, produce, and amplify organizations' communication campaigns and those who consume the communication campaigns' content. Hence, communicators must develop skills and incorporate necessary additional steps when creating and amplifying messages so that perspectives of organizational insiders who have privilege do not obstruct the importance of message content designed for external publics who do not enjoy privileges (Vardeman-Winter et al., 2013b). Yet, organizations routinely can fail to consider social identity differences when Caucasian/Whiteness—or homophily—serves as the dominant standard for working with external publics. For example, the city of Hialeah in Miami-Dade County, Florida, communicated during a crisis via a Caucasian/White spokesperson even though the majority population in this area of the state identifies as members of the Hispanic or Latinx communities (Landis, 2019). Public relations researchers long have advised organizations that during a crisis people prefer to hear information from individuals similar to themselves (e.g., Liu & Pompper, 2012). Therefore, this chapter underscores how remarkably important it is for organizations to recognize intersectionalities of social identity dimensions represented among their external publics.

Marketing and advertising campaigns wherein for-profit organizations promote products and services also communicate about social life and this must be done accurately and respectfully. In other words, organizations' communication practices make brands and services knowledge-making institutions (Rosa-Salas & Sobande, 2022). Therefore, these organizations can play a significant role in society by considering intersecting social identity dimensions and marginalized people's histories *and* lived experiences that include oppressions such as classism, homophobia, racism, sexism, xenophobia, and more. Organizations produce ideas for listeners and viewers through their advertising when they classify people into target markets (Rosa-Salas & Sobande, 2022).

So, discovering and understanding intersecting social identity dimensions among external publics is an essential step for marketers and advertisers to respectfully communicate with them—and there are plenty of examples of ways organizations are coming around to this reality. For support, organizations such as the Unstereotype Alliance, unstereotypealliance.org, a thought and action platform that seeks to eradicate harmful stereotypes in all media and advertising content, are available to work with the advertising industry (About the Unstereotype Alliance, n.d.) An organization that seeks to direct its advertising messages toward an Islamic community must follow Islamic cultural traditions such as avoiding offensive sexual appeals (Ani & Yusoff, 2021). In their 2021 Super Bowl ads, brands such as Michelob Ultra, Logitech, Squarespace, Klarna, and DoorDash featured African American/Black actors and represented LGBTQ communities (Poggi, 2021), Weather Tech featured real employees representing multiple ethnic backgrounds, and Toyota incorporated Paralympian Jessica Long's story about her adoption from a Siberian orphanage by an American couple (AdAge, 2021). The year before, TurboTax featured diverse actors and actresses representing various ages, ethnicities, genders, and two deaf women who sang along in their 2020 Super Bowl ad (AdAge, 2020). Procter & Gamble's advertising messages are guided by an understanding of traditions among American Latinos whose mothers washed clothes with Tide (Landis, 2019). Toyota features actors representing a wide variety of ethnic and gender identities (Maheshwari, 2017), explaining: "[I]f a person of any group is looking for communication that is like them, that looks like them specifically, the good news is because of the breadth of something like a Camry campaign, they can find it" (Maheshwari, 2017, para. 6).

Fenty Beauty, a cosmetics brand created by international pop star Rihanna in 2017, offers another example of for-profit advertisers and marketers carefully considering intersecting social identity dimensions of gender and ethnicity/culture/race. This brand has experienced great success featuring diverse and inclusive images in its communication campaigns. Rihanna not only wanted to make her brand available to women everywhere around the world at the same time (Saputo, 2019), but she expanded the traditional palette of skin tone shades to number 50 (Fetto, 2020). According to Saputo (2019), this was "the first time underrepresented, underserved women and cultures were featured in a global prestige beauty campaign" (para. 1). Fenty Beauty became the biggest cosmetics brand launch in YouTube history and was named one of the 25 Inventions of the Year in *Time* Magazine of 2017 (Saputo, 2019). *Time* magazine (2018) reported: "Fenty's unabashed celebration of inclusivity in their makeup campaigns put an unprecedented spotlight on the need for diverse beauty products" (para. 1). Fenty Beauty's ads also featured models representing multiple ethnic groups (McKinnon, 2022) and served as an example for competing cosmetic brands that began extending their skin tone shade ranges for a wider palette (Fetto, 2020).

LEGO carefully considered social identity intersectionality dimensions (age, gender, sexual orientation) among the large external public of consumers when it launched an inclusive campaign called *A–Z of Awesome* designed to be welcoming to LGBTQ+ families. The toy brand offers a Pride-themed colorful alphabet of identities and definitions made from LEGO bricks (Glenday, 2022) and aims to make conversations and vocabulary about LGBTQ+ identities more accessible by building a queer-helmed alphabet from A to Z such as *L is for Lesbian*, and *I is for Intersex* (DiBenedetto, 2022). Alero Akuya, vice president of brand development, said:

> We also know people love talking about what they build, so we thought it would be a great medium for sparking important and sometimes difficult conversations about identity. We want to show people that with more love and understanding people can be their true selves.
>
> (The A–Z, 2022, para. 5)

Another example of marketers and advertisers embracing intersecting social identity dimensions among external publics is the event labeled *Black-Owned Friday*, the brainchild of Google, the U.S. Black Chambers, Inc., and ad agency Bartle Bogle Hegarty. By considering the traditional first holiday shopping day after Thanksgiving as Black-Owned Friday—instead of simply Black Friday when retailers can turn sales deficits (red) to gains (black)—these three organizations considered the intersecting social identities of ethnicity/race and SES in seeking to support reversal of a negative trend. In 2020, an estimated 41% of Black-owned businesses had to close their doors in 2020 due to the COVID-19 pandemic. The campaign successfully increased Black-owned businesses' online conversation by 300%, created half a billion impressions, and contributed to 3000% sales growth for stores spotlighted (Bartle Bogle Hegarty, n.d.).

Finally, M&M Incorporated is another corporation taking into account social identity intersectionalities among external publics—age, gender, sexual orientation, SES—with M&Ms' introduction of its first new character in a decade, Purple. Purple, the new inclusive spokescandy, has charm and is quirky, self-aware, authentic, and confident (MARS, 2022). The brand introduced Purple with a music video called "I'm Just Gonna Be Me" and donated $1 for every stream of the song up to $500,000 to the nonprofit organization Sing for Hope, which has worked since the 9/11 events to bring creative programs to people in hospitals, schools, care facilities, refugee camps, transit hubs, and other community spaces (About Sing for Hope, n.d.; Mendoza, 2022).

All these examples of brands respecting social identity intersectionalities among consumers were successful, illustrating how being morally respectful also can translate to for-profit organizations accomplishing their commercial aims, too.

Nonprofit organizations also benefit from communicating about social life accurately and respectfully by acknowledging social identity intersectionalities. For example, a U.K.-based nonprofit organization called Relate helps people of all ages and life stages to strengthen their relationships by including a wide variety of age, ethnic/racial, and gender groups in its advertising campaign about what sex and intimacy mean in older age. The nature of the campaign's message made respectfully considering social identity dimension intersectionality supremely important (Yates, 2021). A COVID-19 public education campaign (e.g., WeCanDoThis, 2022) was designed to reach out to high-risk African American/Black and Latinx communities where COVID-19 hit most seriously during the pandemic (Cyrus et al., 2020; Pereida, 2022) since some members of these communities have limited or no access to healthcare, experience financial challenges, occupy migrant status, and/or experience health literacy challenges (e.g., Pedraza et al., 2022; Vasquez Reyes, 2020). The WeCanDoThis campaign included ads featuring trusted African American/Black and Latinx doctors, engagement with Black and Latinx media, community outreach vaccination events, and partnering with organizations embedded in these communities such as Women's Missionary Society Foundation, The Links, Inc., National Coalition of 100 Black Women, Black Women's Agenda, and more. To date, earned media efforts included more than 60 total television, radio, podcast, and print interviews, with 1.6 billion impressions. Similarly, Pereida (2022) discovered how Oregon health officials carefully tailored COVID-19 messages and advertising campaigns across Hispanic/Latinx communities using traditional and social media channels.

Next are two more related examples of how communication practitioners directed attention to disparities of disease and its effects on publics along intersecting social identity dimensions—ethnicity/race, gender, and sexual orientation. Equality California, a civil rights organization, campaigned to get COVID-19 vaccine information to LGBTQ Angelenos (Greenspon, 2021). Research findings suggest that LGBTQ people of color are twice as likely as Caucasian/White non-LGBTQ people to test positive for COVID-19 (Sears et al., 2020). Therefore, this nonprofit organization created a bilingual campaign to provide COVID-19 vaccine information, including an online Help Center and helpline to support LGBTQ+ Californians with the resources needed (Equality California, 2021). Jorge Roman, Director of Clinical Services at the San Francisco AIDS Foundation, explained:

COVID-19 health disparities we witness among LGBTQ+ communities, especially intersecting with immigrant communities, and Black, Indigenous and all communities of color, are not new. It is of paramount importance that we eliminate these health inequities, end discrimination and stop the marginalization of queer Black and Brown people.

(Equality California, 2021, para. 4)

In 2021, the Centers for Disease Control and Prevention (CDC) launched the Say Yes! COVID Test health campaign targeting underserved and historically marginalized communities, specifically focusing on SES dimensions—in parts of North Carolina and Tennessee. The campaign goal was to convince local communities to involve home kits in their everyday routines (Cha, 2021) and to scrutinize whether providing quick access to at-home testing reduces the COVID-19 spread (Brooks, 2021).

Both for-profit and nonprofit organizations morally do the right thing when they consider people's intersecting social identity dimensions and stand to gain the benefits of embracing uniqueness among external audiences. A person's social identity affects their experience and there is no guarantee that all experiences within social identity groups are similar or the same (Appiah, 2018). As we explain throughout this book, thinking of everyone as the same—*universality thinking*—can result in negative outcomes such as stereotyping, out-grouping, and marginalization. These effects build bias and discrimination in organizations' structures, negatively impact relationships, and foster misunderstandings and unequal treatment among people. Read in Sidebar 6.2 about considering social identity intersectionalities in a context of funding decisions for the Paralympics Games.

Sidebar 6.2   Funding issues for the Paralympics Games

Tugce Ertem-Eray

Realities of the COVID-19 pandemic in conjunction with activist and social justice movements have forced organizations to consider intersecting social identity dimensions among people collectively known as *external publics*. In earlier years, brands simply defaulted to the monolithic demographic term, *general public*, without usually thinking about ways to further refine understanding of such a large group of people. Failure to consider groups of people outside of organizations according to ways they are unique undermines an organization's DEI efforts. One case study for examining how

Figure 6.2 Men's 100m in Tokyo, Japan, 2020, Paralympic Games.

organizations may consider ways they respect external publics such as the disabilities communities is to examine funding dynamics associated with the 2016 Paralympics Games.

The Paralympic Games is a major international sports competition for athletes with disabilities such as physical, mental, and sensory disabilities, including mobility disabilities, amputees, visual disabilities, and people with cerebral palsy (Disabled World, 2022). The events are staged according to winter games and summer games and in the same city hosting the corresponding Olympic Games. The Paralympic Games take place every four years following the Olympic Games with a record for driving social inclusion (Olympics, n.d.). They are the world's third biggest sports event in terms of ticket sales after the Olympic Games and the FIFA World Cup (Olympics, n.d.). Examining exactly how the Paralympics Games and athletes with disabilities are funded offers an example of how systemic discrimination and unequal treatment among athletes can happen.

Even in the most progressive societies, people with disabilities face inequality in sports and physical activity because of the many barriers they encounter, such as accessibility, less media interest, and finding trainers and equipment (Zaitsava, 2022). One of the barriers to participation in sports activities that was identified by young people with disabilities between the ages of 6 and 16 was a lack of financial resources (College Sports Scholarship, n.d.). In addition, the National Center on Health, Physical Activity & Disability (NCHPAD) indicated that youth with a disability have lower physical activity levels and their obesity rate is 38% higher than the general population (Solomon, 2020). Therefore, people with disabilities may experience a greater need to have access and equal opportunities for sports and physical activities.

Over the past several decades, for-profit organizations have lent financial support to charitable organizations through matching gifts programs, volunteer grants, and human labor for volunteer programs, including those that work to meet the needs of people with disabilities. Sixty-five percent of Fortune 500 companies offer a matching gift program and 40% offer a volunteer grant program (Double the donation, n.d.). Corporate donations can support Paralympians with disabilities who face funding challenges en route to achieving their dreams. For example, the Toyota U.S. Paralympic Fund works in partnership with the U.S. Olympic & Paralympic Committee. The company offers support to all eligible athletes with disabilities to pursue their dreams (Toyota, n.d.).

The 2016 Paralympics in Rio faced major budget cuts due to poor ticket sales and existing financial challenges in a recession-battered Brazil (CNBC, 2016). Funds originally intended for the Paralympics were spent on the Olympics (Green, 2016).

In some cases, athletes with disabilities also face systemic factors limiting equal access. Kim Fawcett-Smith, a para triathlete who is an above-the-knee amputee, could not compete in the 2016 Paralympic Games in Rio de Janeiro, Brazil, because of the high cost. She could not afford club fees, coaching fees, equipment costs for two specialized prosthetic legs, and competition costs (Para Day, 2016). The Canadian Paralympic Committee only recruits people with disabilities between the ages of 19 and 35 (Para Day, 2016). Also, some companies shy away from sponsoring Paralympic athletes: "Major companies like Coke, Nike, etc. want Usain Bolt promoting their products and not the guy with cerebral palsy who may not look as 'cool' as Usain in their shoes or drinking their soft drink" (Para Day, 2016, para. 23).

Thus, organizations must think very carefully about ways privilege interplays with their charitable giving and sponsorship programs. Focusing on exclusively able-bodied spokesathletes and events excludes and marginalizes athletes with disabilities who may not share the same set of privileges. Supportive corporations such as Toyota can serve as inspiration for additional organizations who seek to meet their social responsibility for considering external publics according to intersecting social identity dimensions—with a goal of affecting broader positive social change. Revising an organization's infrastructure, creating policies, and making decisions that impact external publics requires careful and respectful consideration about what makes nuanced understanding of people possible for maximum respect and understanding.

Resources

Botan, C. H. (2023). In the age of publics: Evolving understanding of theory and publics. In C. H. Botan & E. J. Sommerfeldt (Eds.), *Public relations theory III* (pp. 11–22). Routledge.

College Sports Scholarship. (n.d.). Report reveals that disabled children take part in less sport than their able-bodied counterparts. https://www.college sportsscholarships.com/disabled-children-sports.htm. Accessed August 11, 2023.

CNBC. (2016, August 20). Paralympics faces 'major budget cuts' to hit all teams amid weak ticket sales. CNBC. https://www.cnbc.com/2016/08/20/paralympics-faces-major-budget-cuts-to-hit-all-teams-amid-weak-ticket-sales.html#:~:text=The%20IPC%20said%20it%20has,like%20this%2C%22%20Craven%20said. Accessed August 11, 2023.

Disabled World. (2022, August 21). Paralympic Games: Information, news, and events. *Disability News*. https://www.disabled-world.com/sports/paralympics/ Accessed August 11, 2023.

Double the donation. (n.d.) Top corporate donation statistics. Downloaded November 30, 2023 from https://doublethedonation.com/companies-that-donate-to-nonprofits/.

Green, J. T. (2016, August 22). For disabled people like me, it's clear that the Paralympics are nothing more than an afterthought. *Independent*. https://www.independent.co.uk/voices/rio-2016-paralympics-funding-ticket-sales-disabled-athletes-just-an-afterthought-a7203691.html. Accessed August 11, 2023.

Olympics. (n.d.). History of Paralympic Games. https://olympics.com/en/sports/paralympic/. Accessed August 11, 2023.

Para Day. (2016, September 16). Paralympians face unique funding challenges in achieving their dreams. Yahoo! Finance. https://ca.finance.yahoo.com/news/paralympians-face-unique-funding-challenges-in-achieving-their-dreams-120254955.html. Accessed August 11, 2023.

Solomon, J. (2020, June 15). For kids with disabilities, sports will return much more cautiously. *Project Play*. https://projectplay.org/news/2020/6/15/for-kids-with-disabilities-sports-will-return-much-more-cautiously. Accessed August 11, 2023.

Toyota. (n.d.). A legacy to honor the power of sport. https://www.toyotamobility.com/. Accessed August 11, 2023.

Zaitsava, V. (2022, June 3). What are the main barriers people with disabilities face in sports? https://verv.com/what-are-the-main-barriers-people-with-disabilities-face-in-sports/. Accessed August 11, 2023.

Falling short of social identity intersectionalities thinking

Often, organizations fail to consider external publics' entire social identities when they do not consider ways people's social identity dimensions intersect. For example, when concentrating only on gender, organizations must recognize differences between sex (biological) and gender (social) (e.g., Wood & Fixmer-Oraiz, 2019). Considering gender identities as social dimensions enables organizations to respect fluidity—change over time in a person's gender identity, expression, or both—across audiences who do not accept gender binaries (Katz-Wise, 2020). Moreover, considering gender and sexuality more broadly opens opportunities to connect with and respect transgender people whose "gender identity is different from the gender they were thought to be when they were born" (Understanding, 2023, para. 2). Ways that gender social identity dimensions intersect with age, ethnicity/race/culture, disabilities, faith/religion, and many other dimensions is central to communicating respectfully and accurately among audiences.

When communication practitioners and the organizations they work with have difficulty seeing beyond only one social identity dimension, they tend to forget we have *multiple intersecting* social identity dimensions that uniquely shape us. For example, some people with disabilities worry that they are considered as *only* their disability—to the detriment of being considered wholly in conjunction with all of their intersecting social identity dimensions (Drew, 2023). To address this, Stephen Thomas Smith, an activist who creates social media content on TikTok to reflect on his life with cerebral palsy as a gay man, confronts ableism and other forms of discrimination as part of his work (Drew, 2023; Wilson, 2021).

In particular, discovering and understanding intersecting social identity dimensions among external publics can be vitally important when health and safety issues are at play. For example, the U.S. National Heart, Lung, & Blood Institute sought to inform women of color about heart health with a communication campaign called the Heart Truth, but campaign designers forgot to consider ways social identity dimension intersectionalities—particularly gender, ethnicity, and socio-economic status (SES)—can impact health and safety communication campaigns' success rates (Vardeman-Winter & Tindall, 2010b). Campaign materials suggested that women eat fresh fruits and vegetables and exercise daily; behaviors that may be uncommon among some Latinx women concerned about high cost of fresh fruits and vegetables and how this health advice would translate in their own traditional meal preparation recipes. Another public health campaign that considered age in addition to other intersecting social identity dimensions of gender, ethnicity, and SES was a Gardasil HPV/cervical cancer vaccine communication campaign. Vardeman-Winter (2010) found that campaign awareness and vaccination rates were lowest among low-SES, non-Caucasian/White teen girls—even though they were those more likely to experience HPV/cervical cancer. Again, campaign designers overlooked opportunities to tailor their campaign messaging by considering social identity intersectionalities of age, ethnicity, gender, and SES. Overall, women attend to health messaging uniquely depending upon their age, ethnicity/race, and SES (Vardeman-Winter et al., 2013b), so policymakers and health message creators must carefully consider social identity intersectionalities. Plainly, people's lives depend on the degree to which organizations and their communicators consider social identity intersectionalities when working with external publics.

Organizations that overlook opportunities to engage in inclusive communication practices risk alienating people and this may manifest in failed communication campaigns through lack of engagement, potential backlash, negative publicity for organizations, and failed goals to grow brands and market share (Fongang, 2023; Kavon, 2023; Kular, 2021). Moreover, organizations also can risk losing loyal customers if they do not pay attention to DEI among external publics. When an organization loses a public, it can cost the organization five times as much to acquire a new public (Kavon, 2023).

Social identity intersectionalities and activism

Some people are more aware of the *intersectionality* concept in recent years since it has been associated with social justice movement activism amplified across social media platforms. Activist and social justice movement organizers have pressured organizations to pay attention to disparate, unequal treatment of people along social identity dimensions in conjunction with George Floyd's murder. Many corporations began using their social media platforms to support the #BlackLivesMatter movement for confronting systemic racism (Jan et al., 2021). Among nonprofit organizations aligning social activist goals is Black Health Matters—a group that provides information about health and well-being for African American/Black people – urging organizations to consider people's social locations and intersecting social identity dimensions (age, ethnicity/race, gender, SES) that play out in terms of health insurance access, systemic inequalities healthcare treatment, and lack of awareness about disease prevention (Vardeman et al., 2023). In the U.S., African American/Black people are at a higher risk for developing nearly every illness or dying from it in greater numbers (Black Health Matters, n.d.).

Collectively, nonprofit and for-profit organizations' communication campaigns that carefully consider publics' intersecting social identity dimensions can enrich and save lives, merely by respecting whole people rather than limitedly defining people as *consumers* or *general public*. Organizations must continue to apply a *intersectionality thinking* to remain true to DEI commitments.

Searching for solutions: advancing intersectionality thinking for DEI

Incorporating intersectionality thinking about social identity dimensions into ways organizations consider external audiences and publics is one way for-profit and nonprofit organizations demonstrate a real commitment to DEI. As covered in Chapter 3, "How intersectionality in social identity works . . . at work" and Chapter 4, "Power differentials in organizations and society," it is important to understand that organizations and communication practitioners recognize their own privilege so they may develop empathy for those without privilege (Amaechi, 2020). Moreover, organizations and communicators must interrogate their own personal biases that can affect their work (Vardeman-Winter et al., 2023). Being equipped with insights about privilege promotes challenging systems and engrained biases so that meaningful change and actual DEI can happen (e.g., Tulshyan, 2022). Taking an intersectional approach, means communication practitioners embrace commitments to anti-racist and anti-sexist practices when creating, implementing, and assessing their communication campaigns and take action to center the needs of marginalized people (e.g., Vardeman et al., 2023).

The success of nonprofit groups and social movements have illustrated ways that people with privilege who are external to organizations can be committed to supporting people who do not have privilege. The Trevor Project offers an example of a nonprofit organization taking an important social problem—high suicide rates among LGBTQ+ young people—and applying intersectionality thinking for respectful and successful DEI work. Through allyship and education, this U.S.-based organization supports transgender and nonbinary young people of all genders, ethnic/race, and SES groups by recognizing the complexities of their social identity dimensions across their lived experiences. The Trevor Project tracks legislation across the U.S. that could impact LGBTQ people and builds networks for funding, advocating against anti-LGBTQ laws/policies, connecting LGBTQ peers, and conducting research about LGBTQ young people's lives (The Trevor Project, n.d.) The #BlackLivesMatter social movement also grew into a *global* event, including Caucasian/White people, for widespread support in addition to support among BIPOC communities. Men also attended the Women's March across the U.S. and globally to oppose Donald Trump's misogynistic campaign that demeaned women and "essentially every minority group in the country" (Shavin, 2017, para. 9). People from the Global North work to reduce poverty in the Global South (Mahali et al., 2018). These nonprofit organizations and global social movements offer evidence that people with privilege external to organizations are committed to improving the lives of people who do not have privilege (Radke et al., 2020).

Overall, communication practitioners must incorporate DEI and social identity dimension intersectionality thinking about external publics into their communication plans. When organizations design a communication campaign, they must do the necessary research to discover as much as they can about their publics' intersecting social identity dimensions. As mentioned in previous chapters, listening is an important skill for advancing DEI when working with external publics, such as those who are marginalized (e.g., Place, 2022). Communication practitioners occupy a space wherein they may hear both their organizations and external audiences with a goal toward including multiple perspectives and shifting identities embedded within socio-economic, sociocultural, and sociopolitical contexts (Place, 2022). Using new technologies and social media platforms as listening tools for gathering feedback among diverse publics enables communicators to discover what they need to know about intersecting social identity dimensions (Vardeman & Sebesta, 2020). Indeed, an intersectionalities approach means organizations must probe beyond any one-size-fits-all solution to discover uniqueness of external publics.

Concluding thoughts

The purpose of this chapter is to understand how intersectionality across social identity dimensions plays out among organizations communicating with external publics—by moving beyond homophily thinking and moving toward considering multiple intersections across social identity dimensions—with a goal of finding solutions. We began by defining the concept of publics, or audiences and underscoring the importance of intersecting social identity dimensions among external publics. Then this chapter offered numerous examples of ways organizations have made mistakes while others have discovered how to apply intersectionality thinking by moving to the center those people who traditionally have been relegated to the margins. Overall, communication practitioners must apply social identity intersectional thinking approaches—to identify external publics, discover what their needs are, and explore what motivates them—given the global, cultural, and technological trends shaping external publics and audiences today. Disregarding publics' diverse, intersecting histories, backgrounds, and lived experiences means focusing on a shallow or myopic view. Using an intersectionality approach enables communication practitioners to best explain publics (e.g., Aldoory, 2009; Canfield et al., 2020).

Today's sociopolitical and sociocultural environment requires that communication practitioners think more about intersectionality when they create communication campaigns and messages concerning different meanings around risks, rights, and policies (Vardeman et al., 2023). Hence, both for-profits and nonprofits must keep DEI thinking at the forefront of their marketing and advertising campaigns to ensure that everyone feels that they belong and are accurately represented in communication campaigns (Fear-Smith, 2021). Diverse and inclusive advertising can create positive brand and social effects (Eisend et al., 2023). Organizations must confront privilege as part of this journey, given organizations' social responsibility to use their power to affect positive social change.

Next, Chapter 7, "Social media as a tool and as a weapon" continues the conversation about how new tools, ethically applied, can support communication practitioners at the forefront of making DEI a reality across organizations and among their publics.

Key words

Audiences—Audiences are individual receivers of communicated messages (Hallahan, 2000; Livingstone, 2005).

Market segments—Market segments are a group of people who share similarities along specific particular demographic, psychographic, or geodemographic dimensions. Marketers use this information to speculate that such people are likely to behave or respond to organizational actions or messages similarly (Hallahan, 2000, p. 501).

Organizational goals—Organizational goals refer to the anticipated outcomes of a nonprofit's or for-profit's activities.

Publics—Publics are defined as "groups of people with shared interests related to organizations" (Kelleher, 2018, p. 2). Also, publics are "an interpretive community engaged in an ongoing process of developing a shared understanding of its relationship with a group or organization that can differ substantially from that of the organization" (Botan, 2018, p. 59).

Discussion questions for deep engagement

1. Think deeply about your favorite brand. In what ways do you see evidence that this brand considers intersecting social identity dimensions when communicating with publics?
2. Think deeply about a nonprofit organization where you volunteer—or one you greatly admire. In what ways do you see evidence that this nonprofit organization considers intersecting social identity dimensions when communicating with publics?
3. Visit the website of your school or university. What evidence do you see that it uniquely shapes messages communicated to unique social identity groups?
4. Use Google to discover cases of organizations offending individuals or groups of people according to social identity dimensions. What might these organizations have in common?
5. What advice might you offer to an organization that you suspect continues to amplify a homophily thinking approach?

Resources

About the Unstereotype Alliance. (n.d.) *#Unstereotype Alliance*. Downloaded November 30, 2023 from https://www.unstereotypealliance.org/en/about.

About Sing for Hope. (n.d.) Downloaded November 30, 2023 from https://singforhope.org/about/.

AdAge. (2020, March 2). Turbotax "All people are tax people". AdAge. https://adage.com/video/turbotax-all-people-are-tax-people. Accessed August 18, 2023.

AdAge. (2021, December 24). Toyota "upstream". AdAge. https://adage.com/video/toyota-upstream. Accessed August 18, 2023.

Aldoory, L. (2009). The ecological perspective and other ways to (re)consider cultural factors in risk communication. In R. L. Heath & H. D. O'Hair (Eds.), *Handbook of risk and crisis communication* (pp. 227–246). Routledge.

Amaechi, C. (2020, November 17). Privilege blinds us to plight of others who lack it. *Financial Times*. https://www.ft.com/content/e394fd7b-5bdb-4d96-8375-a10a24e960c2. Accessed July 10, 2023.

Ani, N., & Yusoff, M. (2021). A systematic literature review on advertising from non-western perspective. *Academy of Strategic Management Journal*, 20(6S), 1–15.

Appiah, K. A. (2018). *The lies that bind: Rethinking identity*. Liveright Publishing Corporation.

Bartle Bogle Hegarty (BBH) (n.d.). Google Black-Owned Friday. How we turned a day of shopping into a day to support Black-Owned businesses. https://www.bartleboglehegarty.com/google-black-owned-friday. Accessed August 1, 2023.

Becker Digital. (2022, February 28). Communicating with diverse audiences online. https://www.becker-digital.com/blog/communicating-diverse-audiences. Accessed August 16, 2023.

Benjamin, C. (2023, May 8). Intersectionality in marketing: 5 ways brands can embrace diversity and inclusion for better results. https://www.benamic.com/blog/inclusive-marketing-for-campaigns-that-truly-resonate/. Accessed August 19, 2023.

Black Health Matters. (n.d.). About us. https://blackhealthmatters.com/about-us/. Accessed August 1, 2023.

Botan, C. H. (2018). *Strategic communication theory and practice: The cocreational model.* Wiley Blackwell.

Botan, C. H. (2023). In the age of publics: Evolving understanding of theory and publics. In C. H. Botan & E. J. Sommerfeldt (Eds.), *Public relations theory III* (pp. 11–22). Routledge.

Brooks, K. J. (2021, April 28). States test at-home COVID-19 testing program. CBC News. https://www.cbsnews.com/news/covid-19-vaccine-test-pitt-county-north-carolina-tennessee-cdc/. Accessed August 2, 2023.

Canfield, K. N., Menezes, S., Matsuda, S. B., Moore, A., Mosley, A. A. N., Dewsbury, B. M., Feliú-Mójer, M. I., McDuffie, K. W. B., Moore, K., Reich, C. A., Smith, H. M., & Taylor, C. (2020). Science communication demands a critical approach that centers inclusion, equity, and intersectionality. *Frontiers in Communication*, 5. Downloaded June 24, 2023 from https://shorturl.at/DHITW. Cha, A. E. (2021, April 28). The future of coronavirus testing is in Greenville, N.C. *Washington Post*. https://www.washingtonpost.com/health/2021/04/28/new-coronavirus-testing-strategy-home-kits/. Accessed August 2, 2023.

Cyrus, E., Clarke, R., Hadley, D., Bursac, Z., Trepka, M. J., Dévieux, J. G., Bagci, U., Furr- Holden, D., Coudray, M., Mariano, Y., Kiplagat, S., Noel, I., Ravelo, G. J., Paley, M., & Wagner, E. (2020). The impact of COVID-19 on African American communities in the United States. *Health Equity*, 4(1), 476–483. https://doi.org/10.1101/2020.05.15.20096552.

Dewey, J. (1927). *The publics and its problems.* Holt.

DiBenedetto, C. (2022, June 1). LEGO builds up LGBTQ awareness with new Pride campaign. *Mashable*. https://mashable.com/article/lego-a-to-z-awesome-pride-month. Accessed August 1, 2023.

Drew, C. (2023, May 7). 15 examples of intersectionality. https://helpfulprofessor.com/examples-of-intersectionality/. Accessed August 17, 2023.

Dunn, L. (2021, April 26). Can regular at-home testing slow the spread of COVID? One N.C. county is trying to find out. NBC News. https://www.nbcnews.com/health/health-news/can-regular-home-testing-slow-spread-covid-one-n-c-n1265093. Accessed August 2, 2023.

Eisend, M., Muldrowb, A. F., & Rosengren, S. (2023). Diversity and inclusion in advertising research. *International Journal of Advertising*, 42(1), 52–59. https://doi.org/10.1080/02650487.2022.2122252.

Equality California. (2021, March 2). Equality California Institute launches bilingual public education, outreach campaign with state promoting vaccine, testing. https://www.eqca.org/lgbtq-covid-19-bilingual-education_vaccine/. Accessed August 2, 2023.

Examples of company failure due to cultural mistakes. (2020, October 13). Chron. https://smallbusiness.chron.com/examples-company-failure-due-cultural-mistakes-70712.html. Accessed August 17, 2023.

Fear-Smith, N. (2021, March 16). The importance of intersectionality in marketing campaigns. Hello Partner. https://hellopartner.com/2021/03/16/the-importance-of-intersectionality-in-marketing-campaigns/ Accessed August 17, 2023.

Fetto, F. (2020, April 20). How Fenty Beauty changed the state of play in the industry. *British Vogue*. https://www.vogue.co.uk/beauty/article/rihanna-fenty-beauty-diversity Accessed September 15, 2023.

Fokina, M. (2023). Online shopping statistics: E-commerce trends for 2023. Tidio. Downloaded November 28, 2023 from https://www.tidio.com/blog/online-shopping-statistics/.

Fongang, F. (2023, May 24). Challenges and solutions for implementing inclusive marketing strategies. https://www.linkedin.com/pulse/challenges-solutions-implementing-inclusive-marketing-fongang/. Accessed August 19, 2023.

Glenday, J. (2022, June 6). Lego launches A-Z LGBTQ+ inclusivity campaign. The Drum. https://www.thedrum.com/news/2022/06/06/lego-launches-z-lgbtq-inclusivity-campaign. Accessed August 1, 2023.

Greenspon, C. (2021, March 3). Campaign aims to get vaccination info to the LGBTQ community. Laist. https://laist.com/news/campiagn-vaccine-lqbtq-community-vaccination. Accessed August 2, 2023.

Hallahan, K. (2000). Inactive publics. The forgotten publics in public relations. *Public Relations Review*, 26(4), 499–515. https://doi.org/10.1016/S0363-8111(00)00061-8.

Heath, O., & Joyner, L. (2021, November 9). Amazon's Christmas advert 2021 focuses on the kindness of strangers. House Beautiful. https://www.housebeautiful.com/uk/lifestyle/a24634544/amazon-christmas-advert/. Accessed August 17, 2023.

Holland, T. (2019, January 7). Inclusive brand marketing: 4 ways to foster a more diverse Audience. Skyword. https://www.skyword.com/contentstandard/inclusive-brand-marketing-4-ways-to-foster-a-more-diverse-audience/. Accessed August 16, 2023.

Jan, T., McGregor, J., & Hoyer, M. (2021). Corporate America's $50 billion promise. *TheWashington Post*. Downloaded November 30, 2023 from https://www.washingtonpost.com/business/interactive/2021/george-floyd-corporate-america-racial-justice/.

Jensen, E., Jones, N., Rabe, M., Pratt, B., Medina, L., Orozco, K., & Spell, L. (2021, August 12). The chance that two people chosen at random are of different race or ethnicity groups has increased since 2010. https://www.census.gov/library/stories/2021/08/2020-united-states-population-more-racially-ethnically-diverse-than-2010.html. Accessed August 16, 2023.

Katz-Wise, S. L. (2020). Gender fluidity: What it means and why support matters. Harvard Health Publishing. Downloaded November 29, 2023 from https://rb.gy/eb1pu2.

Kavon. (2023, March 29). Diversity marketing: Pros and cons of implementing diversity and inclusion. PHU Concepts. https://phuconcepts.com/diversity-marketing-pros-and-cons-of-implementing-diversity-and-inclusion/. Accessed August 19, 2023.

Kelleher, T. (2018). *Public relations*. Oxford University Press.

Kular, R. (2021, November 30). Diversity in marketing: What are the advantages? https://wp.wwu.edu/rosekular/2021/11/30/diversity-in-marketing-what-are-the-advantages/ Accessed August 19, 2023.

Landis, K. (2019, March 19). The public relations industry is too white and the solution starts with higher education. Insight into Diversity. https://www.insight-intodiversity.com/the-public-relations-industry-is-too-white-and-the-solution-starts-with-higher-education/. Accessed July 28, 2023.

Liu, B. F., & Pompper, D. (2012). The 'crisis with no name': Defining the interplay of culture, ethnicity, and race on organizational issues and media outcomes. *Journal of Applied Communication Research*, 40(2), 127–146. https://doi.org/1 0.1080/00909882.2012.654499.

Livingstone, S. (2005). On the relation between audiences and publics. In S. Livingstone (Ed.), *Audiences and publics: When cultural engagement matters for the public sphere* (pp. 17–41). Intellect Books.

M&Ms (n.d.). We help people feel included by championing fun as a way to share our true-self and connect with others. https://www.mms.com/en-us/explore? Accessed August 1, 2023.

Maheshwari, S. (2017, October 12). Different ads, different ethnicities, same car. *The New York Times*. https://www.nytimes.com/interactive/2017/10/12/business/ media/toyota-camry-ads-different-ethnicities.html. Accessed July 28, 2023.

Mahali, A., Lynch, I., Fadiji, A. W., Tolla, T., Khumalo, S., & Naicker, S. (2018). Networks of well-being in the Global South: A critical review of current scholarship. *Journal of Developing Societies*, 34(4), 373–400. DOI: https://doi. org/10.1177/0169796X18786137.

McKinnon, T. (2022, May 3). How Rihanna's Fenty Brand is leading in diversity & inclusion. Indigo Digital. https://www.indigo9digital.com/blog/fentydiversity-inclusion. Accessed September 15, 2023.

Mendoza, J. (2022, October 3). For the first time in over a decade, a new M&M color: Meet Purple, who represents 'acceptance'. *USA Today*. https://www.usa today.com/story/money/food/2022/10/03/purple-m-and-m/8169936001/. Accessed August 1, 2023.

Nikolova, R. (2023). Growing audiences—and your media business—through diversity. DCN. Downloaded June 24, 2023 from https://shorturl.at/fmrEX.

Pedraza, L., Villela, R., Kamatgi, V., Cocuzzo, K., Correa, R., & Zylberglait Lisigurski, Miriam. (2022). The Impact of COVID-19 in the Latinx Community. *HCA Healthcare Journal of Medicine*, 3(3), Article 5. https://doi. org/10.36518/2689-0216.1387.

Pereida, S. (2022). Health literacy and information access for Hispanic/Latinx communities: A timely investigation in the time of COVID-19. (Unpublished master's thesis). University of Oregon, Portland.

Place, K. R. (2022). Toward a framework for listening with consideration for intersectionality: insights from public relations professionals in borderland spaces. *Journal of Public Relations Research*, 34(1–2), 4–19. https://doi.org/10.1080/10 62726X.2022.2057502.

Poggi, J. (2021, February 5). Super Bowl LV advertisers tackle diversity, inclusion with mixed results. AdAge. https://adage.com/article/special-report-super-bowl/ super-bowl-lv-advertisers-tackle-diversity-inclusion-mixed-results/2311981. Accessed August 18, 2023.

Rakow, L. F. (2018). On Dewey: Public relations and its eclipse of the public. In Ø. Ihlen, & M. Fredriksson (Eds.), *Public relations and social theory* (pp. 315–333). Routledge.

Rawlins, B. L. (2006). Prioritizing stakeholders for public relations. Institute for Public Relations. https://www.instituteforpr.org/wp-content/uploads/2006_ Stakeholders_1.pdf. Accessed July 27, 2023.

Radke, H. R. M., Kutlaca, M., Siem, B., Wright, S. C., & Becker, J. C. (2020). Beyond allyship: Motivations for advantaged group members to engage in action for disadvantaged groups. *Personality and Social Psychology Review*, 24(4), 291–315. https://doi.org/10.1177/1088868320918698.

Relate. (n.d.). Let's talk the joy of sex in later life. https://www.relate.org.uk/lets-talk-joy-later-life-sex. Accessed August 8, 2023.

Richardson, N. (2022). The democratic household: Why kids hold the key to household purchasing decisions. Open Mic. Downloaded November 28, 2023 from https://rb.gy/4r2m98.

Rosa-Salas, M., & Sobande, F. (2022). Hierarchies of knowledge about intersectionality in marketing theory and practice. *Marketing Theory*, 22(2), 175–189. https://doi.org/10.1177/14705931221075372.

Saputo, S. (2019, June). How Rihanna's Fenty Beauty delivered 'Beauty for All' — and a wake- up call to the industry. Think with Google. https://www.thinkwithgoogle.com/future-of-marketing/management-and-culture/diversity-and-inclusion/-fenty-beauty-inclusive-advertising/. Accessed September 15, 2023.

Sears, B., Conron, K. J., & Flores, A. R. (2021). The impact of the Fall 2020 COVID-19 surge on LGBT adults in the US. Report. https://williamsinstitute.law.ucla.edu/publications/covid-surge-lgbt/. Accessed August 2, 2023.

Shapiro, J. P. (2023). The thinking error that makes people susceptible to climate change denial. *The Conversation*. Downloaded November, 28, 2023 from https://rb.gy/e5b968.

Shavin, N. (2017). Men at the women's march? You bet. Here's why they came. *Vox*. Downloaded November 30, 2023 from https://www.vox.com/identities/2017/1/22/14347710/men-womens-march.

Sommerfeldt, E. J., & Heath, R. L. (2023). OPR and its corruption of "publics": A critique. *Public Relations Review*, 49, 102369. https://doi.org/10.1016/j.pubrev.2023.102369.

Sommerfeldt, E. J., & Iannacone, J. (2023). A "public" by any other name. Reclaiming public theory, and liberating publics from "OPR". In C. H. Botan & E. J. Sommerfeldt (Eds.), *Public relations theory III* (pp. 23–37). Routledge.

Switching from stakeholder (n.d.) Research impact Canada. Downloaded November 29, 2023 from https://rb.gy/qu9cpo.

The Trevor Project. (n.d.). Guide to being an ally to transgender and nonbinary young people. https://www.thetrevorproject.org/resources/guide/a-guide-to-being-an-ally-to-transgender-and-nonbinary-youth/. Accessed August 3, 2023.

The A–Z of Awesome—Because self expression and identity matter (2022). LEGO. https://www.lego.com/en-us/aboutus/news/2022/may/the-a-z-of-awesome-because-self-expression-and-identity-matter. Accessed August 1, 2023.

The Unstereotype Alliance (2021). Beyond gender 2: The impact of intersectionality in advertising. https://www.unstereotypealliance.org/en/resources/diversity-and-inclusion/2021/10/beyond-gender-2. Accessed August 3, 2023.

Time Magazine. (2018, October 3). Fenty Beauty. https://time.com/collection-post/5412503/fenty-beauty/. Accessed September 15, 2023.

Tulshyan, R. (2022). *Inclusion on purpose: An intersectional approach to creating a culture of belonging at work*. The MIT Press.

Tumin, R. (2022). Same-sex couple households in U.S. surpass one million. *The New York Times*. Downloaded November 28, 2923 from https://rb.gy/0k5cat.

Understanding transgender people: The basics. National Center for Transgender Equality. Downloaded November 29, 2023 from https://transequality.org/issues/resources/understanding-transgender-people-the-basics.

Vardeman-Winter, J. (2010). Using the cultural studies approach to understand health decision making among a teen public. *Public Relations Review*, 36(4), 383–385. https://doi.org/10.1016/j.pubrev.2010.06.004.

Vardeman, J., & Sebesta, A. (2020). The problem of intersectionality as an approach to digital Activism: The women's March on Washington's attempt to unite all women. *Journal of Public Relations Research*, 32(1–2), 7–29. https://doi.org/10.1080/1062726X.2020.1716769.

Vardeman-Winter, J., & Tindall, N. T. J. (2010a). Toward an intersectionality theory of public relations. In R. L. Heath (Ed.), *The Sage Handbook of public relations* (pp. 223–236). Sage.

Vardeman-Winter, J. & Tindall, N. T. J. (2010b). "If it's a woman's issue, I pay attention to it": Gendered and intersectional complications in The Heart Truth media campaign. *PRism*, 7(4). Available at: http://www.prismjournal.org/fileadmin/Praxis/Files/Gender/VardemanWinter_Tindall.pdf.

Vardeman-Winter, J., Tindall, N. T. J., & Jiang, H. (2013a). Intersectionality and publics: How exploring publics' multiple identities questions basic public relations concepts. *Public Relations Inquiry*, 2(3), 279–304. https://doi.org/10.1177/2046147X13491564.

Vardeman-Winter, J., Tindall, N. T. J., & Jiang, H. (2013b). Information-seeking outcomes of representational, structural, and political intersectionality among health media consumers. *Journal of Applied Communication Research*, 41(4), 389–411. http://dx.doi.org/10.1080/00909882.2013.828360.

Vardeman, J., Tindall, N. T. J., & Smith, L. (2023). Revisiting intersectionality. The stray, strain, and performativity for social identity dimensions in public relations over the past decade. In D. Pompper, K. R. Place, & C. K. Weaver (Eds.), *The Routledge companion to public relations* (pp. 74–88). Routledge.

Vasquez Reyes, M. (2020).The disproportional impact of COVID-19 on African Americans. *Health and Human Rights*, 22(2), 299–307.

Weber, L. (2001). *Understanding race, class, gender, and sexuality: A conceptual framework*. McGraw-Hill.

WeCanDoThis. (2022, September 19). Covid-19 public education campaign. Campaign approach to reaching Black audiences. https://wecandothis.hhs.gov/resource/campaign-approach-to-reaching-black-audiences. Accessed July 28, 2023.

Wilson, C. (2021, January 22). Disability: 'People assume I can't be gay because I'm disabled'. BBC. https://www.bbc.com/news/stories-55586657. Accessed August 17, 2023.

Wood, J. T., & Fixmer-Oraiz, N. (2019). *Gendered lives*. Cengage.

Yates, C. (2021, December 7). Regardless of how woke a brand is, portraying intersectionality is tricky. The Drum. https://www.thedrum.com/opinion/2021/12/07/regardless-how-woke-brand-portraying-intersectionality-tricky. Accessed August 8, 2023.

Part III

Advancing communication and positive organizational change processes

7 Social media as a tool and as a weapon

Tugce Ertem-Eray

The dichotomy of social media's double-edged sword as a useful tool may be most pronounced in a context of DEI issues, which rarely are uncontroversial. On the one hand, social media platforms offer useful communication media for organizations to reach audiences—yet those audiences also can use social media as a platform for communicating messages designed to damage an organization's reputation. Both for-profit and nonprofit organizations forfeited the ability to maintain some modicum of control over messages communicated about its products and services with the introduction of social media platforms in the late 20th century.

In recent decades, perhaps the most controversial social media campaign involving DEI issues to backlash against a company was Pepsi's ad featuring model Kendall Jenner handing a can of Pepsi to a police officer during a protest event (Hogan, 2017). Many people remarked on the ad's explicit references to the #BlackLivesMatter movement and claimed the ad trivialized systemic racism (Pepper, 2022). The ad was designed to reach out to millennials and Pepsi pulled the ad following intense social media criticism (Handley, 2017).

Because social media platforms enable organizations to engage with, reach, persuade, and target diverse publics effectively, social media tools have been seamlessly integrated into marketing, public relations, and communication practices (Freberg, 2022). As communication tools, social media platforms enable organizations to build, maintain, and foster relationships with their publics (Luttrell, 2018) across a variety of backgrounds and perspectives. Social media platforms empower people to participate in conversations to an extent unseen previously among traditional media users (Freberg, 2022). However, when social media platforms are used as a weapon by publics and activist groups at relatively low cost for building coalitions against organizations (Mundt et al., 2018; Singer & Brooking, 2018), even seemingly minor episodes can spiral into full-blown crises. Therefore, it is important to listen to and respond to publics' concerns through social platforms.

DOI: 10.4324/9781003279129-10

Figure 7.1 Members of the #BlackLivesMatter movement were highly successful in using social media tools to organize protests in Miami, Florida, and other areas around the globe in 2020 to protest the murder of George Floyd.

This chapter explores DEI in a context of social media, including a background of how various social media platforms became popular throughout recent years. Then it covers how organizations can use social media platforms to reach out, connect, and engage with their diverse publics and why considering DEI in conjunction with social media matters. Numerous examples across varying industries are provided. Because publics expect organizations to take a stand and support a social issue that aligns with their values (Hill, 2023), conflict can emerge when organizations waffle, disagree, or choose not to engage. Finally, this chapter concludes with a discussion of issues that organizations must consider to incorporate DEI into their social media strategies. Some key strategies are recommended. Therefore, this chapter covers these key areas: 1) defining social media in a DEI context, 2) connecting with audiences of various social identity dimensions via social media, 3) capitalizing on insights into DEI on social media, 4) considerations for organizations using social media as part of DEI strategies, and 5) concluding thoughts.

Defining social media in a DEI context

A commonly accepted definition of *social media* refers to "activities, practices, and behavior among communities of people who gather online to share information, knowledge, and opinions using conversational media. Social media has become one of the most significant communication tools for both individuals and organizations and has become a mature, established, and vibrant profession in strategic communications over the years" (Freberg, 2022). Social media platforms, such as Facebook, Snapchat, Twitter, Instagram, Pinterest, WordPress, and LinkedIn, are used by more than two-thirds of internet users (Ortiz-Ospina, 2019). Social media includes online platforms, word-of-mouth forums such as blogs, company-sponsored discussion boards and chat rooms, consumer-to-consumer email, consumer product or service ratings websites and fora, internet discussion boards and fora, and social networking websites (Mangold & Faulds, 2009). These platforms are forms of social media that allow users to collect and exchange information through photos, videos, audio files, and content while also cultivating relationships (Luttrell, 2018). For example, some disabled community members use social media to socialize without leaving their houses. They manage their isolation and loneliness through social media platforms by meeting new people and making new friends (Jones, n.d.). Some people experiencing hearing impairments find social media to be an accessible communication vehicle since written communication may be the most accessible way to communicate for deaf people. Social media platforms provide a venue for them to communicate in text with anyone, without them necessarily needing to know sign language (Jones, n.d.).

Social media usage is popular and widespread—and many conversations involve DEI issues. Both organizations and individuals like using social media because these platforms are web- and mobile-based applications and have the power of user-generated content (Freberg, 2022). According to the Pew Research Center (2021), for many users, social media is part of their daily routine and seven in ten U.S. citizens use social media to connect with others, engage with news content, share information, and have fun. While 72% of the U.S. public uses some type of social media, YouTube and Facebook are the most widely used social media platforms (Pew Research Center, 2021). In recent years, there have been ongoing conversations about DEI on social media platforms, and individuals have more opportunities to connect with people of various backgrounds and from different parts of the world with whom they traditionally might never communicate (Thirlwall, 2019).

Among BIPOC communities, around three-quarters of African American/Black, Hispanic, and Asian users indicated that social media helps give a voice to underrepresented groups (Auxier, 2020). Conversational media are web-based applications that make it possible to create and easily transmit content in the form of words, pictures, video, and audio (Luttrell, 2018). Indeed, social media platforms serve as platforms for political engagement and social activism especially for African

American/Black Americans and will continue to be a critical political platform for them (Auxier, 2020).

For organizations, social media "amplified the power of consumer-to-consumer conversations in the marketplace by enabling one person to communicate with literally hundreds or thousands of other consumers quickly and with relatively little effort" (Mangold & Faulds, 2009, p. 361). The power of social media comes from its real-time content creation and the level of engagement it can offer to users across different platforms (Freberg, 2022). For example, social media platforms help young people, especially minorities and the poor to engage with politics. They have used social media platforms to convince others to join in protests such as the Arab Spring, the Occupy Wall Street movement, and the #BlackLivesMatter movement (Luttig & Cohen, 2016).

Over the years, various social media platforms have emerged and changed the world in terms of how individuals access information and organize political change (Ortiz-Ospina, 2019). Historically marginalized communities such as African American/Black and Latino/a young people can discuss and access information through social media networks devoted to young people of color (Luttig & Cohen, 2016). Facebook's parent company Meta Platforms manages the four largest social media platforms with over one billion monthly active users each including Facebook, WhatsApp, Facebook Messenger, and Instagram (Dixon, 2023b). For example, young people of color and low-SES youth can affect organizations and inspire social change through their use of Facebook and Twitter platforms which bypass traditional media gatekeepers (e.g., editors and photographers) and mobilize informal connected networks to exchange ideas and other content (Luttig & Cohen, 2016). Similarly, Black LinkedIn is thriving and brings African American/Black professionals together to be their authentic selves (Martin, 2020). Social video platforms such as YouTube and TikTok also have been gaining popularity among social media platforms (Statista, 2023). These social media platforms usually are available in multiple languages and allow users to connect rapidly with others across geographic and political borders (Dixon, 2023b; Freberg, 2022). For example, a Danish ad that encouraged people to think outside of preconceptions and stereotypes by promoting acceptance went viral on YouTube, with the English version of the video called "All That We Share" being viewed more than 9.4 million times online (*The Irish Times*, 2017).

Most of the top-ranked social media platforms originated in the U.S. However, Chinese social media platforms such as WeChat, QQ, and Douyin also have taken their place among mainstream social media platforms in their respective regions. Douyin is one of the most popular video-sharing applications in China has led to the platform releasing the international version called TikTok (Dixon, 2023b). TikTok was launched in 2017 and reached the milestone of three billion downloads worldwide in July 2021. The popular short video platform still ranks as one of the leading social media platforms both worldwide and in the U.S. (Ceci, 2023a) and is forecasted to reach approximately 2.25 billion users in 2027 (Ceci, 2023b). Dancing is one of the fundamental aspects of TikTok. Individuals create their own short dance videos and those videos spread among social media users quickly (Bleu, 2023).

The success of social media platforms underscores the importance of building, maintaining, and growing successful social media strategies for organizations in conjunction with building strong relationships across internal and external publics. Organizations acknowledge the importance of social media in their communication strategies because the social media phenomenon has changed how the world considers DEI and its importance.

Connecting with audiences of various social identity dimensions via social media

Attending to social media in the communication planning mix enables organizations to keep a commitment to DEI goals and to monitor the pulse of public opinion. In 2022, 99% of nonprofit organizations in the U.S. were using Facebook (Statista Research Department, 2023), 77% of small for-profit businesses used social media to connect with customers (Wong & Bottorff, 2023), and by 2021, 91.9% of U.S. companies larger than 100 employees used social media for marketing purposes (Dencheva, 2023). Yet, using social media as tools to connect with existing and new publics is not necessarily intuitive. Organizations and their communication practitioners must develop **social media competence.** There are many ways for organizations to use these social media platforms to reach out, connect, and engage with the diverse publics. For example, organizations can create their own social networking sites on Instagram and users can affiliate with them by following the organizations' Instagram page. For example, in June, which is Pride Month to celebrate LGBTQIA+ communities, organizations use their Instagram page to show their support. NYX Cosmetics, for instance, supports underground ballroom culture, a safe space for LGBTQIA+ community members to "strut their stuff," whereas UGG has used LGBTQIA+ celebrities such as entertainers like Lil Nas X and Hari Nef to host a virtual prom to demonstrate their Pride activism (Demeku, 2021, para. 14). In this way, brands can connect with LGBTQIA+ communities by using social media tools.

Organizations also take advantage of the rising popularity of TikTok to connect with Generation Z (aged 11–26) audiences among their publics. These short-form videos (usually music, dancing) are the most engaging type of content on social media today (Wong & Bottorff, 2023). For example, Chipotle Mexican Grill, the first major restaurant chain to have an official TikTok account, generated around 111,000 video submissions with their Lid Flip Challenge based on a real employee's distinctive burrito bowl assembly style. Chipotle partnered with Slovak internet personality David Dobrik to launch the challenge to celebrate Cinco de Mayo with free delivery for digital orders. In the first six days, videos resulted in 104 million views and a month later the Challenge had 230 million video views. Chipotle not only had record-breaking digital sales but also became one of the most followed brands on TikTok with millions of impressions including coverage on CNBC and BuzzFeed News (Morris, n.d.; Shorty Awards, n.d.). While such strategies may contribute to sales, it is less clear exactly how they enable organizations to address DEI goals, however.

Similarly, organizations increasingly rely on using online **influencers** to connect with publics online, yet despite popular rhetoric that digital platforms promote democratization and level the playing field, collective action among social media influencers is undermined by racial domination (Christin & Lu, 2023). **Influencer marketing** steadily has grown into a $21.1 billion industry (Santora, 2023), perhaps because 70% of teens trust influencers more than traditional celebrities and 49% of consumers depend on influencer recommendations (Digital Marketing Institute, 2021). Partnering with influencers can include going live with influencers on-site at conferences or specific social networking sites, inviting them as a guest on a podcast, creating new content for public consumption, writing a post or blog content, attending and creating content at events, providing reviews for products or services, and talking about the organization (Freberg, 2022). For example, Penguin Teen, a new imprint for young adult books, partnered with influencers in 2022 to promote the book *All My Rage*, a novel about a South-Asian American teenager (Gaillot, 2023).

Yet, inequities persist in social media influencer spheres and corporations are accused of taking advantage of young women and people of color as aspirational labor in a social media economy (e.g., Duffy, 2022). There exists a 29% racial pay gap between White/Caucasian and BIPOC influencers—with a 35% gap between Caucasian/White and African American/Black influencers (MSL, 2021). Overall, influencers of color are less likely than their Caucasian/White counterparts to receive monetary compensation (sometimes only receiving products/services) or be successful in negotiating with brands (Christin & Lu, 2023; Duffy, 2022). Also criticized are discrepancies on the part of the algorithms that social media platforms use. Instagram, TikTok, and others long have been suspected of suppressing African American/Black voices on their platforms (Steele, 2022). For example, TikTok recommends individual accounts to follow with profile pictures that match the same ethnicity/race, age, or facial features as those whom people already follow (Mellor, 2020). Clearly, degrees to which organizations are equitably paying influencers to promote their products and services has been widely criticized for being incongruous with DEI commitments and social media platforms themselves have work to do in hosting equal and inclusive virtual spaces.

Capitalizing on insights into DEI on social media

Too often, organizations primarily consider social media platforms as tools for generating profits more so than platforms for connecting with audiences for relationship building linked to organizations' DEI goals. Incorporating DEI attention into social media strategies enables organizations to capitalize upon insights into various cultures and experiences for the most inclusive messages and communication strategies (Freberg, 2022). Benefits include enabling for-profit organizations to increase product/service sales and sometimes benefits include enabling nonprofit organizations' fundraising efforts. When organizations' communication practitioners consider DEI in social media communication strategies, they should form internal teams of individuals whose social identity dimensions mirror those of publics central to the organization's goals/mission/vision. Taking extra steps necessary to *match* communicators with audience members supports best listening

Figure 7.2 Organizations must form internal teams of individuals whose intersecting social identity dimensions mirror those of publics central to the organization's goals/mission/vision.

practices and decision making required for selecting which social media influencers to contract, which social media platforms to tap, and more.

With regard to communication planning processes inside organizations, communication practitioners must change the organizational mindset. Whereas some organizations once considered attention to marginalized publics as a *last-minute* or *add-on adjunct* to regular communication planning processes, DEI-committed organizations consider DEI *regularly as part of* ongoing operations (e.g., Wallace & Luttrell, 2021). This shift in organizational mindset is necessary for tangibly proving organizations' DEI commitment with action. Organizations that stress attention to and respectfully consider DEI can avoid many of the painful reminders of mistakes made by organizations in the past.

While it seems probable that in modern times organizations can avoid embarrassing themselves and hurting others, that simply is not the case. Clearly, organizations and their communication practitioners still have much to learn. Here are just a few recent episodes underscoring this advice. Communication planners must do better than H&M's "Coolest Monkey of the Jungle" ad featuring an African American/Black boy modeling a hoodie (Stack, 2018), Gucci's *blackface* sweater featuring a blonde Caucasian/White model modeling a black turtleneck with a bright red lip cut out (Held, 2019), and Dolce and Gabbana's ad included an Asian woman eating pizza with chopsticks (Xu, 2018). These ads created a firestorm of outrage and backlash across social media, forcing the retailers to apologize and withdraw the ads or products. Yet, exactly how these incidents could occur in the first place in modern times—given for-profit organizations' access to resources for building employee bases featuring people representing multiple intersecting social identity dimensions and the ability to copy test messaging materials for feedback prior to their external release—means there are no excuses.

Overall, organizations must work with people across communities to ensure messages are consistent with organizational goals but will not cause harm or disrespect people. For example, the U.S. educational children's television series *Sesame Street* long has embracing diversity and inclusion with its Muppets (Pittman, 2017). On *Sesame Street's* online Digital Storybook series, TV, and social media platforms, Julia is a Muppet with autism who does things a bit differently, and that's OK (Papenfuss, 2017) to increase acceptance and inclusion for reduced bias about autism (Papenfuss, 2017; Paynter, 2019; Suskind, 2017). The Sesame Workshop's online initiative See Amazing in All Children educates people about autism for increased acceptance (Anthony et al., 2020). To discover more about how the social media platform LinkedIn introduced the option for members to list their pronouns by creating a more inclusive environment, check out Sidebar 7.1.

Sidebar 7.1 LinkedIn—redefining what it means to be professional

Tugce Ertem-Eray

When the best social media site for business networking (How LinkedIn succeeded as the best social media site for business networking, n.d.) introduced an option enabling members to list their preferred pronouns, rather than relying on the social media platform's users to guess gender based on a photograph, female-sounding, or male-sounding given names, LinkedIn created an inclusive virtual environment for its members. LinkedIn amplified respect for people working in the modern workplace by introducing a new feature for overcoming traditional norms created by the gender binary.

Today, the LinkedIn social media platform boasts 950 million members in more than 200 countries and territories around the globe (LinkedIn, n.d.) LinkedIn's goal is to connect like-minded business professionals as they network by applying and recruiting for jobs and get the latest business-to-business news from organizations across the world. The site launched the pronoun option in conjunction with a What Does it Mean to be Professional campaign to "explore how the modern workforce is changing" (Hutchinson, 2021, para. 5; Wright, 2022). The importance of representation in the workplace gets to the heart of inclusivity in DEI goals. LinkedIn addressed how being *professional* always meant more than how employees look, sound, or their credentials.

Being professional often means employees feel, think, act, and show up differently when they are at work (Ormes, 2021), a consideration for the now-common platform of working from home. The Covid-19 pandemic merged public and private spheres and it became impossible for individuals to offer their partial selves. Thus, LinkedIn launched a campaign indicating what being professional really means by creating inclusive spaces and culture to honor everyone with their unique experiences and perspectives (Ormes, 2021). Its goal is to make the social media site "more inclusive for every member of the global workforce" (Henderson, 2021, para. 3).

The social media platform introduced the option for its members to list their pronouns, such as she/her, he/him, they/them, or select custom pronouns, on their LinkedIn profile and allowed them to share how they wanted to be identified in the United States, Britain, Sweden, Canada, and Ireland (Greenhalgh, 2021; Ormes, 2021). According to LinkedIn (Ormes, 2021), since the company introduced the option, more than 6 million members used this feature and are now sharing their pronouns on their LinkedIn profiles.

LinkedIn considers users' profiles as more than just a career highlight page. Rather, users' profiles offer space where they can share their own stories, and represent who they really are. This could help users show their authentic selves—which plays a fundamental role in acknowledging and appreciating one another, particularly those who may not identify with traditional norms created by the gender binary (Ormes, 2021). Other LinkedIn features that help members feel as though they belong include adding their name pronunciation, updating their profile pictures, and adding a cover story video where they can introduce themselves to other members or employers—or offer other individual touches (Henderson, 2021; Wright, 2022).

This new campaign is seen as an important initiative that indicates how the modern workforce is changing and how important it is to respect all intersecting social identity dimensions. This campaign highlighted the importance of providing a safe place for all to be their authentic selves. As a social media platform for business, LinkedIn took the lead in showing the changing perceptions of work and professional representation (Hutchinson, 2021). Considering pronoun usage potentially reduces the risk of disrespecting people, creating an inclusive environment for those beyond the gender binary.

Resources

Greenhalgh, H. (2021, March 30). LinkedIn embraces global trend for gender pronouns option on profiles. Reuters. https://www.reuters.com/article/us-tech-lgbt-linkedin-trfn/linkedin-embraces-global-trend-for-gender-pronouns-option-on-profiles-idUSKBN2BM2EX/. Accessed September 6, 2023.

Henderson, T. (2021, March 30). You can now add pronouns to your LinkedIn profile. *Pride*. https://www.pride.com/news/2021/3/30/you-can-now-add-pronouns-your-linkedin-profile. Accessed September 6, 2023.

How LinkedIn succeeded as the best social media site for business networking (n.d.) MaRS. Downloaded December 1, 2023 from https://learn. marsdd.com/article/how-linkedin-succeeded-as-the-best-social-media-site-for-business-networking/.

Hutchinson, A. (2021, December 21). LinkedIn launches new campaign to highlight the importance of representation in the workplace. *Social Media Today*. https://www.socialmediatoday.com/news/linkedin-launches-new-campaign-to-highlight-the-importance-of-representatio/616437/ Downloaded. December 1, 2023.

Katz-Wise, S. L. (2021, July 23). Misgendering: What it is and why it matters. *Harvard Health Publishing*. https://www.health.harvard.edu/blog/misgen dering-what-it-is-and-why-it-matters-202107232553. Accessed August 2, 2023.

Macready, H. (2023, February 22). 47 LinkedIn statistics you need to know in 2023. Hootsuite. https://www.linkedin.com/posts/hannah-macready_51-linkedin-statistics-you-need-to-know-in-activity-703966516251719 2704-_DJM. Accessed September 6, 2023.

Ormes, M. (2021, December 21). Redefining what it means to be professional. LinkedIn. https://www.linkedin.com/blog/member/career/redefining-what-it-means-to-be-professional. Accessed September 6, 2023.

Wright, W. (2022, January 24). LinkedIn redefines what it means to be a 'professional' with new campaign. https://www.thedrum.com/news/2022/01/24/linkedin-redefines-what-it-means-be-professional-with-new-campaign. Accessed September 6, 2023.

Some for-profit organizations have sought a social media spotlight for embracing DEI. U.S.-based sporting goods manufacturer, Nike, for instance, has launched films on YouTube to emphasize barriers female athletes encounter (Kantli, 2018) and signed a multi-year deal with former NFL quarterback-turned-activist Colin Kaepernick, making him the face of the company's Just Do It campaign's 30th anniversary (Draper & Belson, 2018; Ebrahimji, 2020). U.S.-based ice cream manufacturer Ben & Jerry's has been involved in social activism for decades (McKinnon, 2021), using social media platforms to support causes such as voting among youth, sponsoring The Martin Luther King, Jr. Center Annual Salute to Greatness Award (Morris, 2021), being vocal about "inhumane police brutality" in George Floyd's murder (McKinnon, 2021, para. 5), and supporting transgender people and #PrideMonth (Ben & Jerry's, 2020). McNeil Laboratories used its Tylenol brand to celebrate diverse families across social media with #HowWeFamily and images including an immigrant family and an LGBTQ couple (Stigliano-Waite, n.d.).

Organizations that hire a diverse workforce (including the communication team), listen to and consult with external and internal publics, and contract with influencers representing multiple and intersecting social identity dimensions are but a few steps organizations may take to actually be authentic in a DEI commitment. Putting mission and vision statements into action creates an inclusive and respectful environment for everyone, making audiences feel as though they belong. Outcomes can include strengthening trust and building organizational reputation among publics. These insights into DEI should be considered highly valuable—beyond just using social media platforms to generate sales or raise funds simply because an organization states that it supports DEI.

Considerations for organizations using social media as part of DEI strategies

Despite cases of organizations making significant mistakes with their communication materials, as mentioned above, there *are* organizations adopting fresh, positive mindsets about DEI—as evidenced by taking action in building authentic relationships rather than focusing exclusively on the financial bottom line. In today's communication climate, it is more critical than ever that organizations pay attention to the social media landscape in order to connect with both internal and external audiences in conjunction with relationship building when promoting products and services—amidst numerous challenges ranging from digital inequalities, biased technology emerging from the tech industry, and cyberbullying, to digital activism. This chapter now focuses on each of these.

Digital inequalities

First, the **digital divide** phenomenon characterizing a "the gap between those who have and do not have access to computers and the internet" (van Dijk, 2006, p. 221) is highly relevant to organizations' communication practitioners who work to ensure that no public is marginalized. Recognizing that a digital divide exists, excluding certain socio-economic status (SES) groups (including those also defined by ethnicity/race, disability, and more), is a significant disadvantage for people and organizations, as explored in this section. Before the concept was applied to social media, digital divide applied exclusively to economic and geographic disparity in distribution of information technology (IT) in all its forms among people who use and need it (e.g., Eubanks, 2011). The concept is rooted in the work of American sociologist, Robert K. Merton, who philosophized that the rich get richer and the poor get poorer (Merton, 1968).

Access and misunderstandings can represent different sides of a coin in the digital world. Regarding social media engagement, some people simply neither have access to the internet, nor do they have access to communication technologies for accessing the internet (Castells, 2002). Moreover, access alone is not enough since some people are ill equipped to critically discern all that is available (Scheerder et al., 2017). Organizations and their communication teams must be savvy enough to realize that there are varying levels of online skills among users (Hargittai, 2002) to avoid assuming that audiences have access to and can fully understand or use messages (Wei et al., 2011). So, even if there are no inequalities in terms of digital skills or internet usage, this does not mean everyone has positive or beneficial outcomes (Scheerder et al., 2017). For example, digital communication technologies have not solved problems of access and full inclusion for people with disabilities since speech-to-text technology used to assist communities who are deaf or experience hearing impairments often feature inaccuracies such as when YouTube's auto caption feature makes errors (e.g., Ellcessor, 2017).

Social media accessibility means creating social media posts that provide a smooth, all-encompassing experience for everyone (Hill, 2023), including people with disabilities, people of multiple cultural backgrounds, people using languages other than English, and people with unique needs (Wong, 2023). More than 40 million people in the U.S. have a disability, with 62% of adults with a disability indicating that they own a desktop or laptop, and 72% indicating that they use a smartphone (Perrin & Atske, 2021). If organizations do not consider disabilities communities as part of their social media strategies, they cannot create inclusive social media campaigns. Moreover, to create inclusive, accessible social media posts, organizations should include alt-texts that provide informative word descriptions of images (Hill, 2023), add captions or subtitles for video posts (Wong, 2023), use emojis consistent with assigned descriptions (Hill, 2023) that could be mistranslated by screen readers (Dakessian, 2022), and check color contrasts (Wong, 2023). Following these steps, which may feel like extra work, quite simply enables people to feel included.

Biased technology and the tech industry

Organizations also have to be aware of built-in biases across the tech industry—ageism, racism, sexism—when they design and implement social media strategies. The tech industry and its products are built on biases that can marginalize people, alienate them, and insult them (Wachter-Boettcher, 2017). For example, in 2015 the Apple Watch marketing team partnered with a fashion brand to design a woman's smartwatch, but there was only one woman on the team. In the end, the smartwatch was designed based on stereotypes about women rather than women's actual needs and the product failed (Wachter-Boettcher, 2017).

Rather, when organizations are workspaces where multiple and intersecting social identities are respected—as consistent with advice offered in Chapter 3, "How intersectionality in social identity works . . . at work"—communication teams can create social media strategies that embrace DEI and respectfully communicate among publics who are made to feel as though they belong. For example, Procter & Gamble (P&G) launched a My Black is Beautiful (MBIB) community-building program created by African American/Black women in 2007 (Public Relations Society of America, 2018). The MBIB program included an ad about African American/Black mothers talking to their children about race and racial bias in society (Chhut, 2019), generating widespread conversations across social media platforms and traditional news fora (P&G, n.d.), and winning the Cannes Lions Grand Prix award (Fenton, 2018). Part of the campaign's success can be attributed to P&G's conducting interviews with its African American/Black employees (Public Relations Society of America, 2018) whose voices were heard and respected from campaign inception through implementation.

Cyberbullying

Organizations' communication practitioners must proactively consider **cyberbullying**, hate speech, and other forms of abuse and toxicity—effects perpetuated across social media platforms by working consciously to avoid inadvertently promoting or encouraging such outcomes on their social media platforms and in their workspaces. Over the last decade, with the increase in internet traffic and introduction of new platforms, social media have become one of the most common tools for cyberbullying—such as sending unkind messages or posting inappropriate images (Giumetti & Kowalski, 2022). Nearly half of American teens indicate that they have been cyberbullied or harassed online (Teens, 2022). Moreover, African American/Black teens perceive that their race or ethnicity makes them a cyberbullying target (Vogels, 2022).

Given that so many people work remotely today, the use of meeting applications, videoconferencing, and social media platforms to connect with co-workers and managers can amplify conditions conducive to cyberbullying effects (Conn, 2020). Too often, cyberbullying targets people's gender, ethnicity/race, sexual orientation, and social identity dimensions—as well as other physical attributes, or personality features, and political opinions (e.g., Breitsohl et al., 2022; Sterner & Felmlee, 2017). Cyberbullying effects via social media can feel more severe since posts stay longer and individuals sometimes mask behind anonymity and feel less accountable/restrained in computer-mediated situations (e.g., Breitsohl et al., 2022). For example, when Nike posted on its Facebook page about a new video commercial some users made offensive comments offending others such as "What country are you from? I am sure your country people are not all as ignorant as you" (Breitsohl et al., 2022, p. 1). Therefore, organizations' communication teams must work diligently to protect internal and external publics from cyberbullying, hate speech, and other forms of abuse and toxicity.

There are some steps that organizations can take to prevent and combat cyberbullying via social media. Organizations can start by establishing zero-tolerance policies and by creating and updating their anti-bullying policies (Jorgensen, 2023). Organizations must educate and train employees to teach them what cyberbullying is to make them understand how to identify it. Employees are more likely to report cyberbullying if there are clear explanations and understanding of what cyberbullying includes (Jorgensen, 2023). Organizations should define what behaviors comprise cyberbullying on social media such as posting or sharing negative, harmful, false, or mean content about someone, as well as digital discrimination—including strategically leaving certain people out of the conversation (Conn, 2020). Moreover, organizations have to be quick to react to complaints and concerns (Conn, 2020), recognizing that the fastest option is blocking social media users within a few clicks. The next step would be compiling documentation and reporting the user to social media platforms (Pavlovic, n.d.). Overall, organizations have to show their publics that they are taking care of people by ensuring safety on digital platforms (Jorgensen, 2023).

Digital activism

Social media platforms offer fora for advocacy and organizing among activist groups, especially among young people (Internet Matters, 2022). Publics expect organizations to take a stand on issues that matter to them, so social media activism is no longer optional for organizations (Newberry & Reid, 2022). Digital activism involves actions people take online via Instagram, Facebook, Twitter, and TikTok to share and discuss degrees of support for social causes, as well as to raise funds for battling social injustices (Auxier, 2020; Internet Matters, 2022). The use of hashtags enables online communicators to find one another online and to coalesce. The **digital activism** term often is used interchangeably with **hashtag activism** (Newberry & Reid, 2022). According to Auxier (2020), about one-third of social media users indicate that they have used social media platforms in the past month to post a picture to support a social cause, searched for information about rallies or protests happening in their area, and encouraged people to stand for an issue important to them.

Hashtag activism dynamics played out globally throughout the COVID-19 pandemic and some organizations have participated, too—by posting hashtags on their social media platforms, as well as issuing statements, and more. Several hashtag activism labels have emerged in recent years, including the ALS #IceBucketChallenge, #ArabSpring, #LoveWins, #MeToo, and #BlackLivesMatter. As one of the most popular hashtag activist movements in internet history so far, the #BlackLivesMatter movement spotlighted racism, violence, and an unjust criminal justice system. Introduced in 2013 following George Zimmerman's acquittal in the shooting death of Trayvon Martin in Florida, hashtag use peaked in the summer of 2020 following the murder of George Floyd by Minneapolis police officer Derek Chauvin (Bestvater et al., 2023). Brands such as Nike, Airbnb, Lego, Glossier, and Sephora, publicly supported the #BlackLivesMatter movement by using the hashtag on their social media platforms (Collins, n.d.), while other organizations issued solidarity statements, made financial contributions, and offered fund-matching for equality education programs. As the world assessed the pain and widespread harm personified by the #BlackLivesMatter movement reaction to discrimination, some organizations showed deeper sensitivity. For example, Lego communicated via Twitter that it had paused marketing for building sets and products that included police characters or are based around a police theme and the White House (Handley, 2020). Netflix also added a Black Lives Matter collection, featuring films and TV shows made by African American/Black filmmakers (Molnár, 2020).

Yet, organizations must use caution when engaging in social media activism because if its past or present actions fail to align with statements, this could contribute to speedy social media backlash (Newberry & Reid, 2022). Enraged publics and activist groups may use an organization's history at *any time* as a weapon to build coalitions against organizations (Liu & Pompper, 2012; Mundt et al., 2018; Singer & Brooking, 2018). For example, the world's largest coffee retailer, Starbucks (2020, 2021), is not immune to social media backlash even though it features statements about its DEI commitment on all its social media platforms, website, and blog. After two African American/Black men were arrested for waiting in a Philadelphia store in 2018 after a worker asked them to leave because they were not making a purchase (Swann, 2020), a 45-second video showing police handcuffing the men was on Twitter received millions of views. The Starbucks employee's action did not align with the organization's statements. Within hours, hashtags "Too Little, Too Latte," "Coffee is Black! Not Blonde," "#BoycottStarbucks," "#BlackLivesMatter" led to Starbucks apologizing and implementing new employee training procedures (Swann, 2020). When an organization promotes itself as embracing DEI, its actions must be consistent across all contexts.

Organizations that appear inconsistent in their DEI support also set themselves up to become social media activism targets. Communication practitioners must reflect on their organization's culture and values before posting anything on social media to avoid an appearance of contradiction (Newberry & Reid, 2022). For example, Disney stayed silent in response to Florida's legislators in conjunction with the Don't Say Gay bill in 2022—yet sent out an internal email to support its LGBTQ+ employees. This dynamic inspired the hashtag #DisneyDoBetter, employees and fans shared their concerns about Disney's position, and made a lengthy public statement indicating its support for the LGBTQ+ community (Newberry & Reid, 2022). Organizations must be consistent in communications across platforms both internally and externally as part of a DEI commitment.

Another key consideration for organizations using social media as part of DEI strategies is to ensure that the organization's actions speak louder than mere social media hashtag use. Real DEI is authentic and honest, with efforts helmed by leader-allies who create DEI-commitment-shaped workspaces filled with a workforce featuring intersecting social identity dimensions reflective of publics that the organization serves. For example, organizations that amplify hashtags while taking little or no action to ensure DEI across all spheres of its influence may be guilty of **slacktivism** because they do not show true commitment to supporting DEI with action. Across social media platforms, organizations must align the language it uses in posts with the language it uses in its DEI statements. Moreover, organizations can measure their DEI goals and report on results (Pompper, 2015), as well as include links to DEI initiatives in social media posts to underscore support and commitment to social issues (Ragan, 2021). Read Sidebar 7.1 to learn more about how the United Nations (UN) Women Australia used TikTok to promote gender equality and women's empowerment around the world.

Sidebar 7.2   United Nations Women Australia empowers TikTok campaign

Tugce Ertem-Eray

With its connective power to link diverse publics—and by using dance as a common language—the social media platform TikTok successfully has attracted organizations' attention, too. This case study explores how United Nations (UN) Women Australia used TikTok to promote gender equality and women's empowerment around the world—one dance video at a time.

Social media platforms have become one of the most powerful communication tools for organizations to build, maintain, and foster relationships with their publics. TikTok has taken its place among mainstream social media platforms (Statista, 2023), amplifying the social media platform's ability to link diverse publics despite geographic, political, and economic borders (Dixon, 2023). One of the fundamental features of TikTok is dancing. Users create their own short dance videos and those videos spread from person to person quickly (Bleu, 2023).

In 2021, the UN Women in Australia launched a new TikTok dance campaign with the hashtag #EmpowerMoves. United Nations Women promotes gender equality and women's empowerment around the world. United Nations Women was established in 2010 to meet the needs of women and girls globally. It aims to expand women's leadership and participation, stop all forms of violence and discrimination against women, and stop poverty by enhancing women's economic empowerment and responding to crises. Women's needs and talents remain at the center of the organization's planning and response (UN Women Australia, n.d.). #EmpowerMoves was not just another TikTok dance.

The #EmpowerMoves dance was carefully choreographed with basic self-defense actions so that girls can show their strength and support for a future that is safe, equal, and empowered (Green, 2021). UN Women Australia's #EmpowerMoves campaign invited girls to celebrate International Day of the Girl, founded by the UN in 2011 to address the challenges girls face and to encourage their empowerment (Cameron, 2021). Creating a dance using TikTok amplified female voices in support of a strong and equal future for themselves (UN Women Australia, 2021).

Girls were invited to film and share their own dance sequences on TikTok using the hashtags #EmpowerMoves and #Dayofthegirl (Cameron, 2021; Cheik-Hussein, 2021). UN Women Australia CEO Simone Clarke said:

> The challenges girls face are unrelenting, some we could have never imagined, but they are resilient and deserve to celebrate their strength. When the world is safe and equal for girls—we will dance for joy. Until then, girls can dance to be fierce, dance to be powerful, and dance to show their voice for the equality they deserve.
> (UN Women Australia, 2021, para. 4)

TikTok influencers and media personalities joined the movement and the song became #3 on the viral TikTok chart. Australian singer-songwriter Wafia, choreographer and entrepreneur Karla Mura, and She Fights Back self-defense classes came together to create a series of basic self-defense movements such as block, roll under, and resist (Cameron, 2021). The #EmpowerMoves campaign generated earned media coverage with a huge ROI. It also had 130 million video views globally, 62 million total reach, and 59 million unique users globally (The Monkeys, n.d.).

The UN Women Australia had a message to share with its audience and knew they could be reached via TikTok. Through the #EmpowerMoves campaign on TikTok, the organization not only amplified its mission, promoted gender equality and empowerment of women around the world, but also reached out to worldwide publics across geographical, political, or economic borders.

Resources

Bleu, N. (2023, July 13). 20 top TikTok video ideas your audience will love (with examples). https://bloggingwizard.com/tiktok-video-ideas/. Accessed August 23, 2023.

Cameron, N. (2021, October 11). Self-defence TikTok dance from UN Women aims for empowerment. CMO. https://www.cmo.com.au/article/691961/self-defence-tiktok-dance-from-un-women-aims-empowerment/. Accessed September 7, 2023.

Cheik-Hussein, M. (2021, October 11). TikTok dance incorporates self-defence moves to mark International Day of the Girl. AdNews. https://www.adnews.com.au/news/tiktok-dance-incorporates-self-defence-moves-to-mark-international-day-of-the-girl. Accessed September 7, 2023.

Dixon, S. J. (2023, February 14). Global social networks ranked by number of users 2023. Statista. https://www.statista.com/statistics/272014/global-social-networks-ranked-by-number-of-users/. Accessed August 22, 2023.

Green, R. (2021, October 11). UN Women Australia launches new TikTok dance campaign #EmpowerMoves via the Monkeys. Campaign Brief. https://shorturl.at/svPQ4 Accessed September 7, 2023.

McLachlan, S. (2022, November 23). 7 inspirational social media campaigns. Hootsuite. https://shorturl.at/cxNR2. Accessed September 7, 2023.

Statista. (2023). Social media & user-generated content. https://www.statista.com/markets/424/topic/540/social-media-user-generated-content/#overview. Accessed August 22, 2023.

The Monkeys, (n.d.). Case study: Empower Moves UN Women Australia https://new.awardshowjury.com/empower-moves/. Accessed September 7, 2023.

UN Women Australia. (2021, October 8). #EmpowerMoves more than just another TikTok dance, reveals UN Women Australia. https://unwomen.org.au/empowermoves-more-than-just-another-tiktok-dance-reveals-un-women-australia/. Accessed September 7, 2023.

UN Women Australia. (n.d.) About us. https://unwomen.org.au/about-us/. Accessed September 7, 2023.

A final key consideration offered here for organizations using social media as part of DEI strategies is to make sure multiple voices and opinions are consulted, heard, and included. Leadership needs to reflect on what they do not know about marginalized communities (Tulshyan, 2022) and listen to their employees to understand the perspectives they are missing to create inclusive social media strategies. As mentioned throughout this book, when deep listening happens, audiences consider themselves partners in achieving shared goals (Place, 2019). Listening also helps organizations not to rush or put out a statement via social media before evaluating all of the facts (Freberg, 2022). For example, the chief communications officer for the Pacific Council on International Policy in Los Angeles pondered whether or not to add a picture of a lotus flower to an official statement about hate crimes against the Asian American/Pacific Islander community. Asking a member of the organization's communication team—who identifies as an Asian American/Pacific Island community member—had first-hand experience with the cultural importance of the lotus and advised that adding the image would be appropriate (Ragan, 2021).

Hence, creating social media campaigns that are sensitive to DEI may be among the most important duties of a communications practitioner who has a responsibility to the organization, as well as society as a whole.

Concluding thoughts

Social media platforms and tools exponentially have increased in importance among a communication practitioner's kit. Not having a social media account is no longer an option for organizations who want to build belongingness among their publics because there are 4.8 billion social media users worldwide (Nyst, 2023). Moreover, social media platforms are constantly changing and organizations need to adjust their communication efforts accordingly to stay in touch across internal and external publics.

There are so many ways for organizations to use social media as tools for communicating with publics—yet there is no room for *automatic pilot thinking*, given the numerous considerations necessary for organizations to ensure their social media engagement is authentic and honest. Perhaps the very best first step is for organizations to make sure they actually feature

DEI among their employees, including the social media team. All social identity dimensions must be included, with special consideration of ways social identities intersect. Social media communication teams must listen to both internal and external publics, considering effects of digital inequalities, biased technology, cyberbullying, digital activism, and accessibility issues. Considering DEI at the outset of communication planning rather than thinking of DEI as something that is tacked on can go a long way in ensuring authentic DEI attention across social media strategies, messages, implementation, and measurement. This work will enable communication team members to think deeply about their own privilege, ferret out bias, and intentionally include DEI thinking in all aspects of communication work (Luttrell & Capizzo, 2022). Organizations need to show what they are actively doing to make DEI a reality—via social media and beyond.

Next, Chapter 8, "Future directions for developing competence as a DEI change manager" offers summary conclusions and recommendations for helping communicators serve as consultants to organizations with regard to DEI.

Key words

Cyberbullying—Cyberbullying is "an aggressive, intentional act carried out by a group or individual, using electronic forms of contact, repeatedly and over time against a victim who cannot easily defend him or herself" (Smith et al., 2008, p. 376).

Digital activism—Digital activism involves using technology such as social media, email, and websites as a form of activism that helps users spread awareness and information about political or social issues (Internet Matters, 2022).

Digital divide—The digital divide, simply, is the gap between those with computer and internet access and those without it. But it is multifaceted and includes many other factors including access, affordability, quality of service, relevance, and digital literacy (Muller & Aguiar, 2022).

Hashtag activism—Hashtag activism is "discursive protest on social media united through a hashtagged word, phrase, or sentence" (Yang, 2016, p. 13). Individuals use hashtags to bring attention to social issues and mobilize publics to take action about the social issue (Ofori-Parku & Moscato, 2018).

Influencer—An influencer is someone who is seen as an authority and has knowledge, position, or relationships with the publics on a specific subject in online spaces to affect the decisions of the publics (Geyser, 2023).

Influencer marketing—Influencer marketing is a practice that involves partnering with people who will help an organization to market its products or services (Geyser, 2023).

Slactivism—Slactivism means a practice of supporting a social cause online such as on social media in ways that involve very little effort (Wigmore, n.d.).

Social media—The *Oxford English Dictionary* (n.d.) defines social media as "websites and applications that enable users to create and share content or to participate in social networking." "Social" refers to the need that individuals have to connect with others whereas "media" refers to the channels through which individuals connect with others (Luttrell, 2018). Social media provides tools for building and maintaining relationships and also allows users to generate content to share with others (Freberg, 2022).

Social media accessibility—Social media accessibility is the ability of a social media application or content to be easily navigated and understood by a wide range of users, including individuals with visual, auditory, motor, or cognitive disabilities (Patrizio, n.d.).

Social media competence—Social media competence refers to how an organization effectively uses social media platforms to connect, interact, and promote trusting relationships with its publics (Luttrell, 2018).

Discussion questions for deep engagement

1. What is your favorite organization that integrates DEI into its social media accounts? Specifically, what does DEI integration there look like?
2. What is your favorite social media campaign that successfully models DEI strategies? Specifically, what does DEI modeling look like in that campaign?
3. What are the challenges and opportunities associated with reaching out to diverse publics on social media?
4. Analyze a recent social media campaign to see whether or not the social media campaign attends to *intersecting* social identity dimensions. How is intersectionality explained or represented?
5. What should organizations do and what should organizations avoid doing on their social media platforms to authentically support a controversial social issue?

Resources

Anthony, B. J., Robertson, H. A., Verbalis, A., Myrick, Y., Troxel, M., Seese, S., & Anthony, L. G. (2020). Increasing autism acceptance: The impact of the Sesame Street "See Amazing in All Children" initiative. *Autism*, 24(1), 95–108. https://doi.org/10.1177/1362361319847927.

Auxier, B. (2020, July 13). Activism on social media varies by race and ethnicity, age, political party. Pew Research Center. https://www.pewresearch.org/short-reads/2020/07/13/activism-on-social-media-varies-by-race-and-ethnicity-age-political-party/. Accessed August 31, 2023.

Auxier, B. (2020, December 11). Social media continue to be important political outlets for Black Americans. Pew Research Center. https://www.pewresearch.org/short-reads/2020/12/11/social-media-continue-to-be-important-political-outlets-for-black-americans/. Accessed September 8, 2023.

Beard, A. (2021, January 13). Why Ben & Jerry's speaks out. *Harvard Business Review*. https://hbr.org/2021/01/why-ben-jerrys-speaks-out. Accessed August 29, 2023.

Ben & Jerry's. (2020, June 23). The criminal justice system has failed transgender Americans. Learn more and take action at the link in our bio! #PrideMonth. Instagram. https://www.instagram.com/p/CByCiMJn0Bz/. Accessed August 29, 2023.

Bestvater, S., Gelles-Watnick, R., Odabaş, M., Anderson, M., & Smith, A. (2023, June 29). #BlackLivesMatter Turns 10. Social media, online activism and 10 years of #BlackLivesMatter. Pew Research Center. https://www.pewresearch.org/internet/2023/06/29/blacklivesmatter-turns-10/#fn-30023-1. Accessed August 31, 2023.

Bleu, N. (2023, July 13). 20 top TikTok video ideas your audience will love (with examples). https://bloggingwizard.com/tiktok-video-ideas/. Accessed August 23, 2023.

Braverman, B. (2016). The digital divide: How income inequality is affecting literacy instruction, and what all educators can do to help close the gap. *Literacy Today*, 33(4), 16–20.

Breitsohl, J., Jimenez, N., & Roschk, H. (2022). Investigating consumers' motives for consumer brand-cyberbullying on social media. *The Information Society: An International Journal*, 38(1), 1–12. https://doi.org/10.1080/01972243.2021.1981507.

Ceci, L. (2023a, July 14). TikTok – statistics & facts. Statista. https://www.statista.com/topics/6077/tiktok/#topicOverview Accessed August 22, 2023.

Ceci, L. (2023b, April 6). Global TikTok users 2018–2027. Statista. https://www.statista.com/forecasts/1142687/tiktok-users-worldwide. Accessed August 22, 2023.

Chhut, C. (2019, September 12). What video marketers can learn from 7 Emmy nominated commercials. https://www.cambodiaproperty.info/what-video-marketers-can-learn-from-7-emmy-nominated-commercials/. Accessed August 29, 2023.

Christin, A., & Lu, Y. (2023). The influencer pay gap: Platform labor meets racial capitalism. *New Media & Society*. https://doi.org/10.1177/14614448231164995.

Collins, B. (n.d.). Black Lives Matter: Brands who are doing it right. *The Marketing Society*. https://www.marketingsociety.com/blog-post/black-lives-matter-brands-who-are-doing-it-right. Accessed August 31, 2023.

Conn, R. (2020, December 10). 6 ways to combat cyberbullying and digital discrimination in the workplace. Applied. https://www.beapplied.com/post/6-ways-to-combat-cyberbullying-and-digital-discrimination-in-the-workplace. Accessed August 30, 2023.

Dakessian, D. (2022, January 28). A guide to social media accessibility. World Institute on Disability. https://wid.org/a-guide-to-social-media-accessibility/. Accessed September 1, 2023.

Demeku, A. (2021, May 28). 3 pride events to take note of this year on social media. Later Blog. https://later.com/blog/pride-events/. Accessed September 11, 2023.

Dencheva, V. (2023). Social media market usage rate in the United States from 2013 to 2022. Statista. Downloaded December 1, 2023 from https://www.statista.com/statistics/203513/usage-trands-of-social-media-platforms-in-marketing/.

Digital Marketing Institute. (2021, October 19). 20 surprising influencer marketing statistics. https://digitalmarketinginstitute.com/blog/20-influencer-marketing-statistics-that-will-surprise-you. Accessed August 24, 2023.

Dixon, S. J. (2023a, August 22). Facebook: quarterly number of MAU (monthly active users) worldwide 2008–2023. Statista. https://www.statista.com/statistics/264810/number-of-monthly-active-facebook-users-worldwide/. Accessed August 22, 2023.

Dixon, S. J. (2023b, February 14). Global social networks ranked by number of users 2023. Statista. https://www.statista.com/statistics/272014/global-social-networks-ranked-by-number-of-users/. Accessed August 22, 2023.

Draper, K., & Belson, K. (2018, September 3). Colin Kaepernick's Nike campaign keeps N.F.L. anthem kneeling in spotlight. *The New York Times*. https://www.nytimes.com/2018/09/03/sports/kaepernick-nike.html. Accessed August 8, 2023.

Duffy, B. E. (2022). *(Not) getting paid to do what you love: Gender and aspirational labor in the social media economy*. Yale University Press.

Ebrahimji, A. (2020, May 30). Nike is saying 'Don't Do It' in a message about racism in America. CNN. https://www.cnn.com/2020/05/30/business/nike-dont-do-it-message-trnd/index.html. Accessed August 24, 2023.

Ellcessor, E. (2017). *Restricted access: Media, disability, and the politics of participation*. Sage.

Eubanks, V. (2011). *Digital dead end: Fighting for social justice in the information age*. The MIT Press.

Fanbytes. (n.d.). Which brands delivered their Black Lives Matter promises? (A black history month 2021 review). https://fanbytes.co.uk/black-lives-matter-black-history-month. Accessed August 31, 2023.

Fenton. (2018, June 25). Cannes Lions 2018: Unleashing creativity for the greater good. https://www.canneslions.com/news/creativity-can-change-the-world. Accessed August 29, 2023.

Freberg, K. (2022). *Social media for strategic communication: Creative strategies and research-based application*. Sage.

Gaillot, A.-D. (2023, February 15). 7 examples of the best influencer marketing campaigns. Meltwater. https://www.meltwater.com/en/blog/influencer-campaign-examples. Accessed August 24, 2023.

Geyser, W. (2023, January 20). What is influencer marketing?—The ultimate guide for 2023. Influencer Marketing Hub. https://influencermarketinghub.com/influencer-marketing/. Accessed August 24, 2023.

Giumetti, & Kowalski, R. M. (2022). Cyberbullying via social media and well-being. *Current Opinion in Psychology*, 45, 101314. https://doi.org/10.1016/j.copsyc.2022.101314.

Handley, L. (2017, April 5). Kendall Jenner's Pepsi ad pulled after Twitter backlash. CNBC. https://www.cnbc.com/2017/04/05/kendall-jenners-pepsi-ad-causes-twitter-storm-labeled-disrespectful.html. Accessed September 8, 2023.

Handley, L. (2020, June 4). Lego pulls some advertising for White House and police building sets in wake of George Floyd protests. CNBC. https://www.cnbc.com/2020/06/04/george-floyd-protests-lego-pulls-some-ads-for-police-and-white-house-sets.html. Accessed August 31, 2023.

Hargittai, E. (2002). Second-level digital divide: differences in people's online skills. *First Monday*, 7(4). https://doi.org/10.5210/fm.v7i4.942. Accessed August 23, 2023.

Held, A. (2019). Gucci apologizes and removes sweater following 'Blackface' backlash. *NPR*. Downloaded December 1, 2023 from https://www.npr.org/2019/02/07/692314950/gucci-apologizes-and-removes-sweater-following-blackface-backlash.

Hill, C. (2023, January 17). Why diversity in marketing and social media is non-negotiable. Sproutsocial. https://sproutsocial.com/insights/brand-diversity-in-social-media/. Accessed September 8, 2023.

Hill, C. (2023, February 1). 8 guidelines to make social media posts more accessible. Sproutsocial. https://sproutsocial.com/insights/social-media-accessibility. Accessed September 1, 2023.

Hogan, M. (2017, April 5). Kendall Jenner ad uproar 'shows how far Pepsi has fallen,' marketing exec says. CNBC. https://www.cnbc.com/2017/04/05/kendall-jenner-ad-uproar-shows-how-far-pepsi-has-fallen-marketer.html. Accessed September 8, 2023.

Ingram, E. (2019, March 5). Utilizing the Diversity Wheel for personal and professional development. PRSSA. https://progressions.prsa.org/index.php/2019/03/05/utilizing-the-diversity-wheel-for-personal-and-professional-development/. Accessed August 28, 2023.

Internet Matters (2022, April 21). Online activism, social media and young people. https://www.internetmatters.org/hub/news-blogs/online-activism-social-media-and-young-people/. Accessed August 30, 2023.

Jones, N. (n.d.). Social media as a communication tool for disabled people. https://everyonecan.org.uk/news/social-media-as-a-communication-tool-for-disabled-people/. Accessed September 8, 2023.

Jorgensen, N. (2023, February 15). How to keep employees safe from cyberbullying in the workplace. *Forbes*. https://www.forbes.com/sites/forbeshumanresources-council/2023/02/15/how-to-keep-employees-safe-from-cyberbullying-in-the-workplace/?sh=c518bfd1c075. Accessed August 30, 2023.

Kantli, M. (2018, February 25). "Believe in More" | How a Nike campaign crossed three borders. Medium. https://medium.com/ad-discovery-and-creativity-lab/believe-in-more-how-a-nike-campaign-crossed-three-borders-cbf6381104ed. Accessed August 23, 2023.

Kossinets, G., & Watts, D. J. (2009). Origins of homophily in an evolving social network. *American Journal of Sociology*, 115(2), 405–450. https://psycnet.apa.org/doi/10.1086/599247.

Liu, B. F., & Pompper, D. (2012). The 'crisis with no name': Defining the interplay of culture, ethnicity, and race on organizational issues and media outcomes. *Journal of Applied Communication Research*, 40(2), 127–146. DOI: https://doi.org/10.1080/00909882.2012.654499.

Luttig, M. D., & Cohen, C. J. (2016, September 9). How social media helps young people—especially minorities and the poor—get politically engaged. *The Washington Post*. https://www.washingtonpost.com/news/monkey-cage/wp/2016/09/09/how-social-media-helps-young-people-especially-minorities-and-the-poor-get-politically-engaged/. Accessed September 8, 2023.

Luttrell, R. (2018). *Social media: How to engage, share, and connect*. Rowman & Littlefield.

Luttrell, R., & Capizzo, L. W. (2022). *Public relations campaigns: An integrated approach*. Sage.

Mangold, W. G., & Faulds, D. J. (2009). Social media: The new hybrid element of the promotion mix. *Business Horizons*, 52(4), 357–365. https://doi.org/10.1016/j.bushor.2009.03.002.

Martin, A. M. (2020, October 8). Black LinkedIn is thriving. Does LinkedIn have a problem with that? *The New York Times*. https://www.nytimes.com/2020/10/08/business/black-linkedin.html. Accessed September 8, 2023.

McAuliffe, Z. (2022, March 13). Early MySpace was the peak of social media. CNET. https://www.cnet.com/tech/services-and-software/early-myspace-was-the-peak-of-social-media/. Accessed August 22, 2023.

McKinnon, T. (2021, November 12). 6 reasons why Ben & Jerry's is a leader in diversity & inclusion. Indigo Digital. https://www.indigo9digital.com/blog/benandjerrysdiversityinclusionsocialjustice. Accessed August 29, 2023.

Mellor, M. (2020, February 28). Alumnus Marc Faddoul discovers racial biases in TikTok's algorithm. https://www.ischool.berkeley.edu/news/2020/alumnus-marc-faddoul-discovers-racial-biases-tiktoks-algorithm. Accessed September 11, 2023.

Merton, R. K. (1968). *Social theory and social structure*. The Free Press.

Molnár, N. (2020, June 12). All 53 films and shows in Netflix's new Black Lives Matter collection. Medium. https://medium.com/incluvie/all-53-films-and-shows-in-netflixs-new-black-lives-matter-collection-ce91e41b4ddd. Accessed August 31, 2023.

Morris, C. (2021, October 20). 16 reasons why social media is important to your company. *Search Engine Journal*. https://www.searchenginejournal.com/why-social-media-is-important/285809/#close. Accessed August 22, 2023.

Morris, J. (n.d.). 10 successful Tiktok marketing campaign examples of all time. Taggbox. https://taggbox.com/blog/tiktok-campaign-examples/#chipotle. Accessed August 24, 2023.

Morris, S. E. (2021, August 19). Inclusion hero of the week: Ben & Jerry's demonstrates inclusion is not just a buzzword. *Forbes*. https://www.forbes.com/sites/simonemorris/2021/04/19/inclusion-hero-of-the-week-ben--jerrys-demonstrates-inclusion-is-not-just-a-buzzword/?sh=6c90087b44f3. Accessed August 29, 2023.

MSL. (2021, December 6). MSL study reveals racial pay gap in influencer marketing. *PR Newswire*. https://www.prnewswire.com/news-releases/msl-study-reveals-racial-pay-gap-in-influencer-marketing-301437451.html.   Accessed September 11, 2023.

Muller, C., & Aguiar, J. P. de V. (2022, March 3). What is the digital divide? Internet Society. https://www.internetsociety.org/blog/2022/03/what-is-the-digital-divide/. Accessed August 24, 2023.

Mundt, M., Ross, K., & Burnet, C. M. (2018). Scaling social movements through social media: The case of Black Lives Matter. *Social Media + Society*, 4(4), 1–14. https://doi.org/10.1177/2056305118807911.

Murphy, C. (2020, June 3). Lego pulls advertising for police-related toys, donates $4 million to fight racism and inequality. Vulture. https://www.vulture.com/2020/06/lego-pulls-advertising-for-police-toys-donates-usd4-million.html. Accessed August 31, 2023.

Netflix. (2020, May 30). Twitter. https://twitter.com/netflix/status/1266829242353893376. Accessed August 31, 2023.

Newberry, C., & Reid, A. (2022, September 26). Social media activism in 2023: How to go beyond the hashtag. Hootsuite. https://blog.hootsuite.com/social-media-activism/. Accessed August 30, 2023.

Nyst, A. (2023, July 14). 134 social media statistics you need to know for 2023. *Search Engine Journal*. https://www.searchenginejournal.com/social-media-statistics/480507/#:~:text=Social%20Media%20Statistics%20Worldwide,increase%20year%2Dover%2Dyear. Accessed September 1, 2023.

Ofori-Parku, S. S., & Moscato, D. (2018). Hashtag activism as a form of political action: A qualitative analysis of the #BringBackOurGirls campaign in Nigerian, UK, and U.S. press. *International Journal of Communication*, 12, 2480–2502.

Ortiz-Ospina, E. (2019). The rise of social media. OurWorldInData.org. https://ourworldindata.org/rise-of-social-media. Accessed August 22, 2023.

Oxford English Dictionary. (n.d.). Social media. In *Oxford English Dictionary* online. https://www.oed.com/search/dictionary/?scope=Entries&q=social+media. Accessed August 21, 2023.

Papenfuss, M. (2017, March 20). Meet the new kid on 'Sesame Street': Julia, a muppet with autism. *HuffPost*. https://www.huffpost.com/entry/autism-muppet-sesame-street_n_58cf5f15e4b0be71dcf5b455. Accessed August 29, 2023.

Patrizio, A. (n.d.). Digital accessibility. https://www.techtarget.com/whatis/definition/digital-accessibility. Accessed September 1, 2023.

Pavlovic, D. (n.d.). 10 best ways to prevent cyberbullying online. https://www.hp.com/ca-en/shop/offer.aspx?p=best-ways-to-prevent-cyber-bullying-online. Accessed August 30, 2023.

Paynter, B. (2019, August 8). Sesame Street's autistic muppet, Julia, was a huge success—why some of her developers are now cutting ties. Fast Company. https://www.fastcompany.com/90387368/sesame-streets-autistic-muppet-julia-was-a-huge-success-why-some-of-her-creators-are-now-cutting-ties. Accessed August 29, 2023.

Pepper. (2022, May 4). 5 lessons to learn from the Kendall Jenner Pepsi ad. https://www.peppercontent.io/blog/kendall-jenner-pepsi-ad-failed/. Accessed September 8, 2023.

Perrin, A., & Atske, S. (2021, September 10). Americans with disabilities less likely than those without to own some digital devices. Pew Research Center. https://www.pewresearch.org/short-reads/2021/09/10/americans-with-disabilities-less-likely-than-those-without-to-own-some-digital-devices/. Accessed September 1, 2023.

Pew Research Center. (2021, April 7). Social media fact sheet. https://www.pewresearch.org/internet/fact-sheet/social-media/. Accessed August 21, 2023.

Pittman, T. (2017, March 24). 11 moments on 'Sesame Street' that championed diversity and inclusion. *HuffPost*. https://www.huffpost.com/entry/moments-on-sesame-street-that-championed-diversity-and-inclusion_n_58d5257ae4b03787d3576ba9. Accessed August 29, 2023.

Place, K. R. (2019). Listening as the driver of public relations practice and communications strategy within a global public relations agency. *Public Relations Journal*, 12(3), 1–18. https://prjournal.instituteforpr.org/wp-content/uploads/katieplace_listening.pdf

Pompper, D. (2015). *Corporate social responsibility, sustainability, and public relations: Negotiating multiple complex challenges*. Routledge.

Procter & Gamble. (n.d.). P&G values in action our longstanding commitment continues. https://assets.ctfassets.net/oggad6svuzkv/1U1mmczMAgd4xg892kVvPj/bf5fcdc0a11879fc78972c9df960692b/P_G_Values_in_Action__1_.pdf. Accessed August 29, 2023.

Public Relations Society of America. (2018). P&G + MBIB "THE TALK"—Creating a national movement to end "The Talk" and racial bias. ICCOPR. https://iccopr.com/wp-content/uploads/2019/03/6BW-1802D21261.pdf. Accessed August 29, 2023.

Ragan. (2021). Best practices for inclusive social media. Ensure social posts align with diversity, equity and inclusion principles. https://www.ragan.com/white-papers/best-practices-for-inclusive-social-media/. Accessed September 1, 2023.

Reagans, R. (2005). Preferences, identity, and competition: Predicting tie strength from demographic data. *Management Science*, 51(9), 1374–1383. https://psyc-net.apa.org/doi/10.1287/mnsc.1050.0389

Santora, J. (2023, July 18). 17 key influencer marketing statistics to fuel your strategy. Influencer Marketing Hub. https://influencermarketinghub.com/influencer-marketing-statistics/. Accessed August 24, 2023.

Scheerder, A., van Deursen, A., & van Dijk, J. (2017). Determinants of Internet skills uses and outcomes. A systematic review of the second- and third-level digital divide. *Telematics and Informatics*, 34(8), 1607–1624. https://doi.org/10.1016/j.tele.2017.07.007.

Sephora Accelerate. (n.d.). https://sephoraaccelerate.com/. Accessed August 31, 2023.

Shorty Awards. (n.d.). Chipotle lid flip challenge with superfan David Dobrik. https://shortyawards.com/12th/chipotle-lid-flip-challenge-with-superfan-david-dobrik. Accessed August 24, 2023.

Singer, P. W., & Brooking, E. (2018). *Likear: The weaponization of social media*. Houghton Mifflin Harcourt Publishing Company.

Smith, P. K., Mahdavi, J., Carvalho, M., Fisher, S., Russell, S., Tippett, N. (2008). Cyberbullying: Its nature and impact in secondary school pupils. *Journal of Child Psychology and Psychiatry*, 49(4), 376–385. https://doi.org/10.1111/j.1469-7610.2007.01846.x.

Stack, L. (2018). H&M apologizes for 'monkey' image featuring Black child. *The New York Times*. Downloaded December 1, 2023 from https://www.nytimes.com/2018/01/08/business/hm-monkey.html

Starbucks. (2020, October 14). Our commitment to Inclusion, Diversity, and Equity at Starbucks. https://stories.starbucks.com/stories/2020/our-commitment-to-inclusion-diversity-and-equity-at-starbucks/. Accessed August 31, 2023.

Starbucks. (2021, August 5). We believe we're better together: That's why we're working to advance racial and social equity with our partners (employees) and communities. Instagram. https://www.instagram.com/p/CSNQd5iHipz/. Accessed August 31, 2023.

Statista. (2023). Social media & user-generated content. https://www.statista.com/markets/424/topic/540/social-media-user-generated-content/#overview. Accessed August 22, 2023.

Statista Research Department (2023, May 3). U.S. nonprofit organizations social media usage 2022 by platform. Statista. https://www.statista.com/statistics/1371096/social-media-usage-nonprofit-organizations-platform-us/#:~:text=In%20 2022%2C%2099%20percent%20of,nonprofits%20having%20used%20 the%20platform. Accessed August 22, 2023.

Steel, C. (2022, February 28). How racial inequalities affect influencers. PCMAg. https://www.pcmag.com/news/how-racial-inequalities-affect-influencers. Accessed September 11, 2023.

Sterner, G., & Felmlee, D. (2017). The social networks of cyberbullying on Twitter. *International Journal of Technoethics*, 8(2), 1–15. https://doi.org/10.4018/IJT.2017070101.

Stigliano-Waite, Z. (n.d.). "What if normal is just what you know?" Lonelyleap. https://lonelyleap.com/work/how-we-family. Accessed August 28, 2023.

Suskind, R. (2017, December). Why the team behind Sesame Street created a character with autism. *Smithsonian Magazine*. https://www.smithsonianmag.com/innovation/team-sesame-street-created-character-autism-180967218/. Accessed September 11, 2023.

Swann, P. (2020). *Cases in public relations management: The rise of social media and activism*. Routledge.

Teens and cyberbullying 2022 (2022). Pew Research Center. Downloaded December 1, 2023 from https://www.pewresearch.org/topic/internet-technology/technology-policy-issues/online-harassment-bullying/#:~:text=Teens%20and%20Cyberbullying%202022,a%20relatively%20common%20reason%20why.

The Irish Times. (2017). Video promoting diversity and acceptance becomes viral hit. https://www.irishtimes.com/news/offbeat/video-promoting-diversity-and-acceptance-becomes-viral-hit-1.2966548. Accessed September 9, 2023.

Thirlwall, T. (2019, October 1). Social media as a means to diversity. Strategic Finance. https://www.sfmagazine.com/articles/2019/october/social-media-as-a-means-to-diversity/?psso=true. Accessed September 9, 2023.

Tulshyan, R. (2022). *Inclusion on purpose: An intersectional approach to creating a culture of belonging at work.* The MIT Press.

Van Dijk, J. A. G. M. (2006). Digital divide research, achievements and shortcomings. *Poetics*, 34(4–5), 221–235. https://doi.org/10.1016/j.poetic.2006.05.004.

Vogels, E. A. (2022, December 15). Teens and Cyberbullying 2022. Pew Research Center. https://www.pewresearch.org/internet/2022/12/15/teens-and-cyberbullying-2022/. Accessed August 29, 2023.

Wachter-Boettcher, S. (2017). *Technically wrong: Sexist apps, biased algorithms, and other threats of toxic tech.* W.W. Norton & Company.

Wallace, A. A., & Luttrell, R. (2021, December 28). 4 steps for putting diversity at the forefront of PR. PR Daily. https://www.prdaily.com/4-steps-for-adopting-a-diversity-first-practice-in-pr/. Accessed August 27, 2023.

Wei, K. K., Teo, H. H., Chan, H. C., & Tan, B. C. (2011). Conceptualizing and testing a social cognitive model of the digital divide. *Information Systems Research*, 22(1), 170–187. https://doi.org/10.1287/isre.1090.0273.

Wigmore, I. (n.d.). Slacktivism. https://www.techtarget.com/whatis/definition/slacktivism#:~:text=Other%20examples%20of%20slacktivism%20include, signing%20and%20sharing%20online%20petitions. Accessed September 1, 2023.

Wong, B., & Bottorff, C. (2023, May 18). Top social media statistics and trends of 2023. *Forbes.* https://www.forbes.com/advisor/business/social-media-statistics/#:~:text=77%25%20of%20businesses%20use%20social%20. Accessed August 22, 2023.

Wong, L. (2023, April 24). Social media accessibility: Inclusive design tips for 2023. Hootsuite. https://blog.hootsuite.com/inclusive-design-social-media/. Accessed September 1, 2023.

Xu, Y. (2018). Dolce & Gabbana ad (with chopsticks) provokes public outrage in China. NPR. Downloaded June 4, 2023 from https://shorturl.at/lMN38.

Yang, G. (2016). Narrative agency in hashtag activism: The case of #BlackLivesMatter. *Media and Communication*, 4(4), 13–17. https://doi.org/10.17645/mac.v4i4.692.

8 Future directions for developing competence as a DEI change manager

Donnalyn Pompper

We must build better organizations for a more respect-filled today *and* tomorrow wherever life exists. This final chapter offers summary conclusions and recommendations for helping communicators to serve organizations as consultants on DEI issues so that they may embrace social identity intersectionality thinking. That means taking DEI into consideration every step of the way for all decisions and relationship building internally and externally among key audiences. This is ongoing and necessary work. We imagine that readers pick up this book because they are in training for a career as a communication practitioner (or are working with students). If relationship building matters to you, then DEI concerns matter to you, too. We wholeheartedly believe that understanding and appreciating DEI and its adjacent topics deserves a central role in communication training.

While organizations have made many promises to root out homophily of predominantly Caucasian/White male leadership and authentically embrace DEI in the U.S. (and, hopefully, around the world), much unfulfilled potential remains (Rewers, 2020). Doing this work well involves giving attention to social identity *intersectionalities*, as well as dimensions beyond *only* ethnicity and gender. Overall, organizations built on foundational mission and vision statements guaranteeing DEI still have a lot of work to do so long as organizations' infrastructures and systems remain traditional, inflexible, binary, and mired in blatant disrespect of people's intersecting social identity dimensions. Some people and organizations they work with add a *B* representing *belonging* or *sense of belonging* mindset to the DEI framework to underscore a driving desire or commitment to support social justice.

Supporting organizations through systemic change is a highlight of the *organizational conscience* role of communication practitioners for supporting organizations' social responsibility goals. Look for the evidence. Are an organization's approaches to DEI stale and superficial? Or are they informed and progressive? Are organizations merely addressing symptoms

DOI: 10.4324/9781003279129-11

of bias and discrimination, or are they making deep systemic changes to the organization's infrastructure? When you read an organization's financial prospectus, its social media profile, its web page with vision and mission statements—and you compare promises made to actual evidence of DEI authenticity in spaces like organizations' management table, in the board room, across organization levels internally and externally, and among community outreach work—then the view becomes even clearer as to whether or not an organization genuinely is committed to DEI or merely is offering lip service without positive action for real change and authenticity.

Infrastructural change must be sustainable and measurable. Understanding what DEI is and inspiring true passion about revealing and reversing reasons why organizations are *not* diverse, equitable, or inclusive in the first place (historically) absolutely must be at the forefront of all decisions and activities. In recent years, some powerful bodies linked to organizations' financial success have prioritized DEI accountability. For example, multinational investment bank and financial services company Goldman Sachs announced that it will only underwrite initial public offerings (IPOs) of companies featuring diverse boards (Rewers, 2020). Nasdaq's Board Diversity Rule (2023) requires companies listed on Nasdaq's U.S. exchange to publicly disclose board-level diversity statistics and to explain why they do or do not have diverse directors (while accommodating smaller reporting companies and foreign issuers). Such moves might smack of defaulting to considering DEI's business case—as addressed in Chapter 3, "How intersectionality in social identity works . . . at work"—yet it offers a step in the right direction for accountability in avoiding the perpetuation of lip service with regard to some ethnicity and gender social identity dimensions. In other words, by formalizing accountability without exclusively relying on organizations to voluntarily comply with (often they do not) society's demand for DEI, rules and laws may be able to do what waiting for organizations to do the right thing morally has not.

This chapter summarizes the main points made throughout this book and offers practical advice for communication practitioners. Here are this chapter's sections: 1) remembering to re-think the term *stakeholder*; 2) environmental scanning commitment; 3) the elusive DEI commitment; 4) impact of pandemic life on working with others; 5) future of changing definitions of *organization*; 6) future of changing definitions of *diversity*; 7) steps for communication practitioners; and concluding thoughts.

Remembering to re-think the term *stakeholder*

When adopting DEI as the morally right course of action in organizations—beyond business case justifications—it is useful to consider all audiences or publics involved in terms of roles, impacts, and implications of what an organization does and represents in conjunction with those associated with it. One way communication practitioners in organizations typically have addressed these dynamics is to consider internal and external individuals, groups, and entities who are touched by an organization. An organization's success depends on relationships as part of planning communication strategies and crafting messages about and by the organization for sharing among those audiences. In public relations work, specifically, theories in application enable communicators to manage relationships with people (e.g., Ulmer & Sellnow, 2013).

Considering audiences has been an important part of managing DEI in organizations, as well as an important step in dismantling homophily. By considering feedback from internal audiences about work conditions, suggestions from external audiences such as the surrounding community members who live near manufacturing facilities, working with advocacy groups who lobby lawmakers and policymakers, negotiating with retailers who sell the organization's products and services, and so on, organizations show their respect with and for all. Organizational communication experts argue that for-profit and nonprofit organizations are responsible to individuals and groups across society beyond stockholders or those "prescribed by law or union contract" (Jones, 1980, p. 60). Stakeholder theory has been rooted in principles that emphasize corporate rights (May & Roper, 2014). More recently, Merskin (2021) added non-human species to the matrix since most animals are impacted by humans' existence around the globe for a mindset that emphasizes what Kant qualified as *respect* (Hill, 1998) for all living things.

Yet, inconsistencies and disconnects in outcomes associated with organizations' attention to DEI endure. Let's take a look at Walmart, for example. May and Roper (2014) explored ways that Walmart has been charged with "union busting, illegal and unfair labor conditions, exploitive global trade, community sprawl, corporate welfare," but has sought to collaborate with the National Fish and Wildlife Foundation, "for the public good" (p. 771). Also, Walmart has been sued for gender and ethnic/race discrimination by the Equal Employment Opportunity Commission (EEOC) (Segal, 2022). As considered in our Chapter 5, "Social responsibility in corporations and nonprofits," strategic management that incorporates attention to those affected by an organization should be managed for *everyone's* benefit and not just those who stand to gain financially by their association with the organization, as stockholders are. Rather, representatives of individuals and groups affected by an organization should have a role in its policy- and decision making. Too little is known about *if* or exactly *how* this happens.

In recent years, use of the word *stakeholder* among communication researchers and practitioners has been called into question. Critics suggest the word is embedded with "policy-speak or jargon that people in power often abuse" (Reed, 2022, para. 1), while others object to the word's racist and colonial connotations (e.g., Banerjee, 2003; Sharfstein, 2016). Reed (2022) persuasively argued that "the word should be avoided on the basis of its use in colonial times, when settlers used wooden stakes to claim land prior to any treaty or land negotiations with Indigenous groups" (para. 2). As we outlined in Chapter 6, "Universality thinking about publics and its pitfalls," the term *stakeholder* is considered offensive across several communities given its etymological roots illustrating "the person who drove a stake into the land to demarcate the land s/he was occupying/stealing from indigenous territories" (Switching from stakeholder, n.d., para. 3). Instead, Reed and Rudman (2022) suggested substituting the word *stakeholder* with *interested/affected groups* or *parties* so as to also include all living things. In this book we choose to use *audiences* and *publics* unless citing terms someone else has used. We encourage this reconsideration when working in advertising, strategic communication, and marketing-related fields, too. For organizations that care about authentic attention to DEI, simply using an alternate word or phrase seems a relatively simple and straightforward action. Thus, remembering to re-think the way organizations traditionally have communicated with and among individuals and groups—based on specific word choices—can go a long way in communicating respect and willingness to change in moving forward.

Now and in the future, communication workers also must consider important contexts—environments—inhabited by and affected by where people live and work—in addition to carefully considering terms and language used when communicating with and among individuals and groups of people.

Environmental scanning commitment

One technique for keeping a finger on the pulse of public opinion as addressed in Chapter 4, "Power differentials in organizations and society," is environmental scanning. This is a highly useful tool that helps organizations' communication professionals accomplish DEI goals and to benchmark against competitor organizations for additional insights. Perhaps the most visible organizational leader in a for-profit setting is the CEO and in a nonprofit setting it is the director. As noted in Chapter 1, "DEI and social identity intersectionality in organizational communication," CEOs as activists have become more vocal and visible in amplifying their personal opinion and position about social issues. The prevalence, nature, and impacts of CEO activism will continue to evolve as younger CEOs and a higher proportion of women take the helm (Branicki et al., 2021).

Another means for keeping a finger on the pulse of public opinion via environmental scanning is to consider an organization's history—particularly when planning social media strategies and campaigns. Many DEI experts warn organizations about repeating history when they fail to improve conditions to make DEI a reality (e.g., Stovall & Clark, 2022). For example, when Liu and Pompper (2012) interviewed crisis managers, they learned how influential history can be since present behaviors are contextually situated. In other words, what happens today is rooted in what happened in the past. So, if community members boycotted a business in the 1950s for polluting a neighborhood of low-SES BIPOC people, then issues of inequity as experienced by that community today include effects of what happened decades ago. People do not forget injustice and organizations cannot easily separate from their roots. Disregarding publics' diverse, intersecting histories, backgrounds, and lived experiences means operating from a shallow or myopic view. Applying social identity intersectionality thinking means moving to the center those people who, historically, have been relegated to the margins.

The elusive DEI commitment

Collectively, organizations' communicators can change the world for the better, offering a positive route forward consistent with the #ThereIsNo-PlanetB movement. When prioritizing authentic DEI commitment by backing up promises with action, by measuring goals for accountability, and by adhering to high ethical standards, communication practitioners possess significant power for doing good. We already know how useful social media tools can be in spurring **grassroots activism**. The positive spirit and talent of good communicators who know how to pressure elected officials and organizations' leaders is an unbeatable combination for enabling organizations to reverse elusive DEI commitment trends of the late 20th century and early 21st century. Yet, while social media platforms offer useful communication tools for organizations to reach audiences, those audiences also strategically can use social media as a platform for communicating messages to impact an organization's reputation.

Being committed to DEI also means adhering to high ethical standards for treating all people fairly and equitably. As explored in Sidebar 8.1, the use of big data has created ethics problems for healthcare providers, researchers, and patients—so considering power dynamics of pharmaceutical companies in tension with patient privacy along intersecting social identity dimensions of age, ethnicity/race, and gender reveals one facet of big data's limitations despite many people's celebration of big data as a marketing gold mine (e.g., Data-driven innovation, n.d.)

Figure 8.1 Communication practitioners possess significant power for doing good by supporting organizations that prioritize an authentic DEI commitment when backing up promises with action, such as those responding to the #ThereIsNoPlanetB movement.

Sidebar 8.1 When DEI dimensions and patient privacy clash in the age of big data

Tugce Ertem-Eray

Interplay among intersectional social identity dimensions, big data, and privacy concerns have serious implications for people and for ways organizations operate. This case study explores these dynamics in a healthcare context.

Big data means data sets that contain greater variety, are available in increasing volumes, and arrive with growing velocity (What is big data?, n.d.) These large data sets contain people's personal information more readily available than ever before, given digital file keeping and people's willingness to exchange privacy for convenience (Reily, n.d.) Marketers use large data sets to reveal patterns and trends related to human behavior and interactions (*Oxford Lexico Dictionary*, n.d.) that have become essential for improving healthcare by evaluating healthcare quality and efficiency (Price & Cohen, 2019).

Organizations can collect their customers' data easily by directly asking them for it, indirectly tracking them, or overlaying additional sources of customer data appended to the organization's own data files—sometimes without people's awareness or permission. In our digital world, it is easy for organizations to pull in multiple data sets from nearly every corner (Freedman, 2020) and organizations make decisions through data-driven models that can significantly affect people's lives. Having a plethora of information is important in a healthcare setting because it can offer solutions to improve patient care, facilitate stronger assessments of healthcare efficiency, and generate profits (Pastorino et al., 2019; Tom et al., 2020).

Yet, the use of big data *also* has created ethics problems for healthcare providers, researchers, and patients (Terry, 2012). Examining power dynamics of pharmaceutical companies in tension with patient privacy along intersecting social identity dimensions of age, ethnicity/race, and gender reveals one facet of big data's limitations despite many people's celebration of big data as a marketing gold mine (e.g., Data-driven innovation, n.d.)

Novo Nordisk, headquartered in Denmark, is a multinational pharmaceutical company that manufactures and markets diabetes care medications and devices. Novo Nordisk uses a Digital Health Platform, a diabetes management system, to store and analyze data and give real-time feedback to patients and their caregivers (Novo Nordisk, 2017). Novo Nordisk believes that technological innovations such as artificial intelligence and big data help it to have more accurate data on individual behavior and medication usage which could positively affect people living with diabetes (Kite-Powell, 2021). These technological innovations, however, come along with substantial concerns and potential threats such as breached patient privacy, invasive marketing, and discriminatory practices (Cohen & Mello, 2018; Price & Cohen, 2019).

While Novo Nordisk has not admitted to misconduct in some recent settlement cases (Reuters, 2011), it has entered into a civil settlement agreement to pay the U.S. and several states $1.725 million to resolve allegations that the company accessed and misused private patient information and filed false or fraudulent claims to the Medicaid program in connection with its marketing of diabetes drugs (Anderson, 2011; Meyerowitz, 2011). It is said that Novo Nordisk's sales representatives paid pharmacists for access to confidential patient information (Anderson, 2011). According to the agreement, the pharmacists and Novo Nordisk sales representatives identified patients who were candidates for diabetes drugs and asked physicians and pharmacists to encourage these patients to use the drugs (Anderson, 2011). Novo Nordisk also entered into a Corporate Integrity Agreement with the Department of Health and Human Services, Office of the Inspector General, to revise its internal compliance guidelines.

This was not an isolated incident, either. For example, in 2016, an estimated 3.47 million patients were victimized because of the data breach of healthcare ID card-issuer, NewKirk Products. Hackers had access to sensitive information such as primary care provider information, patients' ID numbers, names, and dates of birth (Lord, 2020).

The use of a social identity dimension intersectionality lens—categorizing lower-SES African American women over age 65 with diabetes, for example—may be helpful in marketing drugs to this specific group of patients, but doing so also carries a responsibility for not abusing power dynamics to exploit patients with high prices (Lou & Yang, 2020; Yang, 2019). Use of such information could end up discriminating against certain patient groups when they are overcharged for prescriptions and other healthcare products (O'Neill, 2016; Williams et al., 2018).

So, health organizations must use big data ethically (Whaley & Cheung, 2020).

When data are validated and blended, healthcare organizations need to address process- and policy-related issues (NEJM Catalyst, 2018). Healthcare organizations must carefully engage with healthcare data aggregation, manage processes ethically, and use these data responsibly. Public relations researchers have warned communicators about the need to balance big data's potential with trust building among their organizations' publics (Damschroder et al., 2007; Wiencierz & Röttger, 2019). More specifically, public relations practitioners use ethics guidelines to protect vulnerable publics who may be most affected by potential harm derived from big data-driven initiatives (Gregory & Halff, 2020). Organizational decision makers must be well informed to avoid privacy violations and protect their healthcare organizations as well as the patients they serve from digital privacy breaches (Brumis, 2016).

In the U.S., the HIPAA (Health Insurance Portability and Accountability Act) pertains to healthcare organizations' need to protect patients. HIPAA "requires healthcare organizations that conduct transactions electronically to develop and implement controls to ensure the privacy of patients and security of healthcare data is safeguarded" (Alder, 2018, para. 1). The HIPAA Privacy Rule requires healthcare providers, health plans, and healthcare clearinghouses to protect virtually all individually identifiable health information that is created, stored, maintained, or transmitted by them (Alder, 2018). The HIPAA Privacy Rule also requires written patient authorization to disclose identifiable health information.

Resources

Alder, S. (2018, March 31). What is protected by HIPAA? *HIPAA Journal*. https://rb.gy/6zzp9p.

Anderson, H. (2011, June 13). Fraud case involved privacy violations. https://rb.gy/g7fuuh.

Brumis, A. M. (2016). The right to privacy in a digital age: Reinterpreting the concept of personal privacy. *Inquiries Journal*, 8(09). http://www.inquiriesjournal.com/a?id=1450.

Cohen, I. G., & Mello, M. M. (2018). HIPAA and protecting health information in the 21st century. *JAMA*, 320(3), 231–232. https://doi.org/10.1001/jama.2018.5630.

Damschroder, L. J., Pritts, J. L., Neblo, M. A., Kalarickal, R. J., Creswell, J. W., & Hayward R. A. (2007). Patients, privacy and trust: Patients' willingness to allow researchers to access their medical records. *Social Science & Medicine*, 64(1), 223–235. https://doi.org/10.1016/j.socscimed.2006.08.045.

Data-driven innovation. (n.d.) LinkedIn. Downloaded December 2, 2023 from https://uk.linkedin.com/company/data-driven-innovation-initiative.

Freedman, M. (2020, June 17). How businesses are collecting data (and what they're doing with it). https://rb.gy/nlua1n.

Gregory, A. & Halff, G. (2020). The damage done by big data-driven public relations. *Public Relations Review*, 46(2), 101902. https://doi.org/10.1016/j.pubrev.2020.101902.

Kite-Powell, J. (2021, February 14). How hardware, data and artificial intelligence are changing diabetes care. *Forbes*. https://rb.gy/kxsovv.

Lord, N. (2020, September 28). Top 10 biggest healthcare data breaches of all time. https://rb.gy/jojofk.

Lou, S., & Yang, M. (2020, August 11). A beginner's guide to data ethics. https://rb.gy/lpn34n.

Meyerowitz, S. A. (2011, June 13). Novo Nordisk settles claims that sales reps paid pharmacists for access to confidential patient information. https://www.reuters.com/article/idUSTRE75965S/.

NEJM Catalyst. (2018, January 1). Healthcare big data and the promise of value-based care. https://rb.gy/hf1t6m.

Novo Nordisk. (2017, July 12). Novo Nordisk and Glooko advance their digital health collaboration with launch of unique integrated app for improved diabetes management. PR Newswire. https://rb.gy/kbipoc

O'Neill, C. (2016). *Weapons of math destruction: How big data increases inequality and threatens democracy.* Broadway.

Oxford Lexico Dictionary. (n.d.). Big data. Retrieved from https://www.lexico.com/en/definition/big_data.

Pastorino, R., De Vito, C., Migliara, G., Glocker, K., Binenbaum, I., Ricciardi, W., & Boccia, S. (2019). Benefits and challenges of Big Data in healthcare: An overview of the European initiatives. *European Journal of Public Health*, 29(3), 23–27. https://doi.org/10.1093/eurpub/ckz168.

Price, W. N. 2nd, & Cohen, I. G. (2019). Privacy in the age of medical big data. *Nature medicine*, 25(1), 37–43. https://doi.org/10.1038/s41591-018-0272-7.

Reily, J. (n.d.) Privacy or convenience: What's the tradeoff? Publicis Sapient. Downloaded December 2, 2023 from https://www.publicissapient.com/insights/privacy-or-convenience--what-s-the-tradeoff.

Reuters. (2011, June 10). Novo Nordisk settles U.S. probe for $25 million. Reuters. https://rb.gy/ntyk6c.

Terry, N. P. (2012). Protecting patient privacy in the age of big data. Indiana University Robert H. McKinney School of Law Research Paper No. 2013–04, *University of Missouri-Kansas City Law Review*, 81(2). http://dx.doi.org/10.2139/ssrn.2153269.

Tom, E., Keane, P. A., Blazes, M., Pasquale, L. R., Chiang, M. F., Lee, A. Y., Lee, C. S. (2020). Protecting data privacy in the age of AI-enabled ophthalmology. *Translational Vision Science & Technology*, 9(36), 1–7. https://doi.org/10.1167/tvst.9.2.36.

Whaley, R., & Cheung, D. (2020, October 22). Applying an intersectionality lens in data science [Data Con LA]. https://www.latech4good.org/news/intersectionality.

What is big data? (n.d.) Oracle. Downloaded December 2, 2023 from https://www.oracle.com/big-data/what-is-big-data/.

Wiencierz, C., & Röttger, U. (2019). Big data in public relations: A conceptual framework. *Public Relations Journal*, 12(3), 1–15.

Williams, B., Brooks, C., & Shmargad, Y. (2018). How algorithms discriminate based on data they lack: Challenges, solutions, and policy implications. *Journal of Information Policy*, 8, 78–115. https://doi:10.5325/jinfopoli.8.2018.0078.

Yang, K. M. (2019). Emerging ethical issues in managing real world data. *Healthcare Informatics Research*, 25(4), 237–238. https://doi.org/10.4258/hir.2019.25.4.237

There are multiple tools available to communication practitioners to support DEI commitment and accountability work—from setting goals, organizing people, spreading awareness of problems/opportunities, and then measuring success in accomplishing DEI goals. Some social movements can smolder and extinguish before they can catch on while others blaze to flashpoint and change the world (e.g., Meyer, 2021). Having specific, measurable DEI goals is a great way to start because degrees of success in accomplishing goals seem more real when they are visible and can be tangibly measured. Developing DEI awareness campaigns that rely on communication with other like-minded individuals, as well as creating websites, blogs, and other virtual spaces for organizing pushback and protest are among communication practitioners' staples. Individuals and organizations with a budget also can take out ads to inspire social change and spread awareness of injustices.

While the #BlackLivesMatter social movement has moved organizations to create departments headed by DEI officers to back up their commitment to the 2020 social justice outcry following George Floyd's murder (Corley et al., 2022), some fear it's not nearly enough. For example, since 2020, there have been a significant number of high-level resignations of DEI officers in the U.S. entertainment industry at Disney, Netflix, Warner Bros. Discovery, and the Academy of Motion Picture Arts and Sciences underscores the burnout/hard work required and/or organizations' tepid commitment to DEI if the "support, love, advocacy" (Gallupo, 2023, para. 10) required for diversity leadership is lacking. Research findings have suggested that chief diversity officers (CDOs) last only a couple of years in their position due to lack of support, resources, and organizations' authentic DEI commitment (Darden, 2023). In other words, too many organizations offer an *illusion of inclusion*. Without making DEI a thread woven throughout organizations' mission, culture, and values, CDO officers may move on (Melaku & Winkler, 2022). Moreover, one executive warned that the pool of talent for coordinating DEI goals in organizations is still too small and that organizations must integrate DEI thinking throughout organizations rather than simply designating one department devoted to DEI: "Interest and passion are important, but expertise and experience are also necessary . . . it is not a tangential topic . . . not a specialty department" (Gallupo, 2023, para. 14).

The entertainment industry is not alone in struggling to hold onto CDOs and to deal with organizations' DEI commitment backsliding. Deep change takes time, yet the degrees of actual change since 2020 in organization's infrastructure and systems that fuel inequities have been "largely cosmetic, performative, and perfunctory" (Kalita, 2023, para. 5). Kalita (2023) qualified the U.S. Supreme Court's 2023 ban against considerations of race in school admissions as both a symptom and outcome of inauthentic attention to DEI among majority White/Caucasian communities. So, the perfect storm of racial justice protests, the COVID-19 pandemic, and a polarizing presidential campaign have not been enough to make DEI an *actual* top priority across organizations. Ryan (2023) reported that CDO position turnover was high even before 2020 or the #BlackLivesMatter movement, adding that this latest exodus may be triggering "backlash against diversity and inclusion initiatives" (para. 4).

Often, a question of financial commitment to supporting DEI goals becomes the scapegoat for wavering actual DEI commitment among for-profit organizations. The monster.com Work Watch Report noted that 11% of employers said that DEI programs "are among the first to go when they are forced to cut costs" (2023 Monster, 2023). In 2022, Nike hired its fourth diversity head since 2020, Uber's diversity head was placed on leave in 2023 (Ryan, 2023), and CDOs working in many other industries have quit (Cutter & Weber, 2020). Shi and colleagues (2017) found that S&P 500 firms seem more likely to hire a CDO when they are helmed by a female top management team, located in legalized gay marriage states, and when CDO hiring rates are high in their respective industry.

On the positive side, the high CDO turnover rate phenomenon seems to have inspired the publication of a number of self-help books about DEI so organizations may navigate the course for themselves and/or hire a consulting team. For example, guidebooks with recommendations posit that communicators must be "conscious" in order to "add depth to your organization's communications" (Stovall & Clark, 2022). An authentic DEI commitment remains elusive for organizations that do not back their mission/vision statement promises with action. Therefore, the self-help books rooted in realism and experience offer the greatest promise.

Organizations committed to DEI also stand to gain from the wisdom of DEI-minded entrepreneurs who offer workshops and blogs full of advice based on their lived experience. For example, nurturing a global perspective can go a long way in supporting communications practitioners working to help organizations to achieve DEI goals because embracing multiple viewpoints is "a strategic imperative" best served when multiple voices join the conversation (Akintonde, 2023, para. 4). Communications practitioners are essential to making sure leaders build the *organizational muscle* of inclusive communications with audiences (Brown, 2021) and ensure that messaging is authentic throughout the company culture and talent processes (Jacobs, n.d.)

While organizations may be inspired to attend to some social identity dimensions, it is important that they consider as many as possible and the ways they intersect, as discussed in Chapter 3, "How intersectionality in social identity works . . . at work," and elsewhere throughout this book. For example, Hennekam and Dumazert (2023) explored challenges experienced by transgender individuals with an ethnic minority background, including intersectional invisibility (feeling isolated and excluded with unmet needs) and intersectional hypervisibility (feeling vulnerable and scrutinized especially at the beginning of the transition). Overall, this is an understudied population and greater insights are needed to create more inclusive workplace environments by removing multiple layers of stigma transgender individuals experience due to prevailing dominant (cis)gender norms and racism.

Impact of pandemic life on working with others

While being gainfully employed or volunteering for organizations during the COVID-19 pandemic involved significant downsides, one positive outcome was an opportunity to work from home for people who otherwise experience discrimination and bias when working face to face in organizations. For example, Slack Technologies Inc. (2023) reported in its Future Forum that some BIPOC members ("Black, Asian, Latino," Kalina, 2023, para. 11) prefer working at home at higher rates than their Caucasian/White counterparts, with employers expecting employees to return to a face-to-face environment without fully investigating why/how to solve the infrastructural DEI problems. Yet, the reality of organizations being unable or unwilling to live up to any DEI promises made on their websites has been brought into sharper focus in the COVID-19 pandemic context.

Transitioning to remote and hybrid work environments illuminated just how poorly some organizations actually attend to DEI—with initiatives that fall far short of goals and actually end up doing more harm than good. For example, only 17% of LGBT employees strongly agree that their organization cares about their wellbeing (Dupreé & Robison, 2022). Richmond (2022) posited that there exists a wide divide separating appreciation for remote workers who are as productive as (or more productive than) in-office-based co-workers. DEI managers are challenged to do their job as transformational leaders when organizational leadership is not authentically committed to change. Being a figurehead with little real authority is a recipe for inauthenticity.

Working through the pandemic taught all of us that working face to face, from home, or in some blend of modes is in store for many employees in the future—and these dynamics impact all of us in ways few anticipated. Futurists predict that by 2025, 32.6 million Americans (22% of the workforce) will work remotely—a doubled pre-pandemic figure (American workforce will be remote by 2025, 2020). Key benefits of remote work include reduction of non-essential meetings, increased schedule flexibility, no commuting distance/time, and increased productivity (American workforce will be remote by 2025, 2020). How and where DEI fits into this crystal ball gaze, however, remains to be seen. What is certain is that communicators who know how to build frameworks for asking the right questions and pursuing DEI as a position of strength for actual social justice are at the forefront of the change. Remember to invest resources in discovering what you don't know by using formal and informal research tools such as interviews, focus groups, surveys, and more. Organizations that fail to follow the law and morally address members' perceptions with real and supportive actions run the risk of tarnishing their reputation in the public sphere.

Organizations may consider merits and drawbacks of the TAB acronym as a means for expanding thought processes and decision making for accommodating wide ranges of people who identify according to multiple and intersecting social identity dimensions, including disability, as explored in Sidebar 8.2.

Sidebar 8.2   TAB: a stigmatized acronym for awareness raising?

Donnalyn Pompper

A *New York Times* editor convincingly pleaded with the U.S. Congress to provide funding to "fix the disability program" with a call-to-action headline "To: The Temporarily Able-Bodied" (2007). The TAB acronym serves as a reminder that every person most likely will experience a physical or mental disability at some point in their lives. Today, however, some critics argue that even though the disability community came up with the TAB acronym, there may be better means to explain why "accessibility and understanding of disability issues are important" (Crippledscholar, 2015, para. 5). For example, Maggio (n.d.) warned that even though the disability community created the TAB acronym, it is a label imposed upon a group that does not self-identify this way.

One might argue, however, that it can be useful for some people to self-identify as TAB when it comes to making decisions and policies, communicating among internal and external audiences, and crafting messages. Organizations' communicators have this power and responsibility. Building understanding around the experiences of people with disabilities must happen at the organization level.

For example, I once worked in a strategic communication program department at a university and participated in a faculty meeting discussion about conference meeting room renovations. The space was relatively small, and the department chair wanted to buy a large immovable table that nearly filled the whole room, leaving very little space around the perimeter to accommodate a wheelchair. The doorway was not wide enough to accommodate a wheelchair, either.

When I expressed these concerns, the chair retorted that we had no faculty members in the department who *actually used* a wheelchair. I reminded her that *not yet we didn't*—but that we *did* routinely use the space for faculty applicant interviews and presentations, as well as graduate student thesis presentations. Also, I pointed out that we faculty researchers sometimes used the room for data collection purposes (e.g., focus group meetings) and showcases for graduate student work (e.g., dissertation defenses, research fairs). At the time, I advised a capstone project for a graduate student who analyzed the content of a television reality show about living with disability. She often shared stories about her own experiences living with cerebral palsy that included navigating lack of curb cuts with her wheelchair. I had become more acutely aware of insufficient accessibility accommodations on two campus locations and did my best to support her.

I tried to be persuasive in my plea that education spaces must accommodate everyone.

Unfortunately, I was unsuccessful in my campaign to educate the department chair about why it was so important to accommodate every person who may use our conference room now and in the future. She bought the large table and never had the door widened.

Thinking about TAB as a tool—or filter—for ensuring equity in social spaces and workplaces offers a new way of thinking about ways we consider people and their experiences now and for years to come. The likelihood that people will experience a disability at some point in the lifecycle is high, whether the disability is short-lived or lasts the rest of one's life. A disability may be a manifestation of genetic circumstances, accident/disease, or naturally occurring aging processes.

The TAB acronym also emphasizes that a definition of *disability* changes over time and is defined according to individuals' and organizations' needs and contexts. Every person's value in terms of physical and mental ability, talents, and skills should not bound by degrees of their body's ability (Pompper, 2014). Edison and Notkin (2010) warned against overusing the TAB acronym or conflating *disabled* with *old*, but rather using TAB as a means for engaging in conversations about disability by dedicating time and space for elaborating why and how such acronyms are or are not used.

Globally, nonprofit organizations and awareness groups strive to educate people about how and why it is important to respect and accommodate what may be the largest, most diverse social identity group of people—people with disabilities. According to the World Bank, about 1 billion people (15% of the global population) experience a significant disability today (Disability inclusion, 2023). The World Health Organization (WHO) (n.d.) estimated that the number is growing due to an increase in noncommunicable diseases and the fact that people are living longer.

Moreover, persons with disability is a highly diverse group according to dimensions of age, ethnicity, faith/religion, gender, sexual orientation, and socio-economic status which impact their lived experiences and health needs (WHO, n.d.). Providing access and avoiding discrimination by defaulting to accommodations only for able-bodied-right-now people are two linked goals that should be fundamental and essential to every organization's mission/vision and backed up with action.

Applying the TAB acronym to organization circumstances—both paid work and volunteer work—can be a useful means for nurturing and developing competence among communication practitioners who respectfully amplify a need to advocate for accommodating people who live with a disability now or may do so in the future.

Resources

Crippledscholar (2015, April 27). Can we please stop calling able-bodied people TABS. Crippledscholar. Downloaded August 15, 2023 from https://crippledscholar.com/2015/04/27/can-we-please-stop-calling-able-bodied-people-tabs/

Disability inclusion (2023). The World Bank. Downloaded August 15, 2023 from https://www.worldbank.org/en/topic/disability.

Edison, L. T., & Notkin, D. (2010, February 3). Guest post: Temporarily able-bodied: Useful, but not always true. FWD/Forward. Downloaded August 15, 2023 from https://disabledfeminists.com/2010/02/03/guest-post-temporarily-able-bodied-useful-but-not-always-true/.

Maggio, R. (n.d.) Temporarily able-bodied (TAB). Women's Media Center. Downloaded August 15, 2023 from https://womensmediacenter.com/unspinning-the-spin/temporarily-able-bodied-tab.

Pompper, D. (2014). *Practical and theoretical implications of successfully doing difference in organizations*. Emerald Group Publishing.

To: The Temporarily Able-Bodied (2007, May 1). *The New York Times*, A22.

Future of changing definitions of *organization*

Traditional ways of thinking about *organization* have been morphing—thanks to new technologies. Where once an organization was something we thought of as a bricks-and-mortar structure sheltering people from the elements (e.g., rain, snow), today we know that an organization can exist without a building and people who work face to face every day. Across both for-profit and nonprofit organization types, people work together to form or accomplish something. However, artificial intelligence (AI) increasingly plays a greater role in communication practitioners' day-to-day responsibilities, with ChatGBT and other AI-based tools becoming more popular across the communication industry. These technological developments have significantly impacted ways we think about what an organization is and does.

Among researchers around the globe who build theory about and study organizations, many have focused on *networks* and *institutions* and ways both support or hinder embracing DEI according to people's social identity dimensions (e.g., Perrow, 1991). For example, people who find insufficient support at work for people like them who practice a specific faith system, experience a physical disability, or adhere to cultural customs may reach out to others across other networks with whom they feel comfortable in search of mentoring and career advancement advice (e.g., Pompper, 2011; Yang, 2023). Researchers who have supported a more abstract definition of *organization* (e.g., Aherne & Brunsson, 2011; Weick, 1969) may not have realized that because organization can take place in many ways, this actually supports embrace of DEI goals, too. For, when people come together to mentor one another, solve problems, and share ideas, social interactions can become more just, humane, and people centered rather than profit centered.

Importantly, we also now recognize that some organizations are better understood as a *partial organization*. Much of the contemporary global order is characterized by partial organization (Aherne & Brunsson, 2011) that includes groups like customer loyalty clubs, resistance movements, and more. What makes such organizations *partial* is that each possesses the degree of order necessary for their existence—and nothing more. In the case of customer loyalty clubs, these people receive the benefits promised by their airline or grocery store and they are satisfied with that. In the case of resistance movement organizations, people work together to raise awareness of their cause and to affect social change—with no desire to become a formal arm of organizations they are resisting against. Thus, the *partial organization* concept is broad for greater inclusivity.

Regardless of an organization's size (global or local), economic basis (nonprofit or for-profit), or degrees of completeness (full or partial), all organizations need to include people who advocate for others. From CEOs (e.g., Branick et al., 2021) through rank-and-file employees (e.g., Harris & Lee, 2019), organizations that *are* diverse, equitable, and inclusive include people who serve as role models, mentors, and advocates for all people working to achieve their own goals and maximum potential.

Future of changing definitions of *diversity*

As noted at the outset of this chapter and other spaces in this book, organizations must look beyond predominantly considering ethnicity and gender as sole markers of DEI. Both of these social identity dimensions and their intersectionalities *are* important. However, as this book's chapters have illustrated, DEI includes embracing so many more social identity dimensions. Society and its organizations must respect and embrace *all* social identity dimensions and their intersectionalities.

In organizations and beyond their structural walls, the word *diversity* takes on a variety of meanings. Sadly, not everyone agrees that respecting people and treating everyone well should be organizations' priority. Consequently, not all sources of social stigma—or the ways people negatively react to certain kinds of people—are visible (Goffman, 1963) and we must not forget that many social identity dimensions are invisible. For example, like social identities shaped by interior qualities, sexual identity largely is imperceptible to others. Sometimes co-workers consciously choose to not reveal their sexual identity for fear of experiencing bias that could jeopardize their job and/or their career. Membership in a stigmatized group with an invisible social identity dimension means that people must decide whether to "display or not to display; to tell or not to tell; to let on or not to let on; to lie or not to lie; and in each case, to whom, how, when, and where" (Goffman, 1963, p. 42). People who remain closeted report guilt associated with lying (Schrimshaw et al., 2013), yet opening up about one's sexual orientation, for example, risks igniting discrimination behaviors by employers and coworkers (Dowd, 2021). Three particular strategies may be used when revealing one's LGBTQIA sexual identity at work: 1) *signaling*, which involves offering clues or hints; 2) *normalizing*, which involves making an invisible sexual identity seem ordinary; and 3) *differentiating*, which involves redefining an invisible sexual identity as an asset (Clair et al., 2005).

Also, *culture* often can be an invisible social identity dimension. Beyond clothing and other appearance-related markers such as hairstyle and makeup, culture may be invisible so that we may risk unknowingly offending someone's culture. So ubiquitous is the social identity dimension of culture, that it is used to differentiate among Western culture, Eastern culture, Latin culture, Middle Eastern culture, and African culture. *Culture* is paired with other nouns to describe milieu such as celebrity culture,

Figure 8.2 Colleagues in India maximize globalism trends that link multinational organizations with countries where they do business.

political culture, youth culture, protest culture, lifestyle subcultures, countercultures, and myriad ethnic cultures such as Black culture. Given permeability of geopolitical boundaries and ways that globalism trends inextricably link multinational organizations with countries where they do business, often as part of the work of exploiting developing nations and their cultures (Munshi, 2005), national cultures "rarely develop in isolation" (Ashcraft & Allen, 2003, p. 15). Indeed, *culture* is a highly complex social identity dimension.

Too often, the visible social identity dimensions become what Anand (2019) and others have qualified as "checkbox diversity" (para. 3) that ends up being a "shallow" (para. 4) interpretation of identity that organizations use as a quick fix. Checkbox thinking about DEI may temporarily increase numbers of certain populations being represented in the organization, but it also can result in unfulfilled expectations of both employees (who are either fired or quit) and employers. For example, when a person with a disability is hired in an HR department to officiate policies and serve an outward facing function to the community, the risk of **tokenism** can be high. When BIPOC community members are hired to make an organization look good to funders or other publics (**window dressing**), they may doubt they were hired for their talent and feel insecure and less confident on the job. Rather, Anand (2019, para. 12) advised organizations to:

> embrace people's different approaches to problem-solving that are shaped by their unique lived experience. It will take patient participatory

practice, including a genuine desire to lower egos, listen attentively, and understand what marginalization—beyond the stereotype—means. It will entail combatting entrenched mindsets and behaviors that have led to poor understandings of hegemony and marginalization. It will require instituting the rights for creating sustainable shifts in power.

While the ways *diversity* is defined may change based on context of people's lived experiences, organizations must embrace its fluidity and complexity while acknowledging that people's ways of learning always evolve and that decision making involves multiple moving parts. Internally, an organization's attention to DEI must go beyond only hiring people. Everyone must be supported, retained, and enabled to collaborate with others for personal growth. For example, celebrating each person's assets, talents, learning styles, communication styles, resilience, and personal goals in the job supports their sense of belonging as a valuable organization member. Moreover, many encourage organizational leaders to confront their own and the organization's systemic biases, stereotypes, and marginalization habits head on (e.g., McIntosh, 1989). Rather than celebrating a checkbox, we must celebrate people (Anand, 2019).

Organizations fully appreciating human beings means taking a multi-perspectival normative assessment (e.g. Wessler et al., 2022) approach. In other words, when identifying the normative challenges associated with a hurdle to authentic DEI at work, prioritizing competing values, and developing a set of normative expectations, communicators must offer recommendations for organizational change. For example, in organizations unwelcoming to trans people, the communication manager could first engage in a fact-finding mission to discover tensions of discomfort among trans-identifying employees and co-workers via in-depth interviews or focus group meetings. Second, research results should shed light on precisely which values seem to be at odds, such as comfort/safety/respect versus efficiency/distraction. Third, identifying employee expectations for their environment with co-workers could result in, finally, recommending ways to improve interpersonal relationships and change the organization with new policies/procedures for respecting employees' social identities. Similarly, to address DEI hurdles manifest in workplace age gaps, fact-finding missions to discover work style differences among younger (e.g., entry-level) and older (senior-manager) workers should result in new ways to embrace the value that both employee sets bring to problem solving and decision making.

Consider the virtues of embracing the "you don't know what you don't know" approach to using research tools in the service of DEI goals as a communication practitioner, as explored in Sidebar 8.3.

Sidebar 8.3   When you don't know what you don't know

Donnalyn Pompper

So, what do organizations' communicators do when developing strategies and objectives for campaigns but want to be sure that the words, images, and ideas being amplified in their work is respectful and will not offend or damage any group's social identity? In other words, how can we ever really know in advance if our headline, video, or new logo won't insult a particular faith group, ethnic community, or culture's sense of history?

The short answer is: We don't. However, what we *can* do is work to minimize harm by consulting in advance with people who identify according to those social identity dimensions to ask them for feedback on preliminary messages and designs. In other words, asking people what they think about a campaign *before* it is released via social media or across traditional or social media channels can buy organizations time to make changes before releasing communication materials.

Respecting the feedback loop

Feedback is an invaluable tool; one communicators have relied upon for a very long time. Since the mid-20th century, theorists like Wilbur Schramm explored the information-sharing aspects of communication's source → message → destination path, underscoring the importance of feedback loops (Littlejohn & Foss, 2009). Schramm's non-linear illustration of the way communication works in real life emphasized a feedback loop connecting a person who sends a message and a person who receives the message. When someone communicates something with us, we can react to it and provide information to the person who communicated. When an instructor asks students if they'd prefer an extended deadline, students may resoundingly respond in the affirmative and then the due date can be changed. When a brand asks consumers what flavor combinations they'd like to see produced in their favorite chip, snackers can respond and the manufacturer can produce it.

Here's another way of thinking about the importance of feedback in applied communication jobs. When a soft drink manufacturer develops an ad that uses a celebrity spokesperson and borrow imagery from a social movement—and does not ask people closest to the movement in advance to offer feedback—the manufacturer risks possibly offending people. This is what happened in 2017 when Pepsi was accused of trivializing protests and police killings of Black people, so the company apologized and pulled the ad (Victor, 2017)—as addressed in Chapter 7, "Social media as a tool and as a weapon." When organizations test their strategies, objectives, and communication plans with people in advance, they can learn degrees to which groups may be offended by any proposed creative treatment or delivery vehicles.

Communicators working in strategic and creative fields know how important it is to solve organizational problems and maximize opportunities, but exactly how to reach those destinations requires research. Sometimes we work with people—like the #BlackLivesMatter (BLM) protest movement participants—who can offer feedback on communication plans in the form of advice and insights. Sometimes we must go beyond organizations' walls to meet people in the field where they live and work.

Formal and informal research tools

Research is a common tie that binds strategic communicators, scholars, and students around the globe. Knowing how to collect and analyze data has a practical application that is useful regardless of specialized area of communication students are preparing for as their future career. Informal research is nonscientific, casual, and includes performing tasks to keep a finger on the pulse of public opinion, such as by scanning social media feeds to see what people have to say about current events. Formal research, on the other hand, is scientific, reliable, and findings may be generalizable. Formal scientific research methods involve explicit procedures and steps for yielding the most reliable data.

The best time to use the focus group research method is when lived experiences among people who share an identity, history, or goal (Tracy, 2019) are needed by communicators seeking to help solve a problem or identify an opportunity. Returning to the above example of a 2017 celebrity ad campaign for a soft drink manufacturer, inviting

#BLM members to participate in an online focus group and sharing a draft of the ad storyboard to gauge people's reaction could have gone a long way in discovering important feedback long before investing resources in executing the campaign and making media buys. A focus group is not unlike group interviewing (Babbie, 2007) and looks like a conversation among about five to seven people controlled by a moderator who guides the exchange by asking questions, showing stimulus materials (e.g., images), and recording responses. After conducting a series of several focus group sessions, the researcher then culminates all data and discovers patterns among those data that are used to respond to formal research questions.

Similarly, media relations experts interview clients by asking questions to fully understand a business or service, apply insights about news production processes, closely scrutinize the content of what media are publishing, and maintain relationships with journalists to pitch stories to them over time.

Using formal research methods helps communicators like you to discover what you don't know. Discoveries among data collected, hopefully, enable organizations to avoid hurting and disrespecting people according to their intersecting social identity dimensions such as age, disability, ethnicity, faith/religion, gender, sexual orientation, socio-economic status, and more.

Resources

Babbie, E. (2007). *The practice of social research* (11th ed.). Thomson Wadsworth.

Littlejohn, S. W., & Foss, K. A. (2009). *Encyclopedia of communication theory*. Sage.

Tracy, S. J. (2019). *Qualitative research methods: Collecting evidence, crafting analysis, communicating impact*. Wiley Blackwell.

Victor, D. (2017, April 5). Pepsi pulls ad accused of trivializing Black Lives Matter. *New York Times*. Downloaded November 12, 2023 from https://www.nytimes.com/2017/04/05/business/kendall-jenner-pepsi-ad.html.

Steps for communication practitioners

Throughout this book, we have written about ways readers may harness the power of theory as a tool to make DEI an authentic reality. We have advocated for communication practitioners to assume the role of insider-activist, as outlined in Chapter 5, "Social responsibility in corporations and nonprofits." Throughout this book, we have advised communication practitioners to facilitate deep listening among CEOs and all other organizational leaders as a key step in embracing DEI and intersectional social identity thinking practices. Facilitating awareness and understanding enables communicators to help organizations and their audiences to better embrace what DEI is, really *get* how it works, and move beyond merely invoking this acronym as a trendy buzzword. Rather, DEI must be supported with positive action. A warm embrace of DEI must underpin everything an organization *does* and *is* so that an organization's systems and infrastructure are rooted in fairness and social justice. In the words of one of the modern founders of social, organizational, and applied psychology in the U.S., Kurt Lewin, "the best way to understand something is to try to change it" (Greenwood & Levin, 1998, p. 19). In other words, one of the ways to rid organizations of their microaggressions, bias, and discriminatory ways that thwart some people's attempts to achieve their maximum potential is to change the ways organizations are actually organized! Who better to support this good work than communication practitioners?

DEI commitment by walking around

Begin by taking a look at an organization's surroundings and by talking with people across the organization—not just managers—and people outside the organization who are impacted by it. Too often, DEI efforts fail in organizations because managers become trapped in hiring people who look and think like them. Before they know it, the organization's homophily becomes further entrenched and **group think** dominates (Whyte, 1952). Risk-averse organizations strive to reduce conflict in decision making and seek discussions that minimize any critical evaluation which has the potential for conflict. Yet, communication practitioners must overcome this hurdle in organizations by explaining the benefits of DEI thinking.

DEI commitment by being deliberate

DEI thinking means being a deliberate communication practitioner by clearly defining problems/opportunities, articulating the organization's position, and doing what matters. Organizations must eradicate homophily thinking by living and breathing the concept of social identity intersectionalities in order to understand, explain, and predict behaviors among diverse internal and external publics as part of ongoing communication practices. Taking on a large social problem may be beyond the scope of any one organization, yet it is important to remember that "no individual company can solve the audacious issue of systemic racism, but by being deliberate, they can develop and deploy actionable efforts aimed at specific aspects of the issue" (Stovall & Clark, 2022, pp. 44–45). These DEI consultants advise communicators to "[cut] through the BS to get to the point" (Stovall & Clark, 2022, p. 44) to define real problems and things organizations actually can do about them, or, "extracting an actionable problem from the audacious issue" (p. 44). For example, acceptance of the trans community in the U.S. and many corners of the world continues as a social challenge as these people face severe discrimination, stigma, and systemic inequality (Understanding the gender community, n.d.) There is much diversity among the trans community, a term characterizing people whose gender identity differs from the sex assigned to their birth; people who have "existed in every culture throughout recorded history" (Understanding the gender community, n.d., para. 2). Organizations' communicators can work with leadership to amplify acceptance and respect of the trans community in policy making, communication such as speeches and other talks, and materials such as annual reports, websites, internal newsletters, and press releases. Being a deliberate communicator in supporting DEI by linking social justice issues to DEI and organizational goals enables communicators to serve and lead. Eventually, the cycle becomes continual, consistent, and habitual.

DEI commitment by being accountable

All organizations—whether their raison d'être (French for *reason for being*) is to generate financial profit or not—must accept a responsibility of being accountable to DEI promises beyond lip service (e.g., Logan, 2021). Too many organizations seem to think celebrating March as Women's History Month (n.d.) without enabling women to work as leaders throughout the year represents a hollow DEI commitment. Similarly, merely serving tacos in the company cafeteria in celebration of Hispanic Heritage Month or posting a dancing taco gif on a website can be "extremely embarrassing and racist," inspiring social media backlash (Talbot, 2021). Rather, organizations must carefully consider their role in awareness and visibility campaigns designed to respectfully represent and show pride and support while simultaneously working to change systems and infrastructures that prevent people from achieving their maximum potential and can hurt them in the process by limiting human rights and creating health problems. Moreover, communication practitioners must stay current with social media platforms because they are fluid and constantly changing. Organizations must adjust their communication efforts accordingly to remain accountable across internal and external publics.

A DEI commitment also must be at the forefront of all organizational thinking beyond crisis moments such as murders and other violence and injustices steeped in social identity difference around the world. For example, in the wake of George Floyd's death, corporations have been found limited in using their power to affect social change like eliminating systemic racism (Jan et al., 2023). Rather, large banks (e.g., JPMorgan Chase, Bank of America) offer loans or investments supposedly committed to addressing racial inequality. Said institutions could stand to profit from such loans and investments in the form of mortgages (Jan et al., 2023). Such realities raise skepticism about organizations' authenticity in supporting social change related to DEI.

Organizations' communicators can help leadership avoid pushing back against DEI goals overtly or inadvertently by defunding DEI and prioritizing other goals instead. Consistently demonstrate and illustrate how and why DEI is important to organizational goals and morally the right thing to do. DEI and ways we advocate for and communicate about it cannot be some convenient, trendy afterthought. Sometimes bringing in external DEI experts can help raise consciousness for changing behavior and systems or processes. Guaranteeing that checkbox diversity (Anand, 2019) does not result in inauthentic DEI commitment in organizations and that DEI communication does not become "*the* marketing plan," but rather becomes "*part* of the marketing plan" (Stovall & Clark, 2022, p. 165, italics included in original) also is the communicator's job. Moreover, the organization's communicator can play a tremendous role by ensuring key audiences have technology access, that languages used are appropriate, that cultural translations are respected and used, and that accessibility is ensured for all. Be willing to admit what you don't know and practice humility in seeking support, promoting the sharing of ideas, and working hard to build coalitions advocating for DEI.

Concluding thoughts

Supporting DEI in organizations by keeping DEI goals at the forefront of day-to-day work may seem daunting until it becomes habitual. This book offers many suggestions and tools. Understanding communication's role in supporting DEI and social justice in organizations can be greatly facilitated by employing social constructionism, social identity theory, social learning theory, and other theories. We must recognize ways social identity dimensions intersect to produce people's highly complex realities. Such lenses enable communicators to be clear and respectful when representing social identity dimensions interpersonally in organizations and across media platforms. Simultaneously, dismantling homophily by rebuilding infrastructural systems that preserve power and limit people's ability to achieve their maximum potential means recognizing White/Caucasian privilege and unpacking the invisible knapsack, as discussed in Chapter 1, "DEI and social identity intersectionality in organizational communication." While communication practitioners cannot eliminate the political, social, and economic context from the interactions organizations have with people who are identified as out-groups, with respect, knowledge, and skill, they can help to significantly minimize bias that can negatively affect people's lives.

Communication practitioners must recognize and remember that all organizations have global implications, whether they are an international corporation or a local nonprofit organization. Globalization trends mean multicultural environments have become increasingly important as contexts for embracing DEI across nonprofits, NGOs, and for-profit organizations. Indeed, multicultural realities include both benefits (e.g., profit, harmony) and challenges (e.g., ethnocentrism, stereotyping), so we advocate for intercultural competence and acculturation approaches when using communication tools as part of counseling organizations. All organizations must critically examine their practices and systems to root out ethnocentrism, stereotypes, and harmful attitudes and approaches that negatively impact workplaces, communities, and the planet's environment, as addressed in Chapter 2, "Factoring in globalization, (mis)trust, risk, and sociopolitical contexts." Enabling audiences to feel genuinely respected requires work beyond merely trying to reduce conflict, a mantra that has undergirded most corporations that believe conflict interrupts operations and risks the financial bottom line (Rao, 2011). There is more at stake than financial spreadsheets. DEI is, morally, the right thing to do so that people feel they belong.

Communicators who incorporate the concept of social identity intersectionalities into their DEI thinking and commitment are well on their way toward building organizational cultures and relationships steeped in trust, engagement, innovation, and ethics—because it is morally the right thing to do. Creating an inclusive environment where everyone feels valued and respected requires time and patience. So many of the negative outcomes of lacking DEI are rooted in power differentials, so recognizing the role of power's import across structures and functions can help communicators to advocate for supplanting business case thinking with advocating for social justice case thinking. By working as an insider-activist social change agent, communicators committed to DEI support attention to marginalized voices from within, or inside, organizations. Being willing to confront an organization's DEI shortcomings and working to make organizations authentically embrace DEI is the focus of Chapter 4, "Power differentials in organizations and society."

Organizations that interpret the *S* in *social* of the ESG acronym as it relates to striving for and achieving meaningful DEI goals are committed to social justice. This means DEI attention is authentic and measurable. Organizational communicators have the power to navigate organizations' leaders and decision makers toward social justice thinking while working to address decolonizing goals and other volatile, uncertain, complex, and ambiguous (VUCA) wicked problem conditions, as well as resisting NIMBY challenges. In addition to working directly with organizations' key audiences, communicators can use social media channels to organize and spread positive messages, write op-eds to advocate for DEI, and overall create collective action to address challenges posed by lack of DEI in organizations and society, as shared in Chapter 5, "Social responsibility in corporations and nonprofits." Also, social media communication teams must listen to both internal and external publics, paying strict attention to digital inequalities, biased technology, cyberbullying, digital activism, and accessibility issues, as explored throughout Chapter 7, "Social media as a tool and as a weapon." In addition to internal publics, organizations must carefully consider how intersectionality in social identity plays out when working with external publics, too. Focusing on only one social identity dimension without considering how people's social identity dimensions intersect limits our perceptions, understanding, and decision-making when using communication tools and counseling decision makers. Creating inclusive environments while working with external publics is a talent worth building and nurturing, as covered in Chapter 6, "Universality thinking about publics and its pitfalls." Social media tools' power to communicate can be a double-edged sword, but Chapter 7, "Social media as a tool and as a weapon" addresses how to use these tools to support DEI goals in organizations.

Finally, Chapter 8, "Future directions for developing competence as a DEI change manager" offers practical advice for communication practitioners like you who are concerned about making DEI a reality. We wish all communication practitioners the very best of success in making this mantra a reality.

Key words

Grassroots activism—Social movements that develop in a given community, district, or region among people who work together to amplify their cause or position in order to affect political or economic change are said to be working from the bottom up, therefore emerging from a grassroots level.

Group think—When group members tend to think alike in the service of promoting conformity and harmony in their group. They strive to agree with one another in order to reduce conflict and to promote group cohesion. This psychological phenomenon results in poor decision making.

Tokenism—Organizations that make a symbolic effort to recruit people from underrepresented groups offer an appearance of DEI, but rarely offer these people the power to fully engage with the job.

Window dressing—People who are hired to make an organization look good (e.g., tokenism) often are displayed as a personification of DEI commitment, but in actuality are hired to play a symbolic role.

Discussion questions for deep engagement

1. List three to five personal qualities you think are necessary for actively advocating for DEI in organizations. Do you possess each quality? How can you further develop each quality? For example, *passion* for DEI might be one such quality.
2. What do *you* think about the word *stakeholder*? Do you think it's a respectful term?
3. What does environmental scanning mean to you? In what ways do you think it can be useful for supporting DEI in your school?
4. Why do you think DEI is so elusive in so many organizations today, when everyone seems to be in favor of DEI according to social media channels?
5. How do you think the term *organization* might change in your future? How might this impact what you think about DEI?

Resources

2023 Monster Work Watch Report (2023). Downloaded July 25, 2023 from https://www.futureofworkhub.info/allcontent/2023/1/20/2023-monster-work-watch-report.

Aherne, G., & Brunsson, N. (2011). Organization outside organizations: The significance of partial organization. *Organization*, 18(1), 83–104. DOI: 10.1177/1350508410376256.

Aherne, G., & Brunsson, N. (2016). Resurrecting organization by going beyond organizations. *European Management Journal*, 34, 93–101. DOI: http://dx.doi.org/10.1016/j.emj.2016.02.003.

Akintonde, S. (2023). Leadership lessons gained from the ever-evolving journey of entrepreneurship. *Forbes*. Downloaded August 21, 2023 from https://www.forbes.com/sites/forbescommunicationscouncil/2023/08/18/leadership-lessons-gained-from-the-ever-evolving-journey-of-entrepreneurship/.

Anand, N. (2019). Checkbox diversity must be left behind for DEI efforts to succeed. *Stanford Social Innovation Review*. Downloaded March 10, 2023 from https://rb.gy/d34ly.

Ashcraft, K. L., & Allen, B. J. (2003). The racial foundation of organizational communication. *Communication Theory*, 13, 5–38.

Banerjee, S. B. (2003). The practice of stakeholder colonialism: National interest and colonial discourses in the management of indigenous stakeholders. In A. Prasad (Ed.) *Postcolonial theory and organizational analysis: A critical engagement* (pp. 255–279). Palgrave Macmillan.

Branicki, L., Brammer, S., Pullen, A., & Rhodes, C. (2021). The morality of new CEO activism. *Journal of Business Ethics*, 170, 269–285. https://link.springer.com/article/10.1007/s10551-020-04656-5.

Brown, J. (2021). *How to be an inclusive leader: Your role in creating cultures of belonging where everyone can thrive*, 2nd ed. Berrett-Koehler Publishers.

Clair, J. A., Beatty, J. E., & Maclean, T. L. (2005). Out of sight but not out of mind: Managing visible social identities in the workplace, *The Academy of Management Review*, 30(1), 78–95.

Corley, T., Pamphile, V., & Sawyer, K. (2022). What has (and hasn't) changed about being a chief diversity officer. *Harvard Business Review*. Downloaded July 25, 2023 from https://store.hbr.org/product/what-has-and-hasn-t-changed-about-being-a-chief-diversity-officer/H0790F.

Cutter C. & Weber, L. (July 13, 2020) Demand for chief diversity officers is high: So is turnover. *Wall Street Journal*. Downloaded July 25, 2023 from https://www.wsj.com/news/author/chip-cutter?page=22.

Darden, Q. (2023). Where have all the chief diversity officers gone? *#evolve Magazine*. Downloaded July 25, 2023 from https://worldatwork.org/resources/publications/evolve-magazine/where-have-all-the-chief-diversity-officers-gone-.

Dowd, R. (2021). One in ten LGBT workers experienced discrimination at work in the last year. Williams Institute UCLA School of Law. Downloaded July 25, 2023 from https://williamsinstitute.law.ucla.edu/press/workplace-discrim-press-release/.

Dupreé, W., & Robison, J. (2022). LGBT employee experiences; here's what we know. *Gallup*. Downloaded August 21, 2023 from https://www.gallup.com/workplace/393983/lgbt-employee-experiences-know.aspx.

Gallupo, M. (2023). After a mass exodus of diversity execs, what's next? *The Hollywood Reporter*. Downloaded July 25, 2023 from https://www.linkedin.com/posts/mia-galuppo-5034b5b4_after-a-mass-exodus-of-diversity-execs-what-activity-7095457875745001472-LP4M?trk=public_profile_like_view.

Goffman, E. (1963). *Stigma: Notes on the management of a spoiled identity*. Prentice-Hall.

Greenwood, D. J., & Levin, M. (1998). *Introduction to action research: Social research for social change*. Sage.

Harris, T. M., & Lee, C. N. (2019). Advocate-mentoring: A communicative response to diversity in higher education. *Communication Education*, 68(1), 103–131. DOI: https://doi.org/https://doi.org/10.1080/03634523.2018.1536272.

Hennekam, S., & Dumazert, J.-P. (2023). Intersectional (in)visibility of transgender individuals with an ethnic minority background throughout a gender transition: Four longitudinal case studies. *Gender, Work & Organization*, 30(5), 1585–1610. DOI: https://doi.org/10.1111/gwao.12992.

Hill, T. (1998). Respect for persons in Kant's ethics. In Respect for persons. In E. Craig (Ed.), *The Routledge encyclopedia of philosophy*. Taylor & Francis.

Jacobs, L. (n.d.) SHRM Speakers bureau events programming, LaQuenta Jacobs. Downloaded August 21, 2023 from https://wwsg.com/speaker-contact/?utm_campaign=WWSG&utm_medium=ppc&utm_source=adwords&utm_term=event%20speakers&hsa_src=g&hsa_grp=148983974577&hsa_ver=3&hsa_mt=p&hsa_cam=816118780&hsa_ad=665269428168&hsa_kw=event%20speakers&hsa_tgt=kwd-265498758&hsa_acc=5473859223&hsa_net=adwords&gad_source=1&gclid=EAIaIQobChMIxPikg9SfhQMViM_CBB3M6g0WEAAYASAAEgL8fvD_BwE.

Jan, T., McGregor, J., & Hoyer, M. (2023, August 24). Corporate America's $50 billion promise. *The Washington Post*. Downloaded August 26, 2023 from https://www.abhmuseum.org/corporate-americas-50-billion-promise/

Jones, T. M. (1980). Corporate social responsibility revisited, redefined. *California Management Review*, 22(2), 59–67. DOI: https://doi.org/10.2307/41164877.

Kalita, S. M. (2023). Looking back on three years of performative diversity efforts. Charter. Downloaded July 25, 2023 from https://time.com/charter/6290473/undoing-workplace-diversity-gains/.

Liu, B. F., & Pompper, D. (2012). The 'crisis with no name': Defining the interplay of culture, ethnicity, and race on organizational issues and media outcomes. *Journal of Applied Communication Research*, 40(2), 127–146. https://doi.org/1 0.1080/00909882.2012.654499

Logan, N. (2021) A theory of corporate responsibility to race (CRR): Communication and racial justice in public relations. *Journal of Public Relations Research*, 33(1), 6–22. DOI: 10.1080/1062726X.2021.1881898.

May, S. K., & Roper, J. (2014). Corporate social responsibility and ethics. In L. L. Putnam and D. K. Mumby (Eds.), *The SAGE handbook of organizational communication: Advances in theory, research, and methods* (pp. 767–789). Sage.

McIntosh, P. (1989). White privilege: Unpacking the invisible knapsack. *Peace and Freedom*, July/August, 10–12. Wellesley College Center for Research on Women.

Melaku, T. M., & Winkler, C. (2022). Are your organization's DEI efforts superficial or structural? *Harvard Business Review*. Downloaded July 25, 2023 from https://hbr.org/2022/06/are-your-organizations-dei-efforts-superficial-or-structural

Merskin, D. (2021). Circle of responsibility: Animals as stakeholders. In D. Pompper (Ed.) *Public relations for social responsibility: Affirming DEI commitment with action* (pp. 103–119). Emerald Group Publishing.

Meyer, D. S. (2021). *How social movements (sometimes) matter*. Polity Press.

Munshi, D. (2005). Through the subject's eye: Situating the "other" in discourses of diversity. In G. Cheney and G. Barnett (Eds.), *Organization communication: Emerging perspectives* (pp. 45–70). Greenwood.

Nasdaq (2023, February 28). Nasdaq's board diversity rule: What companies should know. Downloaded July 19, 2023 from https://listingcenter.nasdaq.com/assets/Board%20Diversity%20Disclosure%20Five%20Things.pdf.

Perrow, C. (1991). A society of organizations. *Theory and society*, 20(6), 725–762.

Pompper, D. (2011). Fifty years later: Mid-career women of color against the glass ceiling in communications organizations. *Journal of Organizational Change Management*, 24(4), 464–486. https://doi.org/10.1108/09534811111144629.

Rao, V. (2011). A brief history of the corporation: 1600 to 2100. Ribbonfarm. Downloaded November 24, 2023 from https://www.ribbonfarm.com/2011/06/08/a-brief-history-of-the-corporation-1600-to-2100/.

Reed, M. S. (2022). Should we banish the word stakeholder? Blog. Downloaded July 25, 2023 from https://www.fasttrackimpact.com/post/why-we-shouldn-t-banish-the-word-stakeholder.

Reed, M. S., & Rudman, H. (2022). Re-thinking research impact: Voice, context and power at the interface of science, policy and practice. *Sustainability Science*, 18, 967–981. DOI: https://doi.org/10.1007/s11625-022-01216-w.

Rewers, A. (2020). Fifteen top DEI experts speak out: Truly addressing diversity in organizations. LinkedIn. Downloaded July 19, 2023 from https://rb.gy/cudwh.

Richmond, J. (2022). The importance of DEI in a post-Covid work world. *Forbes*. Downloaded August 21, 2023 from https://www.forbes.com/sites/forbesbusinesscouncil/2022/10/24/the-importance-of-dei-in-a-post-covid-work-world/?sh=13be14d55ff2.

Rivard, N. (2023, Summer). Saving wild: The power of grassroots activism. *Friends of Animals*, 8–11.

Ryan, T. (2023). Why are chief diversity officers heading for the exits? RetailWire. Downloaded July 25, 2023 from https://retailwire.com/discussion/why-are-chief-diversity-officers-heading-for-the-exits/.

Schrimshaw, E. W., Siegel, K., Downing, M. J., & Parsons, J. T. (2013). Disclosure and Concealment of sexual orientation and the mental health of non-gay-identified, behaviorally bisexual men. *Journal of Consulting and Clinical Psychology*, 81(1), 141–153. DOI: https://psycnet.apa.org/doi/10.1037/a0031272.

Segal, E. (2022). Walmart is sued for gender and race discrimination by the EEOC. *Forbes*. Downloaded July 28, 2023 from https://www.forbes.com/sites/edwardsegal/2022/02/11/walmart-is-sued-for-gender-and-race-discrimination-by-eeoc/?sh=322fc5e75614.

Sharfstein, J. M. (2016). Banishing stakeholders. *The Milbank Quarterly*, 94(3), 476–479. DOI: https://doi.org/10.1111/1468-0009.12208.

Shi, W., Pathak, S., Song, L. J., & Hoskisson, R. E. (2017). The adoption of chief diversity officers among S&P 500 firms: Institutional, resource dependence, and upper echelon accounts. *Human Resource Management*, 57(1), 83–96. https://doi.org/10.1002/hrm.21837.

Slack Technologies Inc. (2023). Research: Our findings on the future of work. Future Forum. Downloaded July 25, 2023 from https://futureforum.com/research/.

Stovall, J. M., & Clark, K. (2022). *The conscious communicator: The fine art of not saying stupid sh*t, adding depth to your organization's communications*. Publish Your Purpose.

Switching from stakeholder (n.d.) Research impact Canada. Downloaded November 29, 2023 from https://rb.gy/qu9cpo.

Talbot, A. (2021). Florida county is slammed for using extremely embarrassing and racist dancing taco to celebrate Hispanic Heritage Month. *Daily Mail*. Downloaded August 26, 2023 from https://www.dailymail.co.uk/news/article-9997851/Florida-county-slammed-using-dancing-taco-celebrate-Hispanic-Heritage-Month.html.

Ulmer, R. R., & Sellnow, T. L. (2013). Stakeholder theory. In R. L. Heath (Ed.) *Encyclopedia of public relations*, 2nd ed. (pp. 872–875). Sage.

Understanding the transgender community (n.d.) *Human Rights Campaign*. Downloaded August 26, 2023 from https://www.hrc.org/resources/understanding-the-transgender-community.

American workforce will be remote by 2025 (2020). Upwork. Downloaded August 21, 2023 from https://www.upwork.com/press/releases/upwork-study-finds-22-of-american-workforce-will-be-remote-by-2025.

Weick, K. E. (1969). *The social psychology of organizing*. Addison-Wesley.

Wessler, H., Althaus, S. L., Chan, C., Jungblut, M., Welbers, K., & van Atteveldt, W. (2022). Multiperspectival normative assessment: The case of mediated reactions to terrorism. *Communication Theory*, 32, 363–386.

Whyte, W. H. (1952, March). Groupthink. *Fortune*. Downloaded August 24, 2023 from https://fortune.com/2012/07/22/groupthink-fortune-1952/.

Women's History Month (n.d.) Downloaded August 26, 2023 from https://www.womenshistorymonth.gov/.

Yang, A. (2023). Stakeholder networks and corporate social responsibility. In D. Pompper, K. R. Place, & C. Kay Weaver (Eds.) *The Routledge companion to public relations* (pp. 253–264). Sage.

Yorks, L. (2005). Nothing so practical as a good theory. *Human Resource Development Review*, 4(2), 111–113. https://doi.org/10.1177/1534484305276176.

Index

Note: Page numbers in *italics* refers to figures.

For Product Safety Concerns and Information please contact our EU
representative GPSR@taylorandfrancis.com
Taylor & Francis Verlag GmbH, Kaufingerstraße 24, 80331 München, Germany